THE BOOMER SURVIVOR KIT

AN INDISPENSABLE GUIDE FOR
YOURSELF • YOUR RELATIONSHIPS • YOUR LIFE

William Courter, M.D.

ISBN: 0988854201
ISBN 13: 9780988854208
Library of Congress Control Number: 2013932289
CreateSpace Independent Publishing Platform
North Charleston, South Carolina

The Boomer Survivor Kit

from

The Boomer Health Institute
Founded by Dr. Courter

The Institute's Mission Statement

To improve the quality of life for baby boomers so that they can, despite financial, professional, medical, personal, and family challenges, redesign their lives to make their upcoming years the best part of their life.

*To my wife Priscilla (Ace),
who embraced our challenges
helping to redesign our lives,
renewing our relationship,
and creating a better life
for both of us*

And to Jeffrey Knight,
a friend who never made it
past his setbacks,
but right before his death
- always giving -
made me promise
to improve the lives of others

CONTENTS

STEP 3

Reshaping Your Physical Activity

STEP 4

Sharpening Your Mental Focus

STEP 5

Creating a New Direction for Your Life

STEP 6

Redesigning Your World

STEP 7

Rediscovering Your Spirituality

STEP 8

Lifting and Maintaining Your Mood

STEP 9
Refining Your Legacy

STEP 1

Accepting the Challenge

"What's dangerous is not to evolve."
Jeff Bezos

Chapter 1

A Friend's Suicide:
A Call for Change

"No one wants to go out mid-sentence."
Johnny Depp

On a Sunday night, as I was sneaking a piece of See's chocolate, I received a call around 10 p.m. from a close, lifelong friend. Numbed with alcohol and slurring his words, he announced that he had called to say good-bye, as he was standing on his fifth-floor balcony ready to jump to the concrete sidewalk. Even though I was trained for such emergencies (I had completed a psychiatric residency before progressing into public health administration), my mouth turned to cotton. The piece of chocolate grew difficult to swallow. Before I could say anything, my friend set the parameters for our telephone call. Although intoxicated, he was still mentally sharp. He explained that he would talk to me on two conditions. First, I had to promise that I would not attempt to call 911 with any behind-his-back attempt to abort his suicide. Second, I would not try to talk him out of his jump. So, with those demands, what would you do? Accept the ultimatum and talk as a friend? Or make an attempt to call for assistance?

I elected to meet his conditions. Over the next hour and a half on the phone, as I moved from our kitchen into our empty living room, I sat in the dark, making no attempt to call 911, nor any attempt to talk him out of his suicide. Instead, I simply listened, offering a sympathetic ear. He talked about the death of his wife (she had died three years earlier) and his lingering grief. He reviewed his life's many setbacks, including his financial setbacks in the stock market crash in 2007, the continued financial losses over the subsequent years, and his current financial predicament as he was behind in his taxes. He shared some of his physical complaints about a replaced hip and a balky knee; and he focused on the depression of his growing age (he was getting ready to turn sixty) with his sense that life was "closing down." He felt as if his attempts at happiness had slipped through his fingers, never to be retrieved. He felt as if he had made too many mistakes with no hope of correcting those missteps or finding a path that would give him a chance for a better life. Too much money had been lost. Health had been wasted. Relationships had been damaged. He expressed concern for his two adult children and their future. His relationship with them had been repaired, but other friendships had disappeared. He saw the concrete as an end to his pain, an escape to the solace of cremation and ashes.

At one point in our conversation, he did not say anything for over a minute. I worried that he might be pouring himself another drink or perhaps climbing the railing, preparing to jump. When he finally spoke, he surprised me. No, he had not changed his intention to leap. Instead, he wanted to discuss the plans for *my* future. He had heard that I was trying to redesign my life and that I was trying to write a survivor's guide (or as he described it "a prescription without any pills") for baby boomers so that they could improve their health and their lives. He listened without saying a word for almost five minutes, as I explained my desire to reshape our baby boomers by offering a guide that did not depend on our medical or pharmaceutical industry. At the end of my rambling, to my surprise, he said my suggestions were the best prescription that he had ever received from a physician and that he had received far too many prescriptions over the course of his life. Then he did something equally unexpected. He demanded a promise: as a lifelong friend (who had picked him up at the airport and rushed him to the hospital for the birth of his first child), would I promise to develop my thoughts, write my suggestions, and publish my guide? Would I consider setting up a company (now The Boomer Health Institute) to help the baby boomers redesign themselves, their relationships, and their lives? He lamented how there were so many struggling individuals, pushed to the brink, who needed a renewal of themselves, their family, and their lives. Sitting in pitch darkness on the living room sofa, I made that promise.

At this point his mood seemed to lift. But did it lift enough? In truth, I would have needed more details and a much clearer, more refined discourse to snap him out of his depression.

Through his cell phone I could hear the noise of passing cars and the barking of his dog. At that point he thanked me for not calling 911; he congratulated me for not trying to talk him out of suicide; and he said good-bye, abruptly hanging up his cell phone. Unsettled and unnerved, I did not call the police. I sat in the dark for an hour and finally went to bed well after midnight, sleeping fitfully. Did my friend, Jeffrey Knight, jump to the concrete that night? In mid morning, as I was finishing my coffee and trying to shake myself out of my doldrums, I received a telephone call. My nerves twisted into an even tighter coil until I finally heard the sound of his voice. No, he had not jumped. He had decided to seek help, and he had just checked into a hospital.

Did his psychiatric treatment rescue him? He spent three days in the psychiatric ward, receiving an antidepressant, a mood stabilizer, and an anti-anxiety agent. On the third day, he did not feel much better, perhaps he even a little worse from the side effects of the psychiatric medications. On that day's rounds the psychiatrist asked him if he were still feeling suicidal. He knew what he had to say. He lied. Once released from the psychiatric unit, he returned to his apartment, opened a bottle of vodka, and resumed drinking. On the next morning, after a twenty-hour alcohol binge, he climbed the railing and jumped to his death. Before this jump, did he place one final call to me? Unfortunately, no. For the next week, I kept asking myself: Why had he not placed just one more call to me? At his memorial service on the beach, the answer came to me. He knew what I had to offer. He liked the basic points of my guide. But without my suggestions more developed, without my prescription better refined, and without my institute up and running, would it have been enough to change his mood or his attitude? At the time of his jump, probably not. But now, with this book finished and with The Boomer Health Institute established, my opinion is different. If time could have been frozen, and if he had called me today, I am convinced that my new survivor kit would have aborted his suicide. With this belief, this book, and this institute, I am keeping my promise to offer you, the baby boomers, a path to a better life so that you too don't have to "go out in mid-sentence."

Chapter 2

Our Initial Challenge

"The longer you wait for your future, the shorter it will be."
Anonymous

There is the story of the golfer and the great ant massacre. A man starts his round of golf with poor scores on the first several holes. On the third hole, he slices a golf ball off the course and into a large field well out of bounds. The golfer, not wanting to take a penalty stroke, climbs over the fence, searches through tumbleweeds, and finds his golf ball on the largest anthill that he has ever seen. Annoyed, he grabs his five iron, climbs the anthill, and takes a swing, missing the golf ball and killing 1,000 ants. He takes a second, third, and fourth swing, each time missing the golf ball and killing another 1,000 ants. Finally, with his temper flaring, he breaks his iron, selects his massive driver, and positions himself for a full-throttle swing. At the top of his swing, two ants emerge from one of the remaining holes to peer up at this towering figure and his enormous driver. Petrified at their circumstances, one ant says to the other ant, "If we want to stay alive, maybe … maybe we should get on the ball."

From my vantage point, we, the generation of baby boomers, are those ants. We are surrounded by historic and economic changes that seem designed to destroy our finances, professions, health, families, and lives. We can see around us a landscape of unexpected devastation. With every broadcast of the news and every headline on the Internet, we watch another unfolding, senseless disaster. At our age, just when we thought we would be facing fewer problems and just when our faculties (and tolerance) seemed strained to the limit, we find ourselves facing more (and larger) stressors than ever. So, let me ask: What is it that is keeping you up at night? Is it concern over finances? Is it worries for your health? Is it anxiety for your aging parents? Or is it preoccupation with your children and their future? For baby boomers, those are three primary areas of late-night worry: finances, health, and family. Well, let me add three more questions to your list of concerns. Have you lived? Have you loved? Have you really made a difference? Those are the questions that keep me tossing and turning, shifting my position from under the sheets to the top of the blankets.

Let's be honest with ourselves. With the world's economic/ethnic/cultural challenges and the growing disparity in wealth distribution, do you think our standard of living is ever going to improve for you or your children? Do you think we are going to enjoy our older years? Or do you think we are going to be forced to work at our current jobs, year after year, until we drop dead? And do you think your health will ever rebound with increased vitality? Or are you anticipating a downward spiral with chronic health problems? And what about your family? Do you see your responsibilities rising higher and higher to your own financial and emotional breaking point? When we were growing up, people referred to their old age as their golden years, the best years of their life. So, what's happened? For the average working man and woman, those dreams now seem beyond our reach. For many of us, the fantasy of an old age with less stress, more relaxation, a secure family, and peace of mind has long since vanished. It's been replaced by a life (and a future) that we don't really want to visualize. And with all this stress, what is our first line of defense? More doctor visits and more pills?

Do you know what makes this picture even more disturbing? For many of the baby boomers, life has seemed like a nonstop, fast-paced treadmill. Didn't we rush through our childhood, rush toward adolescence, rush to (and through) high school, rush to (and through) college, rush toward our career, rush to fall in love, rush to get married, rush to raise a family, and rush to be successful in our career? And now, after countless years of work, don't we find ourselves facing ... well, this chaotic world with all of these unexpected challenges? At some point, didn't we realize we were scurrying along a conveyor belt toward the wrong destination? Didn't we realize that we were just rushing toward a barren life, ending in a vertical coffin? Isn't it sad how people have rushed toward tomorrow without making the most of today? Isn't it equally depressing how people have made repeated personal sacrifices in their quest for 'something' without ever finding greater happiness, either at work or at home? While ruining their health? Isn't it deflating how many people have labored all their lives and missed the real target of life to create a far more meaningful existence? Isn't it time to face those three fundamental questions? Did you live? Did you love? Did you make a difference? And isn't it time, while there is still time, to make some changes?

Ask yourself: Were you satisfied with your three answers? Well, there is good news. You do not have to follow the plight of my friend, Jeffrey Knight. As someone who was always giving, he would have wanted more for you. I remember the day that he moved into the condo beside ours. As my wife and I were rummaging around for some housewarming gift, there was a knock on our front door. It was Jeffrey Knight and his wife bearing gifts with a basket of goods from the Good Earth restaurant. Well, consider this book as a welcoming gift for the next part of your life, a gift for your future and your family's future. Despite all of our challenges, I am convinced that the term "Good Earth" still applies to our future. Why my optimism? No, I do not think our economy is going to rebound without a long, slow recovery. Yes, all economies eventually rebound, despite the political fighting.

A recovery just takes time, sometimes a decade. Or longer. But for your upcoming years, what counts is not your current level of success, or health, or even happiness. What counts is one fundamental challenge: How much of yourself and your life are you willing to change to make your future better? The answer to that question does not lie in any of your old solutions. The answer lies in your willingness to incorporate my suggestions into your new life. Given our enormous, shared challenges, I am confident that you are more than willing to give this guide a chance. I suggest the sooner, the better.

But first, there is an important point that needs to be clarified. This guide was not written to simply extend the length of your life. If that had been my sole goal, I would have titled the book *The Boomer Survival Kit.* Do I think this guide will add years, maybe decades, to your life? Yes. But longevity is not my central focus. If you are reading these pages, you have already been successful at surviving. You have overcome the stress of many years. You have beaten the odds. You have not jumped. I congratulate you. So, for me, you are a survivor. However, at this point, you need to do more than survive. You need to create a better life and a better future. For this transformation, you need something more valuable. Thus, *The Boomer Survivor Kit.* A kit to change your life, not just extend your life. With the tools in this kit, I will help you change yourself, your relationships, and your life. Now which do you want? Another day? Or a better day? For me, the answer is a better day. In truth, I think this kit will give you both. But let's focus on the better day *and* the better life.

Chapter 3

Society's Challenge

"You can't change what you don't acknowledge."
Dr. Phil

In today's world, there are small groups of surviving indigenous tribes, such as the Aborigines of Australia and the Adivasi of India. If you could take a snapshot of their campfire, what would you observe? The tribe would be gathered for the evening and an elder (the oldest member of the society) would hold an honored and venerable position. That person would be treated with respect. That person would be viewed as the guardian of the tribe's traditions, the storyteller of the tribe's history, the protector of the tribe's spiritual core, and the nurturer of the community. When that person spoke, his (or her) voice would not be diminished by the tribe's chatter. Their words would be cherished, valued, and shared throughout the community. Now, how does that response compare with society's response to today's older members of our population? America is worse than most countries, but throughout the world, the older people seem to be more marginalized and less appreciated. That reality presents a societal challenge for all of us baby boomers.

When I was younger, I attended a small liberal arts college, Williams College, in Williamstown, Massachusetts. I would fly from Los Angeles to New York's Kennedy Airport, take a bus into Manhattan, and then catch another bus from the city to the rural college. One year, returning after the Christmas vacation, I climbed into the bus, settled into my seat, and shivered in the cold. The bus started to draw away from the terminal when this gray-haired, elderly woman came hobbling after the bus, begging for it to stop. She was desperate to board, as an extra 30 minutes in the frigid weather, waiting for the next bus, could be a killer. To my surprise and relief, the driver slowed the bus, allowing the old lady, still dragging her luggage, to reach the bus door. The driver opened the door just enough so that he could talk, but not wide enough to allow the old lady to enter. With a face as cold as the winter chill, he scolded her, "Lady, the next time you're in a hurry, take a cab." He closed the door and steered the bus into traffic, leaving the old lady, stunned, standing at the snowy curb. Now, would he have let her in if she were young and beautiful? Who knows? But in our culture that poor lady's age did not convey any advantage for respect or kindness or even sympathy.

The industrial countries, and much of the world, seem captivated by technology. How long do most of our technological devices last? Most of them are designed to last a couple of years. Many devices, like our cell phones, become obsolete well before they have lost their functional value. Many of today's older people fall into that same category. Instead of being valued and appreciated, more and more older people are marshaled into segregated communities or retirement homes. They seem tossed aside, just like an older piece of technology, ready to be scrapped for something newer. The older population is viewed as a burden, a drain on the economy. Worse, much of our society seems focused on youth and beauty, abhorrent of physical signs of aging. This perspective represents a strange paradox. In America we have 74-77 million baby boomers who are entering their older years. For the next 20 years, 10,000 baby boomers will turn 65 each day. Around the world, there is an even larger demographic shift. Some experts call it a demographic earthquake from America to Europe to China. Other experts refer to it as the graying tsunami. In the world's population, the percentage of older people has never been higher, and it is rising rapidly. By the year 2020, 36 percent of the world's population (2.7 billion) will be over 50 years old, and 20 percent of the world's population (1.6 billion) will be over 65 years old. That's an issue that needs to be addressed.

There is an old adage that if you do not value yourself, the world is not going to increase your value. My point? The responsibility of improving our value to the world, as we progress through our upcoming years, starts with each baby boomer. That is the broader challenge. We need to view this challenge as an opportunity. Yes, some of us will have to work longer than we expected. Some of us will have to address far more physical and emotional challenges than prior generations. Many of us will live three decades longer than our grandparents, probably working to the end. Many of us will have to assume new (and changing) family responsibilities. Yes, there is a growing level of stress. And, yes, aging has the potential to bring forth our worst features. But we cannot let ourselves succumb to negativity. As we address our challenges, we must exude a level of responsibility, coupled with a degree of optimism, that surprises society. Simply stated, we need to fight against the world's expectations of older age. People often become what others expect them to become. Now is the time to fight against society's expectations and our own negative self-fulfilling prophecies. Let's fight against the myth of decreased capacity. Let's not allow ourselves to be defined by our loss, diminishment, or disengagement. Let's not become marginalized, disempowered, or invisible. Let's not let anyone close the bus door on us. Let our future show renewed health, higher vitality, greater happiness, deeper family bonds, stronger connections with each other, increased spirituality, and a revamped leadership through sharing, giving, and teaching.

So, let's embrace this challenge, and let's promise, starting with this guide, to make some changes. Together, let's reclaim our historic role as leaders. Collectively, let's make a difference. To accomplish that goal, we will have much to learn as we progress through this book. We need preparation and commitment. We need to convert our experience into a collective wisdom. But we have much to offer. We can offer a better perspective on the real value of life, countering shortsighted beliefs that focus too much on external rewards and achievement. We can mentor the adults and defend the children. We can fight to maintain the world's balance. In the rush of youth, too much of real value gets pushed aside. Let's show them the value of combining passion and purpose. Let's show them the value of things greater than money or fame. Let's show them the importance of living in the world of being, not just doing. What counts, after all, is not what you do, but who you are. So, together, let's start to live, love, and make a difference. Let's teach the world by example. It is time for a societal transformation. For baby boomers, it is not just a societal challenge; it is our social responsibility. Are you willing to accept that challenge?

Chapter 4

A Historic Time for Renewal

"The world is more malleable than you think."
Bono

There are years that are renowned for historic landmarks: 1492, 1776, and 1945. There are many years that were predicted to change history with disastrous results: 1844 (Judgment Day), 1910 (Halley's Comet), and 2000 (Y2K computer bug). Since the 1960s there has been a preoccupation with 2012. Some historians relate it to the Mayan calendar and the completion of its

Long Count, 5,100 year calendar, signaling the end of one cycle of civilization. Some Mayan scholars have predicted an assortment of possible disasters: a planet Nibiru crashing into the Earth, a switch in polarity between the North and South poles (which occurs naturally every 400,000 years), or an explosion of extreme solar storms (which occur on a smaller scale every 11 years). Other scholars have predicted a new, better era in human relationships and a brighter era for the Earth. Regardless of your belief, with all that is happening in our world, don't you think that now is a good time for both a personal and societal renewal?

I have never been much of a believer in prognosticators. I have never placed much emphasis on one single year. I am more of a follower of my own spin on the Elliot Wave Theory, which offers another perspective on the flow of history. The Elliot Wave Theory asks you to imagine a set of five waves approaching the beach, with each wave having a peak and a valley. At the beginning and at the end of this five-wave pattern, there is a severe prolonged economic trough. In terms of American history, this five-wave pattern just covered a time period of 90 years. The previous severe trough occurred in the 1920s; the five waves transpired from the 1930s to the 2000s; and our recent severe trough started with the market crash in 2007. So, what is the value of this theory? Historically, in the first wave of any new cycle, after a severe and prolonged trough, the country experiences a wave of significant changes in government, business, and even general lifestyle. Do you know what was invented in the first wave after the Great Depression in the 1920s? It's an impressive list, including TV, radar, power steering, diesel locomotive, helicopter, ball point pen, the zipper, etc. For today, the situation is remarkably similar. Think of all of the current technological advances, surfacing around the same time and changing our world and lifestyle. So here is my question. If the world is going through a period of turbulent change, shouldn't we follow the world's lead? Shouldn't we be willing to redesign ourselves, our families, and our lives to lead the world past these technologic changes to a truly better future?

I have already highlighted our rapid changes, multiple challenges, and escalating conflicts. According to most of the theories on the flow of history, these changes will be dramatic over the next 20 years before settling into a rhythmic pattern of growth with the natural waves of peaks and valleys. With this context, don't we have a responsibility to try to improve ourselves and the world over these next 20 years? And I am not referring to an economic renaissance. For many of us, these next 20 years will not be our golden years. But we still have a chance to make ourselves better, our lives better, and the world better. Take a look at our history. For our generation of baby boomers, how much impact have we really had on the world? The technological changes may have rearranged our lifestyle, but have they been of sufficient import to change the course of history? Did the ball-point pen or the zipper change mankind? No. Technology is spectacular, but a generation needs to do more than create new tools. The generation before us, which some experts call the greatest generation, changed the world through their sacrifice during World War II. How do you suggest we leave our mark on the world? What can we do that will have true historic impact?

Personally, I would love to see our generation leave a historic mark. How? By changing ourselves in our golden years, redefining our role in society, resetting the values of society, and regaining respect for older people. Let's present ourselves as models for those generations that will follow us; and let's reestablish the historic role for elders for our families and the world. Around 1900, the average person lived into his or her 30s to 40s; today, the average person lives into his or her 80s to 90s. By 2100, those longevity figures will rise even further. According to one insurance company, the first person, who will live until the age of 150 years old, is already alive today. For the sake of all future generations, why not assume this mantel? Let it be our legacy. Do you know what music lasts the longest in the Elliott Wave Theory? It's the music that comes at the mid point of the five-wave period, the music that is most popular at the top of the third wave. Who ruled the music charts at the top of the third wave? The Beatles in the 1960s. And what did they sing about? Living. Loving. And making a difference.

If you pause for a moment and reflect on our baby boomer life arc, it is clear that we made a historic difference back in the 1960s with songs about love and peace, protests against war, and the struggle for civil rights in our country. Yes, we lost our share of leaders. But that era was still one of our generational peaks. We shifted some of our country's values, remember? Recently, we have made some progress on other human rights, including sexual orientation. But we still need another generational peak with even greater societal impact. The world needs us. We need, once again, to reshape the world, but through more than just songs or protests. Again, we need to shape the world by example. Our golden years can be the pinnacle for ourselves and our generation with a consequence that is far superior to any of our earlier actions. Let's take the lead and shift the world one more time. Let's shift their view of aging. Let's shift some of the distorted values. Let's show them how much our generation can still contribute. As the singer Bono asserted in the longer version of the opening quote for this chapter, "The world is more malleable than you think. We can bend it into a better shape." Yes we can. Now, let's do it.

Chapter 5

Are You Interested?

"The scariest moment is always just before you start."
Stephen King

Before you answer the above question, I need to offer a disclaimer. I cannot do anything to change your finances. I don't pretend to offer the false promises of a wizard financier. But I can do something far more important. I can change your life and help you create a meaningful future. If you think your happiness in your upcoming years is dependent on your background, education, achievements, or finances, you are mistaken. If you believe the satisfaction of these years requires retirement, you are mistaken. Your older years, and the meaningful experiences you create in your older years, will rely on our discussions in this book, not on the above factors. Unconvinced? As a physician, I will admit that more education is associated with better longevity. Americans with 16 years of schooling live longer than Americans with less than 12 years of schooling. But education, achievement, and wealth are not as clearly associated with happiness and life satisfaction in your older years. There are other more important factors.

Think of your own life. When were you happiest? When I finished my final year of psychiatric residency, I took a year off and moved to Marbella, Spain. Accompanied by my fiancé (now my wife of three decades), we lived in a tiny villa, spending a total of four thousand dollars for that year. What did I do with that free time? I wrote seven hours a day, seven days a week, crafting my first novel *The Cure*. Okay, so I crashed and burned. The novel was never even submitted for publication. Frankly, I did not think it was quite good enough. Worse, I had alienated my parents, who considered my writing an affront to my medical education. Even my wife suffered consequences. Her father, who hated the idea of her living with someone before marriage, was ready to disown her. He had always warned her (she was a medical intensive care nurse) against two mistakes: don't marry a doctor and don't marry a bum. When we left for Spain, he was convinced that she was about to do both. But you know what? For that year we did not need money to be happy. We did not need achievement to be satisfied. We lived; we loved; and we made a difference to each other. In fact, with just each other for company, we learned an early lesson, which is all too often forgotten. Happiness often comes from activities that are far related from any financial issue.

Do you think the wealthy own the market on happiness? Yes, they will take more fancy trips and have more expensive possessions. But have you examined the financial statistics for daily happiness? The graph of happiness versus income is not a straight linear line, consistently heading upward. Instead, it is a bell-shaped curve. At some point on the curve, additional income does not translate into greater happiness. In fact, at some point on the curve, additional income often leads to reduced happiness. For the people whose income lies in the first half of the bell shaped curve, there is a stress to meet their basic needs. For those people whose income extends beyond the highest part of the bell shaped curve, there is a stress that comes with your sacrifices (in the pursuit of additional income). Reduced freedom. Reduced time with your spouse. Reduced time with your family. Reduced time for other hobbies. My point? A higher income does not always lead to a better life. Remember that money is not the only currency. As we age, time and freedom become more valuable. So, if your goal is to increase your level of happiness and satisfaction with your life (for yourself and your family), you need to choose a path that is different from society's preoccupation with wealth.

Still unconvinced? Well, have you read the tabloids? For the rich and famous, there are a multitude of problems. They buy more, but have less. They purchase a fancier home, but discover it's still a broken home. They ingest more pills, but have reduced wellness. Of the rich and famous, how many of them cycle through multiple spouses? How many of them have dysfunctional families? How many of them have alcohol or substance abuse problems? What about their children? Similar problems? For me, it is obvious. An improved financial portfolio is not the route to greater happiness. Why? Because happiness is not an acquisition; it is a skill. In the same vein, the satisfaction with your upcoming years is also not an acquisition; it too is a skill that can be learned and refined (and shared with those people you love). Now is the time to learn the necessary skills to live, love, and make a difference. Now is the time to embrace, not fear, the coming years. Now is the time to come alive, not numb yourself with alcohol or drugs (legal or illegal). Trust me. You are never too young or too old to benefit from this guide. So, are you interested?

Chapter 6

Is Retirement Necessary?

"Life is not fair; get used to it."
Bill Gates

The answer to the above question is no. For me, there is an important distinction between your golden years and a dream of retirement. A person, who is still employed and struggling to pay bills, may create a much more meaningful life (with the right focus, right priorities, and right skills) than someone who is, in fact, retired. I want to offer a path toward a deeper fulfillment that is greater than a paycheck. From my perspective, your later years should signal a transition from a financially driven, achievement focused life to a broader, more balanced, less stressed, and more meaningful life with a higher level of physical, emotional, and spiritual health, a greater level of personal satisfaction and serenity, and better relationships with family and friends. If you are still working, you just need to shift your focus toward the activities away from the job. Regardless of your employment, your later years should still represent the pinnacle of your life, not a downward slide toward the end of your days.

So, what is necessary if not retirement? Self-help speakers claim motivation gets you going, but it's your habits that get you to your destination. My program is not designed to motivate you. The spiral into older age, by itself, will be motivational. Who wants to grow older? Who wants to die? Some people claim to hate the words golden years. But age forces you to ask yourself: What can you do to make the rest of your life better, more satisfying? From this fundamental question, my approach is designed to direct you to refocus your attention on some core components of your life and redesign your upcoming years with the help of specific habits that will enhance the quality of all aspects of your life, regardless of your finances or employment. Aristotle asserted that "you are what you repeatedly do" and your "excellence is not an act, but a habit." That statement was true 2000 years ago, and it is also true today. For all of us, it is the small habits and the small advantages that lead to the greatest triumphs. That is my core belief. Your satisfaction with your older years will be dependent on your ability to reevaluate certain areas of your life and your willingness to incorporate new crucial habits. If you can absorb the coming suggestions and establish these habits, it is also my belief that you will be able to stand in front of a mirror and proclaim that your older years were golden, and that (during those years) you lived, loved, and made a difference.

To incorporate the new habits, you are not going to have to commit significant hours. In our careers we have all wasted too much time on useless pursuits. I have seen too many workaholics disappear into the night. As you grow older, I do not want you to work harder; I want you to work on the areas of your life that are much more important than any employment. Your new direction will require learning new habits. But don't worry. Unlike your employer, I will not work you to death. Chapters in this book will be short, and your reading time will be brief.

However, I will need your mental focus, your willingness to consider new perspectives, and your commitment to your personal growth. Your initial challenge will be to ignore the other problems in your life. The problems that are taking up so much of your time and energy. What's your biggest problem? What is your most overwhelming stressor? Your job? Your finances? Your health? A specific illness? Some family issue or conflict? Let's agree that life is not fair. Let's move past your current problems to a new focus. So, whatever is your major challenge, I want you to skip that current crisis. We can address that problem later. For now, I want you to focus on my suggestion to gain new insights, learn new habits, and create a new path toward far greater happiness. The time to start is today, not tomorrow. Do you think it is too late? If you have ever pumped a well, you will know one of its secrets: the longer the pumping takes, the cooler the water. You may think that the dream of your golden years has died. I think the dream has just been delayed. These years are well worth the wait. The results can still be wonderful, regardless of your employment status. You just have to learn the skills and the secrets, and then share them with the people you love.

Chapter 7

So, What's The Prescription?

"Nothing like a nighttime stroll to give you ideas."
J.K. Rowling

As a physician, do I possess some secret elixir for each of us to swallow to find happiness? No. But I have a new program for your life. It costs nothing more than effort on your part to follow the recommendations within this book. Are all of my ideas original? Do I claim ownership of all of the specific ingredients? No. But when a physician writes you a prescription, has he invented the specific medicine? No. The physician has utilized his or her own study, training, and acumen to prescribe something to improve the health of the patient. I have tried to follow the same approach. This guide was not written to rid you of a specific ailment; it is not offered to cure you of a specific disease. It cannot change the satisfaction with your job. I am more interested in how you live your life away from your office than how you perform at your work. As a physician, I want to improve the quality of your life, especially the parts that really matter.

What are the ingredients of this prescription? Do they represent technological breakthroughs? Just the opposite. As much as the younger generations are recreating our world in unforeseen ways, there is wisdom buried in our past. Each of us is the product of those people who have come before us. As we grow older, we need to give credit to those people and listen to their wisdom. I am just like many of you who are reading this book. I was worried about my golden years. I had doubts about the quality of my older age. It would be nice to claim this book was written for you; but in truth, it was not. It was written too late for my friend Jeffrey Knight. But it was also written for me. With the death of my friend, I needed these recommendations just as much as he did. I needed to change the direction of my life just as much as you likely need to change the direction of your life. I needed to better embrace life and love. I needed to feel that I had made more of difference. There is good news. The program works. My golden years have unfolded in ways far beyond what I had imagined. Not because of me, but because of this guide. Experts proclaim knowledge is power. For me, clarity is power. My suggestions will give you renewed clarity on exactly how to make the most of your upcoming years. Now how did I concoct this group of recommendations? From where did they arise?

The writings of the early philosophers like Socrates, Plato, and Aristotle offer gems of knowledge. The texts from the great religions (Judaism, Christianity, Islam, Hinduism, Buddhism, Taoism) are worthy of a good read. The common sense books in America's history like Benjamin Franklin's *Poor Richard's Almanac* and Henry David Thoreau's *On Walden Pond* do not show their age. In the 1900s there is a long list of personal development writers/speakers (Dale Carnegie, Napoleon Hill, Earl Nightingale, Norman Vincent Peale, Zig Ziglar, Anthony Robbins, Stephen Covey, Wayne Dyer, Louise Hay, Brian Tracy, Deepak Chopra, Jack Canfield, etc.) who offer guidelines on how best to live your life and achieve happiness. Many of these writers/ speakers provide their own points of view, each highlighting various suggestions. My approach will reflect the core components of the teachings from these people and their sources of wisdom, but it will also offer some new ideas specific to your golden years.

The biographies/autobiographies of successful people are equally enlightening. The life histories of famous political figures like Abraham Lincoln and Nelson Mandela, respected scientists like Isaac Newton and Thomas Edison, and remarkable coaches like Vince Lombardi and John Wooden all showcase similar character traits that enhance the quality of lives. For the coaches, their approach enhanced the quality of their players' performance on the field/ court; but their approach, especially for Wooden's, also enhanced the quality of their players' lives. If you have sufficient time and interest, I encourage you to read some of these books. Wooden, for example, directed his athletes to "drink deeply from good books." For now, I just want you to know that this list of people and their stories are a key part of the central ingredients that were condensed into my recommendations for your future life.

I also want to highlight the medical resources that are equally valuable. Your older years are nothing without good health.

Books like Dr. Andrew Weil's *Why Our Heath Matters* or Dr. T. Colin Campbell's *The China Study* or Donna Gates's books *The Body Ecology Diet* and *The Baby Boomer Diet* or Christopher McDougall's *Born To Run* provide valuable insights into our medical challenges, our health-care system's inadequacies, and our physical/emotional needs for our later years. I love the saying that all readers are not leaders, but all leaders are readers. I do not pretend to fall in the category of a leader. However, my reading of these resources, as well as my own work caring for patients, has provided me with the framework for understanding the need for a new program for your upcoming years. If my recommendations for this period of your life prove effective, and I believe they will be very effective, we should pay respect to the collective wisdom of all of these resources.

Isaac Newton, one of the world's most insightful scientists, once stated: "If I have seen further than others, it is by standing upon the shoulders of giants." I do not offer any pretense that I have seen further than the others. My resources have all been giants in their fields. Louise Hay's grasp of the underpinnings for self-improvement exceeds my own. Jack Canfield's ability to tell heartwarming stories dwarfs my own weak attempts.

Victor Frankl's understanding of human psychology is deeper than any psychiatrist's. Wayne Dyer's discussions of spirituality serve as points of inspiration, not just points of knowledge. Dr. Campbell's research on physical health extends beyond my medical acumen. Donna Gates's investigation of diet, digestion, and health are more thorough than my own research. Christopher McDougall's portrait of exercise is better drawn than I could ever sketch. In writing this book, I have taken many nighttime strolls, trying to take disparate elements to mold them into a cohesive, convincing program. Some points will be old; other points will be new; and some points will seem counter intuitive. I have tried to configure these collective elements, offering a comprehensive program for your golden years that is simple, understandable, and doable. I encourage you to focus on the message, not the messenger. It is the message that counts. In fact, improving the quality of yourself, your relationships, and your life is all that counts.

Chapter 8

If We Want More ...

"To have what you have never had,
you must be willing to do what you've never done."
Seren Destineer Mary Loverde

I am not writing a group of suggestions that are complicated. I am offering some changes that each of us can follow. Like any group of suggestions, their effectiveness may not be transparent within the first few days or the first few pages. For now, give the recommendations a trial. Many people, as they grow older, start chasing an imagined bucket list. I disagree with that approach. In the rush of activity, they lose their direction and miss the chance to make fundamental changes. I encourage you to postpone your bucket list. Not derail it, just delay it. Instead, I encourage you to take a breath, appreciate this turning point in your life, and embrace the possibilities for personal change. I encourage a firm commitment to incorporate the upcoming habits. If you are willing to focus on these new habits, and if you are willing to wait for your bucket list of activities, I promise that your upcoming years will be far better than you expected. I also promise that your life will be far better when you commit to changing yourself.

This is a different type of prescription (or guide) in so many different ways. But you can't swallow the material and expect the medicine to work on its own. There is a reality for all of us. If we want more, we are going to have to become someone better, someone different. That requires that you work on yourself. That demands you make some changes to yourself. That requires that you take steps that you have not so far done. There are significant benefits. The rewards go to you, not to someone else. The world's current problems cannot prevent you from implementing your personal changes. All of those obstacles cannot prevent you from our goals. With any new endeavor, there will be naysayers. Ignore them, just as I ignored my parents and many of my friends when I took off a year to write a novel in my 20s. So what if you crash and burn? In reality, we all crash and *learn*, not just crash and burn. So, become independent of the good (and not-so-good) opinion of others. Focus on yourself, so that you can have a better chance at living, loving, and making a difference.

Remember the saying that there are a thousand excuses for any failure, but never a good reason. There is no reason for not learning and mastering this material. There is no reason for not achieving a wonderful life in your later years. Abraham Lincoln once remarked that if he had eight hours to chop down a tree, he would spend the first six hours sharpening the saw. Well, this book, and its suggestions, is akin to the sharpening of your saw. It will allow you to create new skills to lead you in the right direction. If incorporated, the habits will not only give you a new future; they will make you a better person. They will steer you away from a narrow focus on external success toward an inner focus on things of value. They will lead you toward more meaningful experiences with a chance for a much improved legacy. Your best days are ahead of you. Let's take this opportunity and make a difference. If I can close this preface with a prediction, I will return to my core belief. The material in this book will not be a bitter pill; it will be something you can enjoy. If I have completed my part and successfully presented the wisdom of my elders (with some new insights), my suggestions should be educational and transformative. There is wisdom to be embraced. There is hope to be reignited. A commitment to improve yourself, to become a different type of person, is the starting point for these changes. And don't worry. You will not be alone on this journey. There are many of us taking the same path.

And one final point. Just because I am asking you to make some changes to yourself, that does not mean that you are an inadequate person. Everything you need already lies within you, just outside of your awareness. Your current stress? Your current problems? They are just telling you that it is time to move in a new, different direction. As you transform toward self-improvement, remember that self-acceptance is one of other starting points. In fact, there is a saying that no amount of self-improvement can make up for any lack of self-acceptance. So, what am I suggesting?

I want to help you change, yes. But I do not want you to down-grade or rebuke yourself. I want you to accept the old you; yet, be ready to change and embrace the new you. Don't lose sight of both features of self-acceptance and self-improvement. These components are both crucial to your transformation.

Chapter 9

Sorry, Compliance Is Critical

"Life is 50% what you make it and 50% how you take it."
Oprah Winfrey

Many studies show that the majority of people are not fully compliant with their prescriptions. So, are you one of those people who typically do not ingest all the pills in the bottle? Do you take the medicine for a few days until you feel a little better, and then set aside the remaining pills, buried deep in the medicine cabinet? And has that approach worked for you? My guide, as explained, will not ask much of you, but any prescription does not work if it is discontinued prematurely. My suggestions are not dissimilar. Each new habit will vary in its spectrum and importance, but any new habit needs time to be digested and incorporated. Most habits require at least four weeks to be ingrained in your daily behaviors. Some habits may require more time, depending on the prior habits they replace. So, I have a simple request. Maintain compliance until each new habit becomes automatic. Complete the medicine. Don't stop the prescription or this guide.

When I was in medical school I rotated through the emergency room. There was a patient who had a nickname "Mr. Noncompliant." Initially, he presented with a sore throat. He received a ten-day course of antibiotics, which he stopped on his fourth day because he felt a little better. However, the infection in his throat progressed into his chest. He returned within two weeks with a diagnosis of bronchitis and received another ten-day course of a different antibiotic. Once again, he stopped the pills by the fifth day of treatment because he felt better. A week later he was back in the emergency room, receiving a diagnosis of pneumonia with strict orders to take the full prescription of a new antibiotic. Again, he stopped the pills, apparently around the sixth day. When he returned for the fourth time, guess who he saw for his medical workup? Me. By the time I had finished all the tests, he had progressed from an initial diagnosis of pneumonia to a series of diagnoses, including polycythemia, ketoacidosis, and kidney failure. So, did I prescribe another new antibiotic? Nope. I sent him, and he was not very happy, directly to the medical intensive care unit. He never made it back. Sadly, it could have been avoided if he had simply been compliant with the treatment recommendations.

Compliance with habits is actually far more important than compliance for most medications. You may recall that in the early days of America's astronaut program, NASA designed an experiment to test the physiological response of spatial disorientation, a condition that was expected to occur in space. Each astronaut was required to wear, day and night (even while sleeping), a set of convex goggles that flipped their world upside down. When they stared through the goggles, the floor became the ceiling and the ceiling became the floor. It was a difficult transition, causing marked changes in blood pressure, pulse, etc. However, something unexpected happened during the experiment. Around day 26-30, the astronaut's world, while still wearing the goggles, flipped right side up. Their brain adapted, correcting the disorientation. But there was a critical requirement. The astronauts had to wear the goggles every day and night for that change to occur. If they skipped a single day at any point in this convex goggle experiment, they were back to the starting point, day one; and they had to wait another 26-30 days for the brain's adaption. Well, habits are similar. You need to work on them every single day. But if you make that daily effort, there will come a point around the end of a month when the habit becomes ingrained, no longer requiring any effort. At that point your own world will have flipped for the better.

There's another challenge with habits. Some people are dabblers. Others are obsessive. A dabbler jumps from one enterprise to another, never completing the various projects. An obsessive focuses all of his or her energy onto one project, often to the point of mental exhaustion. I do not want you to jump from this program to another pursuit, nor do I want you to crash and burn from your initial intensity. Instead, I want you to read at a relaxed and thoughtful pace. I want you to learn at your own speed. There are no tests. There is no time limit. Most importantly, as you learn the new habits, I want you to learn to love the plateau. If you are ever going to change, you have to love the plateau. People do not change in a straight linear upward progression. They change a little, and then plateau; they change some more, and then plateau; and then they change a bit further, and then once again plateau. Some people, at times, even briefly regress. Remember: this nonlinear pattern is part of the learning curve. Be patient with yourself. Don't expect old behaviors to disappear overnight. Likewise, don't expect to incorporate these changes and these core habits in one upswing. Expect an upward step and then a plateau. Expect another upward step and then another plateau. Embrace not just the results. Embrace the process of change.

I want to offer another disclaimer. Don't expect fireworks on the first few pages or the first few chapters. The different changes and the different habits are not of equal value. I want you to start small and build a path toward a better future. It is what worked for me. It is what will work for you. If you struggle or falter (for a bit) with a specific component or habit, keep moving forward. Think of Oprah's observation. Yes, we are trying to make your life dramatically better. But how you handle the setbacks and the plateaus will make an enormous difference to your overall progress. So, maintain the daily effort. How do you keep going? Just don't stop reading. Don't stop trying. Keep adding each group of new habits to the prior habits. Climb your ladder. Step by step. Rung by rung. Keep progressing upward to your destination, even if you have to pause to catch your breath. Compliance and persistence (through those plateaus) are your allies. When you reach your destination, your life and your family's life will be far better and far richer (in all the right ways) than you ever imagined.

Chapter 10

Our Partnership for a Better Life

*"Our life does not get better by chance;
it gets better by change."*
Jim Rohn

There are many books that offer a specific list of habits or steps toward some personal transformation: *The 7 Habits of Highly Effective People. The 12 Steps To Happiness. The 7 Spiritual Laws of Success. The 5 Habits for Health Transformation.* The list of these types of books is endless. In this book, I organized nine steps. But I did not highlight the number in the book's title. Why? As a physician, you learn that one standard treatment plan does not work for each patient. A treatment plan has to be individualized to best suit the needs of each person. So, I am going to present a spectrum of nine steps for your consideration, expecting you to select (and prioritize) your own desired habits. Yes, I want *you* to write your own prescription (your own guide) to fit your own needs, not someone else's needs. It's my responsibility to provide you with the sufficient options so that you can rearrange your life and progress toward our specific goals. But the path is yours; and it should be designed by you, not by anyone else.

To help you with this task, I have orchestrated this survivor kit in a particular format. The steps will cover the general areas of your life. Within each step there will be multiple chapters offering various habits, or offering explanations for the habits. On the first page of each chapter, there will be an opening paragraph that provides a snapshot of the topic. I encourage you to peruse each of those paragraphs. Is the subject of interest to you? Does it address any area of your life that may need improvement? If the answer is yes, then you should study that chapter, assessing your need to incorporate the habit. If the answer is no, then you can simply peruse that chapter and move to the next chapter, repeating the same process. From my physician perspective, the chapters are like pieces of a puzzle. They need to be set aside and then merged into a meaningful collection to maximize your new skills and your new path. When you reassemble all of the habits, you will have changed yourself and your life. This progression will go far beyond the initial steps or the first several habits; it will cover the key areas for your golden years, hopefully offering a shift toward new goals.

I want to highlight several other unique features. As stated, I want you to ask the right questions. What steps reflect the topics that resonate the most with you? What chapters address issues that may be valuable for you? Yes, I want you to take the lead and incorporate the habits that seem most useful. But I would not shortchange yourself by failing to explore the full spectrum of potential habits. You should be aware that some habits may not resonate with you today, but they may pique your interest tomorrow (after you have reviewed more chapters). I recommend using this book as a resource, which should be reviewed at different times, reclarifying your need for any additional habits.

As your coach, working to establish the proper fundamentals, I would encourage you to scan the steps and chapters in the order that works best for you. What order will work best? Who knows? But what counts the most is not the order of the habits; it's how you prioritize, incorporate, and implement the habits that match your needs.

Let me close this chapter by repeating several points. The golden years don't just happen. Yes, they arrive of their accord sooner than most of us would want. And for some people, these years are not golden at all. But, if you are going to maximize your happiness in your older years, you need to rise to the challenge of changing yourself to meet your needs. There is a saying in the military that when a challenge confronts a soldier, the soldier doesn't rise to the challenge, the soldier sinks to the level of training. In my opinion, in your older years, you will rise or fall to the level of your new habits. Without these new habits, I do not think you will truly live, love, and make a difference. Without some revision to your old habits, I am worried that you will continue to struggle, possibly spiraling downward like my chest cold patient in the emergency room. That type of end is not so pretty. So, please, examine the steps and chapter headings. If your challenge is not the first habit, maybe it will be the second or third habit. Just keeping asking: What area of your life, excluding your finances, needs the most change? And when that area of your life changes, what other areas might also need to be addressed? After all, difficulties in one area often lead to problems in other areas.

So, prioritize your new habits with care and select them to fit the image of who you want to become. For your entire life, people have been telling you who to be and what to do. Now is your chance to short-circuit that process. Now is the time to write your own program. Now is the time to create your own changes. Now is the time to find and release the real you, the person with the best chance of meeting your needs. Aging does not have to be a negative; it can be transforming and uplifting. It can lead to an exciting journey with personal growth and personal fulfillment. As Picasso said, "It takes a long time to become young." With the right habits, and the right changes, your older years can be a time for a rebirth of the real (authentic) you and a life that truly reflects you, not someone else. If you can maintain our partnership, your life, as you grow older, will not be an arc that rises to a certain level and then plummets to a deep valley. Instead, as some experts have proclaimed, and as many older people have already realized, life can be like a ladder, lifting you and those loved ones around you higher and higher. With your own individualized program of new habits, and your own personal and family changes, you will be ready to live, love, and make a difference. Who knows? You might even be ready for that bucket list.

STEP 2

Reclaiming Your Physical Health

"First, you must last."
Earnest Hemingway

Chapter 11

Your Physical Health Challenge

"By any number of measures, America's health is failing."
T. Colin Campbell, PhD

There's no sense denying the truth. It will be a struggle to reach our goals without reasonable health. So, as your foundation, you will need to improve your physical health and develop the necessary habits for maintaining your physical health. Unfortunately, there are some challenges. If you live in the United States, and if you believe the American health system is the best in the world,

63

you are mistaken. The World Health Organization recently ranked the US health care system as the thirty-seventh best in the world and the worst of any industrial country. That global ranking placed our national health care system on par with Serbia's. That global ranking placed our national health care system behind that of Columbia, Chile, and Costa Rica, but ahead of Slovenia's, Cuba's, and Croatia's. From my perspective, the ranking of our health care system is a national embarrassment and a challenge for each of us.

The broader health care statistics get worse, not better. By any health outcome, infant mortality, rates of chronic illnesses, or longevity, America ranks near the bottom of developed countries. We pay far more per capita for our health care than any industrial nation. Much of our total health bill, around 75-80 percent, is spent on the chronic illnesses that could have been prevented. Who said more equals better? Forget our national pride. Discount what politicians like to tell you. The war on cancer, launched in the 1970s, has done little to reduce our risk for cancer. Our cancer rates are among the highest in the world. If you are male, you have a lifetime cancer risk in the 40 percent range; and if you are female, you have a lifetime cancer risk in the 30 percent range. Those cancer risks are not stacked in your favor; and they do not get lower with age. Our health care system offers one new drug after another, but people are developing cancer at higher rates, not lower rates. If you develop cancer, do not have the delusional belief that our health care treatments will come to your rescue. Some cancers are cured by expensive radiation, chemotherapy, and/or surgery. Unfortunately, even with insurance, many people cannot afford those expensive treatments.

The risks for the other major medical illnesses do not get any better. In the United States, the leading cause of death is heart disease, killing one out of three Americans. Cancer is the second leading cause of death. The third leading cause of death? Prepare for the worst. If you count physician errors, medication errors, and adverse reactions from drugs or surgery, our health care system is our third leading cause of death. Why is that so important to acknowledge? Because a majority of Americans take at least one prescription drug every week. Does that include you? Let me share my mother's health situation. She takes three medications every day. One of the medications is for her high blood pressure; one medication is for her low thyroid; and another medication is for her irritable bladder. When I speak to her in the morning, she feels great. But by noon, after she has taken the medications, she feels markedly worse. She has a strange heaviness in her head; she is often dizzy; and she feels excessive fatigue. Worse, she often has to tolerate the progressive development of blurred vision. My opinion? I think her three medications are making her worse, not better. I think the side effects from those three medications are more problematic than her initial symptoms. Will she stop taking her current collection of pills? Well, I am helping her toward that goal.

Does any of the above sound familiar? If yes, I am not recommending that you immediately stop your medication. But I strongly believe that a drug-free life in your older years is realistic, reasonable, and often necessary. To move toward this goal, I am trying to encourage you to take more control of your physical health. Do you know what happens to some hospitalized patients? They are placed in a drug-free observation period. Do you know what? A number of those patients get better without their group of daily medications, even if they have been taking those medications for decades. The positive effects of those medications are often buried beneath the side effects. So, if you can start to improve your physical health through the upcoming habits, your dependence on medications will decrease. All those side effects can be eliminated. Improving your physical health, not just staying alive, should become an initial step. Without good physical health, are you going to have the energy to redesign your life? Not likely. So, from my perspective, a renewed focus on improving your physical health and slowly reducing your medications should be your first area for new habits.

Let me be especially clear. A renewed focus on your physical health does not mean more dependence on your physician or more dependence on our broken health care system. I want you to see your doctor less, not more. I want you to take fewer pills, not more pills. American physicians, compared to the general public, have higher rates of heart disease, chronic illnesses, and addictions, plus a shorter life span. Physicians do not excel at promoting health, not yours and not their own. They have been trained to diagnose and treat disease, not prevent disease. What's the real problem? Physicians focus on the disease, not on the underlying causes. At this point, as you head into your older years, aim for some fundamental health goals. Work to reverse any current disease and yes, it can be done through the right habits. Take the necessary steps (and establish the healthy habits) to prevent additional diseases, especially heart disease, cancer, and the chronic diseases. That too can be done. With this book, learn to identify the causes of these diseases and then start to initiate the habits to prevent (or reverse) those causes. And the rewards? Fewer doctor visits. Fewer medications. And an improved sense of well being with more energy for changing the direction of your life. That translates (and I know I am repetitive) to a far better life.

Chapter 12

Barriers to Your Physical Health

"Our medical technology is our greatest single asset? It is not."
Andrew Weil, MD

I need to offer a disclaimer. I have never been involved in scientific research on heart disease or cancer. Everything I have learned has come from my reading of the literature and my experience with patients. Nevertheless, I am confident in my level of knowledge. I am also confident that your grasp of what is best for your health and how to achieve your optimum health is significantly distorted. It is not your fault. You are bombarded with too many conflicting messages, from best selling diet books to new products for improved health. At the same time, you are bombarded with advertisements, trying to encourage you to eat whatever they are selling. Those commercials must be working. Two thirds of Americans are overweight and one third are obese. Over one hundred million Americans have high cholesterol. All of these conditions are linked to heart disease and cancer. Even if your physician is telling you that you are just fine, I would remain skeptical. There are too many forces in our country working against you.

If you are not healthy, to whom can you turn? I am sorry to advise you not to place much faith in our medical research societies. Too many of our health studies are funded by organizations that are focused on their profit margin, not your health. The pharmaceutical companies are notorious for advancing those studies that support their drugs. The food companies are equally bad. In my opinion, the National Dairy Council, the American Meat Institute, and the Dairy Management Inc. corrupt the scientific studies on food and health. In my opinion, the Food and Nutrition Board, the Institute of Medicine, and even the American Institute for Cancer Research too often support health recommendations that provide profits for meat and dairy companies. You got milk? What about the scientific fact that one of milk's key proteins, casein, has been linked to cancer and cardiovascular disease? Or what about the fact that numerous dairy products have been linked to diabetes, prostrate cancer, osteoporosis, multiple sclerosis, and autoimmune diseases? Do these negative medical health reports reach the general public? Not often enough. The meat and dairy industries make certain that those types of causes remain unreported. Is America's health care system educating us? No. Most people remain grossly misinformed.

In fact, where do you think is the absolute worst place to receive accurate medical research information? How about the tabloids when you check out at the grocery store? Nope. The worst place for accurate, reliable medical research information is television's evening news. As I was writing this program, I spent several months watching the evening news on television. On one night there was a news flash that everyone should now be tested for hepatitis. There were just too many undetected and untreated cases. In the next news segment they announced this brand new drug, ready to be released, for the treatment of hepatitis. Did anyone miss the clear link between the station's promotion of the new drug after their hype for more testing? It gets worse. Watch the commercials for the evening news. It's one pharmaceutical commercial after another, advertising and promoting one medication after another. And the costs of those new medications? A pill that used to cost a couple of pennies now costs you a couple of dollars. Is the new pill that much better? Only in the carefully selected studies that they decide to release. In my opinion, no. And do you think that all of that advertising income does not unfairly slant the message or impact the medical portions of the news?

In my opinion, you also cannot rely on the benevolence of your health insurance company or your hospital. Do you know the high salaries of the top executives of your health insurance company or your hospital? The CEO of a health insurance company and the CEO of a hospital do not receive multimillion dollar salaries simply for providing excellent, high quality health care. The CEO receives an enormous salary for creating profits. How do you obtain high profits for a health insurance company? By increasing premiums while denying, or at least reducing, access to health services. How do you reap high profits for a hospital? By charging incomprehensible costs for health services. And our health care product companies are not any better. They can produce a medical devise or a medical treatment for three hundred dollars and sell it for three thousand dollars. So, if you are not wealthy, you will have challenges in accessing health care and paying for health care, just when you will have more risk for illnesses. For many people, this stress is worse than the disease and it will drain you of the necessary energy for redesigning your life. So, be aware of these barriers to your health and take a new approach to bypass these barriers. Part of that approach includes a habit of self-education with better understanding of the limits of our health care (or disease care) system. Part of that approach also includes incorporating the upcoming habits for preventing and even reversing many of our prevalent major illnesses. Again, do not rely on medical organizations, research studies, insurance companies, hospitals, or heath care product companies. Instead, rely on yourself, your self-education, and the development of some new healthy habits.

Do you know what I, as a physician, do? I don't see doctors unless absolutely necessary. I don't even have a primary care physician. On my last visit to a primary care physician, almost twenty years ago, I was scheduled for a routine physical checkup. My doctor thought he might have heard a slight mitral valve murmur. Mind you, I had no symptoms. Nevertheless, I received a full medical workup, including an EKG, a stress test, and an echocardiogram. By the time my routine physical exam was finished, I had visited the physician's office three times and spent $1,500 of my health insurance company's money. Yes, the medical technology was excellent, but those additional tests were still absurd. Here is the best part. I was pronounced fine with no medical diagnosis, which is what I would have predicted without spending a cent. So, here is my own plan. I try to educate myself on the causes for poor health; I try to take a preventive approach to avoid the major illnesses; and I try to steer clear of any physician's office. Is our national health care bill rising? The politicians can't blame me. How about you? Do you want to help yourself and the economy of our country? Start learning about the barriers to good health. Start incorporating the right health habits. Learn to take better care of yourself.

Chapter 13

Have You Seen Our Livestock?

"People are not aware of what happens to animals before they get to the plate."
Nicolette Hahn Niman

Have you ever thought about the typical breakfast served at so many restaurants? Let's just order scrambled eggs with some sausage. The hen was most likely stuffed in a cage with no room to move, not even able to flap its wings. Its beak was likely sheared so it could not peck another hen. After a year of constantly laying egg after egg, it was undoubtedly malnourished and sick before it was carted down to another cage where it was slaughtered for potpies, soup stock, or perhaps your frozen dinner. What about the sausage? The pig's life wasn't any better. It's not unusual for 1,000-2,000 pigs to be housed in a single building. Around 20 hogs can be crammed inside an area the size of your bedroom. Day after day, they stand on a hard concrete surface, not mud or hay, producing massive amounts of feces. Some of the feces, thank God, fall through slats. But don't fret. Some of the feces is collected and recycled for other food-chain purposes. It adds to their agricultural profit, right?

Did anyone at the restaurant table order some milk? Tell me, have you ever pictured the life of the cow that produced your milk? A Holstein cow is separated from its babies, confined without exercise, hooked up to a pumping machine, and milked to its production limit. In its three-to-four-year agricultural lifespan (its normal life span should be closer to 20 years), it develops a host of illnesses, including open abrasions, crippled feet, calcium depletion, and infected udders. When it has reached the end of its torturous life of forced milk production, guess what happens? Voilà. It becomes your hamburger, with all its own hidden ingredients. Prefer chicken for lunch? For most of its life span of seven weeks, the chicken was probably squeezed into less than one square foot of living space, confined with 20,000-30,000 other chickens in the same poultry prison. It too stood in its own waste, often referred to as 'cake' or 'poultry litter.' And this waste? You can relax. Again, nothing is lost in the pursuit of agricultural profit. The chicken waste becomes part of some cattle food supplements. Tasty for the cattle and healthy for the consumer, yes?

Now, do you have a clearer snapshot of our livestock? Not yet. Did you know that 80 percent of all antibiotics are used in agriculture? No, the antibiotics are not prescribed from a veterinarian for a sick animal. The antibiotics are prescribed to all the caged animals to promote weight gain and, yes, increase profits. In many parts of the world (and that includes over 50 countries), the use of antibiotics is banned as a growth promoter. Not in America. That would require our government to change its policy and break its alliance with the meat and dairy industries. As stated, that is not likely to happen within either party. In fact, our government already subsidizes a good part of the meat and dairy industries. So, how have those industries changed? At this point, it is estimated that just two percent of our life stock facilities produce 40 percent of our farm animals. We have gone from small local farms to massive livestock complexes. When I was a child, my mother used to drive to the small, local dairy farm every Sunday to pick up our dairy products, including those containers of eggs. I loved those trips. There were chicken darting around the yard and cattle roaming across the grass. Not today. In our lifetime we have lost five million farms and over ten million farmers. Today our country has twice as many prisoners as farmers.

Do you know those commercials where they portray several cattle grazing on a scenic hillside? The commercials where they highlight happy California cows? The commercials were filmed in New Zealand. California's cattle industry is located in the San Joaquin Valley, which is hot and dry. You'd be more accurate if you pictured 100,000 cattle in a single industrial parking lot. Forget the grass grazing. Many cattle never eat a single blade of grass. Instead, imagine them eating (or being forced to eat) hydrolyzed poultry feathers, by products of slaughtered animals, interspecies waste, cement dust, newspaper, and plastic roughage replacement mixed into various types of grain. And cattle are grass eaters, not grain eaters. So, what is the point of this snap-shot? Be aware that our animals are growing fatter; we are grow-ing fatter; and the meat and dairy companies are growing fatter (with their profits). Of course, the animals are sicker and we are sicker. Their lifestyles are worse; and our lifestyles are worse. I am not speaking about a few select animals. Do you know how many animals we kill each year to feed our appetite for meat and dairy products? Ten billion. That's right. We slaughter ten bil-lion animals each year for our food. We kill a million animals per hour. So, see what you are up against? Massive agricultural com-plexes, financially supported by our government, are dramati-cally reducing the quality of our meat and dairy products. So, understand why our risk factors for certain diseases have risen so quickly during our lifetime. And then educate yourself on all of these causes for our declining national health statistics.

In every state, we have laws against animal cruelty. Sounds fair, yes? But do you know which animals are exempt? In each state, the government legislatures, with a financial squeeze from the agricultural lobbyists, have decided to exclude any animals that are destined for human consumption. In other words, these agri-cultural businesses do not incur legal or financial repercussions for cutting off the beaks of hens, stuffing chickens into tight cages, forcing hogs to stand a lifetime on their waste, milking cows until their udders are noodles, or caging cattle in packed stalls. If you or I ever did any of those acts to our household pets, we would be incarcerated for life. Murder? A few months of prison. But cruelty to our pets? Probably a lifetime. But the agricultural companies? They are rewarded with profit. How do you think that reflects on our species? Let me share one random conjecture. If you were an alien, hovering above our planet and observing how we treated each other and our animals, would you stop for a visit? My own suspicion? I think that any alien with enough intelligence to reach our planet would take one glance at us, head back out into space, and not return until humans had improved as a species with more respect for what they eat, greater care of the other species, and a deeper respect for each other. Have any aliens returned? I rest my case.

Chapter 14

Do You Know Agricultural History?

"We don't need cheap food, we need higher wages."
Raj Patel

Do you know the health risks from even the well-treated live-stock? In World War II, Germans occupied numerous countries, always confiscating their livestock. The supply of cattle, sheep, goats, pigs, turkeys, and chickens abruptly disappeared for the local populace. Did their health suffer? Just the opposite. In the occupied countries, despite the stress of the war, the number of deaths from heart attack or stroke dropped. Without their animal food and dairy products, the people grew healthier. And when the war ended and their farms were replenished with livestock, guess what happened in these countries. Their prior rate of heart disease, heart attacks, and strokes returned to their higher levels. So, if you want to keep your imaginary vision of livestock enjoying life on the range, at least accept the medical reality that these animals cause disease and death. Don't forget that it's far worse today because of all of the contaminants.

Realize that the medical risk applies to each of us. Studies of young American veterans, as early as the Vietnam era, have revealed that 80 percent of soldiers have evidence of coronary artery disease. A study of young women, who died from accidents or suicide or homicide, produced similar findings. Facts are facts. If you are born and raised in the United States, by the time you graduate from high school or college, you may have an enriched mind, but you have a diseased body that has already been primed for multiple illnesses. The causes for these diseases have been neglected. Take something as simple and common as regular milk. A cow's milk is great for a calf, but the calf has four stomachs and gains 200 pounds in the first year. Do you? Hopefully not. But with our current intake of meat and dairy products, your coronary arteries are clogged. Your blood pressure is high. You have cholesterol plaques throughout your vascular system. Yes, your body will fight off these conditions for as long as it can (perhaps, if you are lucky, for three to four decades), but the odds are against you, especially as you progress toward your older years. Don't underestimate the destructiveness of our current national diet; and don't underestimate your need to do something about it.

Is there a reason why our government offers subsidies that promote these meat and dairy factories? After World War II, there was a food shortage, especially in Europe. Our government enacted policies (and created subsidies) for the creation of more meat and dairy products, and at a lower cost. With those subsidies, our country's agricultural industry changed. We transformed ourselves from a country where the average farm had twenty cows to an industrial agricultural industry where each site had an average of ten thousand cows. The result was a massive increase in the production of meat and dairy products, coupled with a lower cost for meat and dairy products. A success? Back then, yes. With starving populations in parts of the world, the policy seemed reasonable and logical. But in those days, we did not have today's awareness of the negative health consequences of the meat and dairy products. In those days, America was providing more and more of these foods, but we did not yet know how we were making our population less and less healthy.

Unfortunately, that short-term solution for the World War II food crises became a long-term problem for our population. Close to 99 percent of our agricultural subsidies still go to unhealthy foods. The industrial agricultural companies, primed for growth with these subsidies, have progressively expanded. They have packed the animals into tighter, cheaper quarters; they have added horrific ingredients to the animal feed (like steroids and antibiotics); and their meat and dairy production rates have risen to new heights. That makes the government content, and it certainly makes these food companies financially content. Was there any benefit to the public? Just a superficial benefit. The price of meat and dairy products remain reasonably low. In America, most of us spend around 5.5 percent of disposable income on food. In Germany, it's 11.4 percent; in France, it's 13.6 percent; in Italy, it's 14.4 percent; in South Africa, it's

20.1 percent; and in Mexico, it's 24.1 percent. The figures rise higher in some African countries. But guess what? We pay for our reduced cost of the meat and dairy foods through our taxes. Worse, we pay for the reduced cost of the meat and dairy foods with increased physical illnesses and increased health care costs. So, what is my underlying message? Yes, it is a bit repetitive. But it bears repeating. Take control of your health. Learn which agricultural companies work for your health and which ones work against your health. Learn what foods impair your health and what foods promote your health. If necessary, be ready to spend a little more money on what you eat. And the next time you have a chance to vote on anything related to food production? Vote for higher wages, not cheaper foods. Vote for the smaller farms, not for the huge agricultural conglomerates. The extra pennies spent on the healthy foods just might save your life and a small farmer's livelihood. More importantly, the extra money will improve your level of health so you can focus on improving the other areas of your life. For living and loving, you need vitality. With improved health, you have a far better chance!

Chapter 15

Genetically Modified Organisms?

"Our seed supply is the little unit from which we all come."
Elizabeth Kucinich

There are food companies around the world promising us genetically engineered crops that would grow in drought conditions or saline soils while providing superior nutrition and medicinal benefits. The companies have offered a rosy, almost science-fiction picture of resistant crops with increasing yields, claiming that the food industry will finally be able to feed the entire world. Starvation? Gone. Fear of the consequences of climate change? Gone. Unfortunately, it has been science fiction, pure fantasy. In truth, reality has been difficult to analyze. Scientists have been denied access to the results of genetic engineering. Specifically, scientists have been prevented from studying the genetically modified organisms within the crops. When scientists have persevered and presented unsettling findings of their research, they have been fired, threatened, stripped of funding, and even denied tenure. Why the intensity of these attacks? Why have the companies wanted these scientists silenced? Because their research on genetic engineering has revealed disastrous consequences for livestock and humans.

Let's try to make this issue simple through one hypothetical example. Imagine a company genetically modifies a crop. Imagine the genetic modification allows each cell to release (from its new snippet of DNA) an insecticide. Therefore, when any part of the crop is ingested by an insect, its new defense mechanism is activated in the insect's stomach, releasing toxins and killing the insect. Imagine how this genetic modification protects the growth of this crop. Now imagine how this same company proclaims that the genetically modified crop releases its toxins only in insects, not in the stomachs of any other animals. Imagine how this company is hiding the truth. Imagine how the genetically modified crop actually releases its insecticide poison in the stomach of every animal. Imagine how the released toxins damage the stomachs of every living animal, creating microscopic holes in the intestinal cells and allowing leakage of the toxins to spread through the body, disrupting multiple systems with progressive insult to the multiple organs. Can you imagine the consequences that might develop from an animal's ingestion of a genetically modified crop, or from a human's consumption of an animal that was forced to consume the genetically modified crops?

Now pause for a moment. Can you see the Achilles heal for a genetically modified crop? It's the time period between the planting of the seed and a reasonable growth of the crop. Growth to the point where the crop is sufficiently mature so that its cells are ready to release (whenever ingested) its own insecticide. Until the crop reaches that point, it needs protection against insects and other pests. So what's the cost-effective action for a genetic engineering company? It soaks that ground with the strongest pesticides, making certain that no pest gets to the crop before the crop can protect itself. Good planning, yes. But the result? That genetically engineered crop not only produces insecticides; it is practically soaked in pesticides from its early growth. Pity the bug that takes a bite. Or the animals that later eat its grain. Or the human who eats the animal. Those initial pesticides? They have become strong, really strong. Remember Agent Orange from the Vietnam War? They actually use pesticides that are almost as strong as Agent Orange. Now, if the pesticide doesn't kill the bug (or animal), then the engineered insecticide will finish the task. In the end the genetic engineering company produces a crop that is more chemical than food. But, if you haven't noticed, look up our largest, genetic engineering companies. They are not food companies. They are chemical companies, which now produce food. Or more accurately, they produce grains soaked with pesticides, grains able to produce their own insecticides.

There have been studies that have disclosed the consequences of genetically engineered crops. Animals, ingesting these genetically engineered grains, have shown gastrointestinal problems, reproductive disorders, immune system problems, organ damage, and accelerated aging. Other studies have documented cancer, endocrine disruption, abnormal sperm, and birth defects. Even in healthier animals (animals that have eaten genetically engineered crops but have not yet shown overt disease), there is a reduction in digestive hormones, an increased time to break down proteins, and less nutrient absorption, leaving the animal nutrient deficient. What about us? Studies have confirmed that the majority of humans already have GMOs in their blood stream. Since the development of GMOs and the production of genetically engineered crops, hasn't there been a dramatic increase in humans with food allergies, inflammatory bowel disease, and more chronic illnesses? Some experts even speculate that the GMOs may be a possible factor in the recent rise in autism and the other pervasive developmental disorders.

Be aware that 70 percent of our supermarkets and restaurants, without your knowledge, offer food items that are genetically engineered. Did you know that 90 percent of US corn and soy is genetically engineered? It is true that the great majority of our corn and soybean goes to our animals, but some of those crops still make it to our market. The largest company, Monsanto, has received over seven billion dollars in subsidies from our federal government, supported by you, the taxpayer. Monsanto has spread beyond America into other countries, progressively controlling our foreign food supply. India is a country of incredible agricultural diversity. They grow 200,000 varieties of rice, 4,500 types of eggplants. Monsanto controls 95 percent of their cotton. Unfortunately, as one company dominates an agricultural crop, the diversity within that crop declines. Imagine a company introducing a GMO into the crop in an agricultural community. Imagine that crop cross-pollinating with a neighboring crop. Guess who sues the neighbor? Guess who takes control of the neighboring crop? It's not the little farmer; it's the genetic engineering company. The result? The genetic engineering company gains a larger share of the market; and the public progressively receives more of the genetically engineered crop and fewer of the alternative crops, even when those alternative crops are more varied, better tasting, and healthier.

You should also be aware how the massive companies that produce genetically modified crops have resisted the attempts to require labeling of their foods. There are around 60 countries in the world that require labeling of genetically engineered food. Not our own country. Even though 93 percent of Americans want labeling to warn the public of foods with GMOs. Even though 53 percent of Americans assert they will not eat foods with GMOs. Even though there are phone applications that help the individual go GMO-free. Repeatedly, the federal and state governments have refused to require labeling of GMOs in our food. In fact, in 1997, the US Department of Agriculture tried to claim that genetic engineering should be called organic. That attempt failed. To this date, there have been a number of ballot initiatives for the appropriate labeling of GMOs in foods. But all of those ballot initiatives have failed. The big agricultural companies have spent too much money and secured too many politicians in their pocket. So, until we establish nationwide labeling of GMOs, do not believe what is written on any label. As with so many areas, if you are going to improve your physical health, it will have to come through your own self-awareness.

So, what do I do? When I was younger, I used to love corn on the cob. Add butter and a little salt and I was more than satisfied. Not any more. Not after my research. There are no accurate labels in the market at this time. Whenever you purchase corn and many of our other crops, you cannot be certain that the corn or other crops are not contaminated with GMOs. So, what do I do? I just do not eat any corn. For home, we don't buy it.

At restaurants, I push it aside. Yes, I am depriving myself of something that I enjoy eating. But do I want to contaminate my body with insecticides and pesticides? Do I want to damage my intestinal lining and some of my organs? It is just not worth the risk. So, at this point, I am waiting for accurate labeling for all GMOs. I am trying my best to avoid eating any genetically engineered crops. But here's the bad part. Every time I consume a dairy or meat product, I am probably still ingesting a GMO. If the GMO crop were fed to the animal, then it was fed to me. The GMO just works its way up the food chain to me. And to you. So, it comes back to the original question. What do you really want? Cheap, contaminated food? Or more expensive, clean, healthy food?

Chapter 16

The Food We Eat – It's Killing Us

"I just want to eat a little bit cleaner."
Kathy Freston

Clearly, the food we eat today is not the same food eaten by our grandparents. Imagine yourself, once again, in the board meeting of an agricultural company. What do you think are the executives' primary concerns? How can they keep the animals from getting sick? How can they ensure that their products are nutritious and contaminant free? Or how can they produce the most grain for the dollar? Or how can they make the animals as big and profitable as possible? America's beef and chicken have been fortified with steroids, supplements, and antibiotics; and our food sources has been contaminated by crop pesticides, industrial synthetic chemicals, GMOs, and a host of other pollutants to increase their profits. Our meat and dairy products are a major problem, but not our only problem. Much of our food has been processed, leaving us with more unhealthy components. Today, we eat more calories (62 percent) from refined food; we eat more meat and dairy products; and we ingest more calories than any time in our country's history. Our food is killing us.

Let us assume you have been eating eggs and bacon for breakfast and hamburgers and steaks for dinner. Let us assume you are free of disease as you approach your older years. Do you think you can maintain the same eating style? Sorry, but the correct answer is no. We produce cancer cells within our body every day of our life. Our body repairs itself as those cancer cells are identified, neutralized, and discarded. Think about the following facts. Your stomach cells replace themselves every five days. Your skin cells replace themselves every month. Your DNA replaces itself every six weeks. Most of your skeleton replaces itself every three months. Your brain cells replace themselves each year. Overall, 98 percent of your cells are replaced every year. Now, I do not want to inundate you with the multiple theories of aging from the DNA theory to the free radical theory to the inflammation theory to the mitochondrial theory? No. But it should be understood that your body's cumulative mistakes increase with age while your body's ability to repair those mistakes decreases with age. So, to counter your increasing risk of disease as you age, change your eating style to better prevent (and better repair) the deterioration within your cells (and within your DNA).

There's one more educational fact to consider for your health. More and more studies demonstrate that the health of your intestines plays a crucial role in your overall physical health. Do yourself a favor: take a look at some of the Internet sites (or books) that address this topic. Recent studies reveal that one of the key factors that determine the quality of your physical health is the state of your healthy bacteria in your intestines. If you have healthy bacteria in your intestines, your body is better able to produce what's necessary for your immune system and your overall physical health. If you do not have healthy bacteria in your intestines, your body is less able to produce what's necessary for adequate physical health. Do you know which foods promote healthy bacteria in your intestines? Do you know which foods interfere with those healthy bacteria? Do you know what types of cooking help the healthy intestinal bacteria? Or what types of cooking hurt the healthy bacteria?

Are you aware of the anatomical features of our intestinal tract? Our digestive tract is not similar to that of carnivorous mammals. For those animals, once the ingested food is past the stomach, their digestive tract is relatively short and straight. Our digestive tract is much longer with different sections (small intestines and a colon) with numerous bends and pockets. Our stomach acid completely breaks down vegetables and fruit, but it does not completely break down meat. The undigested meat can be trapped in the bends and folds of our small intestines. The meat, stuck in those tight spots, can putrefy over a period of several days, causing toxicity and delaying elimination. The resulting toxins are dangerous on their own, but those toxins also decrease the digestive system's capacity to assimilate protective vitamins and minerals. With these factors, the digestion of meat increases certain health risks. Are you aware of those risks?

To make matters worse, as we grow older, our intestines begin to leak, allowing toxins to seep through the intestinal wall into our bodies. So, for good health, we need to safeguard ourselves with food choices that decrease, not increase, the risk of such toxins.

For your own self-preservation, I recommend that you make an attempt to educate yourself on these medical facts that doctors overlook. Remember: the average physician receives only two and a half hours of nutrition training in medical school. For your health, the responsibility falls to you. Is your doctor going to tell you that the quality of your food is directly related to the quality of its soil? Is your doctor going to warn you about the reduced nutrients in our soil and the damaging long-term effects from decreasing nutrients and minerals? Is your doctor going to educate you on harmful consequences from pesticides and insecticides? Or the disastrous effects of genetic engineering on both crops and the animals that eat those crops? Is your doctor going to explain the value of locally grown organic foods? I do not want to complicate my guide with too many facts. You do not need to obsess over every item that I have covered. That would be a brain overload. As your physician coach, I will simplify the suggestions. At the same time, you do not have the luxury to be ignorant of these health issues. It's your health, your life. The Internet is packed with educational sites that address all of these important health issues. Read a little. Educate yourself. That habit will be one of the (many) starting points for your physical health. If you can just "last," as Hemingway observed, then you can direct your life toward more meaningful areas. But one of the starting points is to realize that our chronic illnesses are food borne diseases. We need to eat cleaner and healthier. I have seen many patients, simply through changes in their eating styles, dramatically improve the quality of their health. If you still find yourself skeptical, why not give the new eating habits a chance for just two months. Then, after this trial, ask yourself: Are you feeling better? Do you have more energy? From my experience, and from my patients' experiences, the answer will be 'yes'!

Chapter 17

It's Time to Change Our Menu

"Change is not merely necessary for life – it is life."
Alvin Toffler

From my perspective, the great majority of the suggestions for this guide for your golden years are timeless. They would have worked 100 years ago; they should work 1,000 years from now. Their wisdom comes from the ages, not from me. The wisdom is valuable and historic. Science is a different animal. There is the tale of the older professor Albert Einstein. While teaching physics courses at Princeton, he was popular, but he was known to be forgetful. Before the final exams of some courses, he would post the previous year's final exam. One year he apparently posted the previous year's final test with all the correct answers; then he gave the exact same final test for the current year. One student, a bit timid, approached him at the end of the test, explaining the professor's mistake. Einstein responded by reminding the student that this year's questions might be the same as last year's questions, but the correct answers for this year were different from the correct answers for last year. That is science.

Many experts say that the scientific knowledge is doubling every few years. There will be health breakthroughs and new health treatments (traditional and alternative) during your older years. So, with this constantly changing information, what can you do to gain control of your physical health? Well, I can recommend a good starting point. I think we can return to some fundamental, healthy eating habits. These suggestions should work now; and they should work through your later years. I encourage you to incorporate these eating habits into your daily life. Like any habit, they will take some time to establish. You may feel a need to adjust slowly. That is fine. I recommend you give yourself several months to adopt my suggestions for a new eating style, meal-by-meal, bite by bite.

Americans ignore the fact that your best defense against heart disease, cancer, and the multitude of chronic illnesses is a healthy eating style. Most Americans forget that all of the major illnesses, including cancer, can be prevented (even reversed) with a healthy eating style. According to statistics, three-fourths of you reading these words right now will die from a late onset debilitating illness, which could have been prevented with a healthier eating style. With my eating suggestions, I think we can change that outcome. With a healthy eating style, I think we can prevent heart disease, cancer, and the chronic medical illnesses; and if we can prevent those illnesses, we can also save you from our third leading cause of death, those visits to our physicians and the subsequent mistakes made within our own disease care system.

When you listen to physicians and read health announcements, do they discuss the causes of heart disease, cancer, and the chronic illnesses? They often discuss the physical conditions (like obesity or high blood pressure or high cholesterol) that are associated with these conditions. They may even acknowledge that saturated fats in dairy products may contribute to some diseases (but, please note, the saturated fats are not our core problem). But do they directly address the basic causes for these illnesses? Do they address your eating style? Too often they focus only on testing, diagnosis, and treatment. Too often they avoid discussing the crucial, underlying causes that can be corrected. I will not avoid the central causes. I will not neglect my responsibility. But I warn you. You are not going to like what you read. As before, take it with an open mind. See if my points make sense to you. See if my suggestions for healthy, new eating habits just might work for you. I, of course, think they just might save your life.

Of equal importance, I am going to make it simple. Many physicians, if they said anything, would simply tell you to eat less. After all, we are eating 700 more calories per day than we did 20 years ago. Other physicians would tell you to reduce your daily intake of saturated fats. But when you stare at your plate, can you judge the amount of saturated or unsaturated fats? Many other physicians would direct you to reduce your sugar consumption. One hundred years ago the average American consumed

10 pounds of sugar annually. Today we consume around 150 pounds of sugar per year. Worse, it's processed sugar, not natural sugar. But, again, when you glance at your plate, can you determine the amount of sugar? Let's say you are eating a cheeseburger, fries and soda at your favorite fast food restaurant. There is sugar in the bun, the relish, the meat, the cheese, the batter for the fries, and the soda. In fact, your 20-ounce soda will contain around 15 teaspoons of sugar. The ketchup for the fries? It's loaded with high fructose corn syrup. Fructose equals sugar. Corn equals genetic engineered organisms. It might be tasty, but it is not healthy. And the sugar is not easy to count.

So what is my simple healthy eating style recommendation? I want you to notice the general portion of meat and dairy products with each of your meals. I want you to make certain that your animal product or dairy product is the smallest portion on your plate. Why? Because Americans' reliance on meat and dairy products is the underlying explanation for our increasing rates of heart disease, cancer, and the chronic illnesses. This is a scientific reality that will not change. There is too much epidemiologic data to misrepresent the truth. Animal-based protein, any protein that comes from something with a face or feet, is one of the leading causes of our major medical illnesses. We were taught that protein is good for us, right? It is, but only to a certain extent. Americans eat a diet that is around 26 percent animal-based protein. Any diet that contains 10 percent (or higher) of animal-based protein is, according to worldwide epidemiology studies, carcinogenic and disease promoting. How carcinogenic? In laboratory studies, cancer cells can be turned on or off with a diet of high animal protein or low animal protein. So the carcinogenic effect is immediate and powerful, and it needs to be controlled on an ongoing basis. For you, what does that mean? It means you need to reduce your intake of meat and dairy products, and reduce your amount of animal-based foods. Americans currently eat around 160 pounds of meat per year or about half of pound of meat per day. Don't count or weigh anything. Just make certain that the meat and dairy products are the smallest items on your plate. Simple enough?

Is there any easy explanation for the negative impact of meat and dairy products on your physical health? Actually, there are many explanations; but your eating style's impact on heart disease, cancer, and the chronic illnesses is complex. You have already read how our current livestock negatively impact our physical health. You have also read how the current production of meat and dairy products has deteriorated the quality of those foods, creating even more problems for your health. So, let's try to address the blood and guts of the issue. Actually, let's focus on your blood and your genes. Imagine your body as a V-6 engine of a car of your choice. A healthy eating style fills your gas tank with top line gasoline; and the engine runs smoothly with that gasoline. But what happens when you try to pour Diesel fuel into your gas tank? The Diesel fuel is too oily, too thick. Your engine sputters. Your spark plugs misfire. Your exhaust pipe starts spitting black smoke. That's how your body reacts to animal-based food products. Well, that might be a bit dramatic, but you get the idea. Your average blood vessel is only five millimeters in diameter. You don't want oily, thick blood flowing through your arteries and veins. Key nutrients are not absorbed by the appropriate cells. Plaques form along the lining of your blood vessels. Eventually, your blood slows, your motor falters, and your health deteriorates into disease.

Let's examine how animal-based products fundamentally affect your genes. At this point, there appear to be over 500 genes that play a role in the formation of cancers. A high level of animal-based food ingestion appears to damage chromosomes, making them shorter. The shorter your chromosomes, the shorter your life. At the same time, the animal-based foods seem to turn on a significant number of genes that lead to cancer and a host of chronic illnesses while (did you guess this part?) the plant-based foods appear to turn on an equally significant number of genes that help to prevent cancer and other diseases. Those same cancer-preventing genes, turned on by plant-based foods, also help to bolster the immune system, reduce the risk of multiple diseases, and even reduce the speed of aging. Yes, it is complicated. Yes, the facts are often buried. Yes, it's probably not what you want to hear. It is not what the meat and dairy industries want you to hear. But make no mistake. If you want to design the most toxic, least healthy eating style, you would be hard pressed to design any eating style that is worse than what the average American consumes on a daily basis. We, after all, are the country that sends 22 million people every day to McDonald's. As you grow older, if you want to have the health and vitality to redesign yourself and your life, you cannot afford to leave this eating style unchanged.

Chapter 18

More Vegetables, Fruit, Nuts, and Seeds

*"I'm enjoying the taste of healthy food.
It's like I am aging backward."*
Donna Brazile

At this point, you need to consider switching more of your daily

eating to plant-based foods. We all remember the saying that an

apple a day keeps the doctor away. The Chinese proverb ("If you

want to be happy all your life, plant a garden") is closer to the truth. A plant-based meal is what keeps the doctor away. Now, before you slip my prescription into the corner of the medicine cabinet, I am not suggesting that you become a vegetarian. Most of you are going to want to eat some beef and chicken. Or some eggs for breakfast. But why not try to reduce those occasions? Why not aim for more variety with other plant-based food sources? I am arguing that, as you age, you must reduce your consumption of meat and dairy products to lower your risk. A steak may be your favorite food choice, but eating part of a dead animal is not going to keep you alive. Vegetables, fruit, nuts, and seeds form the best, most nutritional meal for keeping you healthy, energetic, and free from heart disease, cancer, and the chronic illnesses.

I know some of you do not care. I know some of you profess that you want to live life, that you want to eat what you want to eat, and that what happens ... well, that is what happens. I get it. I understand your sentiment. But you have not seen the end of the runway. During my internship at USC Los Angeles County Hospital, I had an elderly patient who was admitted to my service with more illnesses than fingers. On her admission, I remember counting up her total number of pills, and it was 17 different medications. Her list of medical diagnoses was slightly shorter. On the days when I was able to complete my rounds and medical tasks, I would pull up a chair by her bed and ask about her life. For me, the hard part was not her sadness about how she was going to miss seeing her grandchildren grow up. The hard part was sitting there, listening to her bones crack as she shifted positions. Among her illnesses, there was bone cancer. She never survived that hospitalization. You want to live your life and eat what you want? Sometimes it does not feel nearly as good as it sounds.

Let's assume you are still set in your ways. Let's assume the American health statistics are not going to be enough to convince you to change your current eating style. How about some individual statistics? They probably won't help either. But if you eat a three-ounce steak daily, your risk for a premature death rises by 13 percent. If you eat two slices of bacon every morning, your risk for a premature death climbs by 20 percent. If you substitute nuts and seeds instead of the red meat, your risk for a premature death drops by 14-19 percent. If you switch from the red meat to more legumes, your risk for a premature death decreases by 10 percent. Even if you substitute fish for the red meat, your risk for a premature death lowers by 7 percent. Simply stated, the health statistics show that the daily intake of meats and dairy products increases your risk for disease and death while a shift of your meals toward vegetables, fruits, nuts, and seeds decrease your risk of disease and an early death. And don't ignore our health trends. In 1960, 95 percent of the visits to a physician were for treatment of an infection. Back then, in 1960, only five percent of physician visits were for the chronic illnesses. Today? Over 95 percent of physician visits are for the care of chronic illnesses. Only five percent of physician visits are for infections. Again, all of those chronic illnesses are food borne diseases, related to your animal-based eating style. So, don't pretend to be ignorant. Don't end up like that old lady in my hospital bed. Trust me: it is not worth it.

To those who still feel continued resistance to these new eating suggestions, I can hear some of you saying: "I can't give up my periodic steaks." Or, "I can't go without eggs and bacon." Let me share a personal anecdote. I am not any different. I love hamburgers and steaks. As I grew older, I thought I was fairly healthy. As I reached my older years, I realized I had been fooling myself. Despite daily exercise, I had gained a pound for every couple of years of employment. With the attempt to write this survivor kit, I refined my eating style. Please note: I did not go on a diet. In fact, I do not want you to go on a diet for the rest of your life. Every year, 50 million Americans go on some type of diet to lose weight. That is an unhealthy approach, the opposite of what I want to recommend. Those diets, at least long-term, do not work. For my golden years, I selected a healthier eating style with the goal of improving my physical health. I switched my own eating habits from animal-based foods to more plant-based foods. In the first six months, I lost 20 pounds (without trying to lose weight); I gained increased vitality; and I improved the quality of my sleep. Today I have better health and more energy than any time in the past three decades. Those results are the benefits that you can receive when you switch to more plant-based foods. They will make you feel great and keep you out of the hospital.

Let me give you one more anecdote, something else I experienced. When you change your eating style, your taste buds change. They really do. I found the new eating style of plant-based foods to be delicious. At the same time, your urges for certain types of food or beverages will change. That does not mean that a barbecued steak will still not smell delicious. It does not mean that a cracking sound of cooking bacon will not start you salivating. But your urge to eat those foods will change as your eating style changes. I used to eat one piece of chocolate late after dinner. Something for my sweet tooth. Now? At times a box of dark chocolate will find its way into our kitchen pantry (hmmm … me?), but I do not feel the same urge for a bite. If you are still worried about an inability to stop your own cravings, I have even better news. There are delicious alternatives to meat and dairy products. Veggie burgers. Veggie sausage. Faux chicken. Meatless burritos. Nondairy cheeses. Nondairy frozen desserts. Vegan ice cream. Vegan cookies. The list is endless and these alternatives are surprisingly tasty. So, you do not need to give up your favorite foods. Just find some healthy substitutes for those foods. You will find this new eating style far, far better than you ever expected.

Chapter 19

Simplify the Multitude Of Diets

*"Try to open a path through that maze,
put a little order in that chaos."*
Isabel Allende

The world does not appear to be getting any simpler. If you walk

into a bookstore or search online, you can find hundreds of diets.

Many of the diets are created for weight loss, and all of them

should be avoided. But there is a subset of diets that are offered

as pathways to improved physical health. Much research has

been done on those people who live the longest. There are blue zones around the world where the population has the longest longevity. The blue zones can be found in areas of Italy, Japan, Greece, Costa Rica, and even in several spots in California. The Japanese island of Okinawa offers the highest concentration of centenarians (people who are 100 years old). The purpose of this guide is not to create more centenarians. The purpose is to help people enjoy their golden years, and that means enjoying optimal health. So, what are some of the healthier eating styles for longevity? What can we learn from these healthy patterns of eating?

First, for the eating styles of centenarians, there are some common features. They eat more vegetables and fruit, and they consume far less meat and dairy products. They tend to eat smaller portions and consume fewer calories. In Okinawa, for example, they eat until they are 80 percent full. Picture a typical American restaurant and its massive servings. Do you think any of their patrons eat until they are only 80 percent full? If you watch those Americans clean their entire plates, it looks like they have gone well beyond a full tank. Restraint? It is something Americans need to learn for their daily eating style. Restaurants may not be conducive to longevity. Centenarians often eat what they grow, and that's without pesticides or contaminants. They eat limited processed foods. They consume less sugar and less salt. Centenarians eat more nuts and seeds. Collectively, they eat a pattern of balanced, plant-based meals with reduced calories, reduced contaminants, and reduced toxins. If you need some good news, centenarians consume moderate amounts of daily alcohol. Additional good news? They visit their doctors less frequently than everyone else. Just like me.

Many of us are well familiar with the Mediterranean diet. It is not associated with the production of centenarians, but it does, in some studies, extend a person's life span by two to five years. Of much greater significance, some studies claim that it reduces the prevalence of those chronic illnesses. The Mediterranean diet is linked with a decreased risk of stroke, heart disease, cancer, and diabetes. The basics of the Mediterranean diet are simple and worthy of consideration for your own eating style. The Mediterranean diet offers increased vegetables, increased fruit, increased fish, and increased nuts and seeds. This collection of foods lead to fresh, organic products with less sugar, less salt, fewer preservatives, and fewer chemicals. Can you see one hidden benefit? For a healthy diet, there has been no discussion of calories. Yes, males should consume around 2200 hundred calories per day and females should consume around 1800 calories per day. But it is the quality of the calories that matters more than the quantity of the calories. I do not want you to count calories. I just want your calories to contain far fewer contaminants, far fewer unhealthy components, and far less dairy/animal sources. Clean healthy eating, with more focus on plant-based foods, is better than reducing calorie consumption.

Many of you may have also heard of the increasing role of cultured vegetables. These are vegetables that have often been cut, ground, or shredded, left to ferment at room temperatures, and then eaten. Raw saltless sauerkraut is one example. Kimchi (bok choy cabbage with carrots, green onions, ginger, garlic, and hot peppers) is another example. The advantage of cultured vegetables is that you are eating an already, pre-digested food. The process of fermentation allows for the breakdown of sugars and starches in the vegetables, turning them into lactic acid. This is the same process that starts with your saliva when you ingest something. At this point you do not need to know the details of the process, nor how it leads to healthy microflora in your intestines. You only need to grasp the central point of cultured vegetables. As we grow older, you want to make it easier, not more difficult, for your digestive system. So, when you examine the multitude of diets, give consideration to which eating styles would be less demanding on your digestive system. The easier something is to digest, the more likely that it will be beneficial for your health. Still uncertain? Try eating a daily salad for one of your meals. Try a lunch bowl filled with lettuce, a cup of raw vegetables, and a topping of mixed nuts and seeds. Your health, vitality, and longevity will all improve.

For me, that's my typical daily salad. On many days, I will grab a bowl from the kitchen cabinet, fill it halfway to the top with different types of lettuce (or green spinach or kale or arugula), and then combine an assortment of broccoli, carrots, mushrooms, red onion, and red peppers, mixed with kidney beans or some other type of beans. Then I will add a scattering of almonds, walnuts, flax seeds, and sunflower seeds, topped by a healthy salad dressing. Now, I realize it is not a hamburger and fries. But step back and look at the two choices. Imagine them side by side on the kitchen table. By selecting the salad, you are not killing another animal. More importantly, you are also not killing yourself. You are choosing more nutrients, more minerals, and more vitamins. They are all easier for you to digest. That hamburger and fries? A year ago, that would have been my first choice. But not today. Today I am eating the salad. Do I feel better? Am I healthier? Absolutely. And, yes, my taste buds have changed. I am enjoying my new lunch. More importantly, I have more vitality to enjoy life.

Chapter 20

The Importance of Hydration

"It's amazing what a little water can do."
Priscilla Salinas

The mythical fountain of youth? It is water. Your body needs water to regulate your cell environment, transport nutrients, remove waste products, and maintain the appropriate chemical, electrical, and magnetic reactions. Young bodies are 80 percent water. Older people are 60-70 percent water. Your brain has an even higher percentage of water. As we age, our bodies (and brains) progressively decrease in their water content. Worse, as we age, we lose our thirst sensation. Many older people do not realize that they are not drinking enough. Many individuals, as they grow older, become chronically dehydrated. When you become dehydrated, most of your water loss comes from your cells, not from extracellular volume. Dehydration leads to ineffective enzymes, impaired physiology, DNA damage, and poisoned cells. Your skin sags, your heart rate increases, your blood pressure rises, your memory fails, and your energy level drops. In short, you experience premature aging. Are you willing to drink a little more water?

Have you ever asked yourself, when sipping some water, "What's the age of this water?" Your water could be 30 days old; it could also be 20,000 years old. If you think the age differential is massive, brace yourself. The quality of water varies tremendously around the world. Scientists have utilized dark-field microscopes to examine different water sources, discovering that water can have markedly different crystalline patterns. Clean, clear water can create a gorgeous landscape of geometric designs. However, contaminated water often shows distorted, twisted geometric patterns that look ominous and destructive. You need to drink, but you need water that is clean, not polluted. With clean water, your energy will lift, your memory will sharpen, and your skin will appear smoother. Appropriate hydration will improve your immune function, prevent physical deterioration (including manifestations of arthritis), and increase the elimination of toxins. You are what you eat; and, no surprise, you are also what you drink.

I suppose I should share that I have many idiosyncrasies. My wife would call that a major understatement. But for many years, I have sipped hot water throughout the day. I would boil the water in the morning, place it in my thermos, and then carry the thermos to my administrative health care meetings, taking a few sips every thirty minutes. I am certain that the various committee members thought I was crazy. Sipping hot water? Most of them were convinced it was vodka. I would attempt to explain how hot water cleansed a dirty dish while cold water simply rinsed over the dish; and I would apply that image to the hot water cleansing the cells of my stomach and intestines. The clean cells lead to increased energy, improved health, and weight loss. But here is the key point. Have you ever boiled different types of water (even different types of bottled water) and sipped the water at high temperatures? Gather your friends. Give it a try. Some of the water, when boiled and sipped at a high temperature, is nauseating. Other hot waters? They actually taste good, clean and refreshing. So, what is the difference in the taste? Those dark-field microscopes don't lie. Some waters are clean, others are packed with contaminants.

So, how much should you drink on a daily basis? The average person loses 10-15 cups of water per day through skin evaporation, regular breathing, sweat, urination, and defecation. If you weigh around 100 pounds, you should be drinking at least four glasses of water daily. If you weigh around 200 pounds, you should be drinking around eight glasses of water daily. You should drink a glass of water thirty minutes before breakfast and a glass of water thirty minutes before lunch. It is much better to drink water thirty minutes before your meal than during your meal. Why? If you drink water while you are eating, the water, especially when it's ice-cold water, will decrease the efficiency of your digestion by decreasing the concentration of your stomach enzymes and lowering the temperature of your enzymatic reaction below their optimum level. Don't believe me? The next time you eat at a restaurant, look around. The fattest people? They will have the tallest, coldest drinks. So, if you want to drink something at meals, try warm tea or at least room temperature water. Perhaps, you can now understand the advantage for Europeans with their habit of drinking room temperature wine with their meals. With moderation, the wine aids digestion better than a drink that is ice-cold and caloric. For alcohol, there are some restrictions. You should imbibe only two drinks of alcohol per day, two glasses of wine or two glasses of beer or two shots. At any higher amount, alcohol will become dehydrating, just what you need to avoid.

Your next challenge? How do you make sure the water is clean without any pollutants or chemicals that can cause you harm? Our challenge with water is the same predicament we have with food. The water we drink today is not the water our grandparents drank. Yes, our water is filtered with the modern technology. Thank God because much of the water in urban areas goes from the toilet to the tap. Did you know that most municipal water systems contain residual amounts of antibiotics and prescription medications? Those residual amounts are not of sufficient dose to be clinically effective, but they are of sufficient dose to be caustic to our digestive system. This problem is growing worse, not better. As our population increases, the demand for water increases. For those of us who live in Southern California and visit Las Vegas, we are told to flush frequently so as to increase our water supply. I guess what happens in Vegas does not always stay in Vegas. That unpleasant fact notwithstanding, you still need to drink water and find clean water. My suggestion? For your next habit, drink plenty of mountain stream fresh water and make certain that it is mountain stream fresh water, not regular water poured into a falsely labeled bottle. Know that certain water bottles contain BPA (bisphenol A), which is banned in many countries (but not, of course, in the United States). BPA can interfere with body hormones and disrupt endocrine systems

We are facing another important problem: the growing shortage of clean water. One of the culprits? Our industrial agricultural complex and its production of animal-based products. In the US we grow 90 million acres for corn, 80 million acres for soy, and only 14 million acres for fruit and vegetables. It takes 7,000 pounds of grain (corn and soy bean) to produce 1,000 pounds of meat. So, 70 percent of our water is currently used to grow animals. Only 30 percent of our water is used to satisfy our thirst. Do you want to correct the future shortage of water? The solution is transparent. Reduce your animal-based foods and you will reduce the waste of water from our industrial agricultural complexes. Shift to more plant-based foods and you will help direct the flow of water back to fruit and vegetables. The country will have more water for you. The country will also have cleaner water for you. For me, that is a win-win scenario.

Chapter 21

Vitamin Supplements?

"I don't pretend to have all the answers."
Arthur C. Clarke

Linus Pauling was one of the most influential chemists in the twentieth century. He was one of only two people to win Nobel Prizes in different fields. In his later years, he completed research on Vitamin C, presenting evidence that high-dose Vitamin C was effective for treating the common cold and cancer. Pauling's opinions created controversy, as subsequent clinical trials did not support his original findings. Pauling attacked those competing clinical trials, calling them fraudulent and misleading. There were many discrepancies between his research and subsequent vitamin research. Pauling used intravenous Vitamin C at high doses; subsequent studies used oral Vitamin C at lower doses. But this debate over the value of vitamin supplements started in the 1960s; and now, 50 years later, the debate continues, with many experts promoting a range of vitamin supplements while other experts proclaiming they offer no benefit at all. So, what should you do?

A new medical opinion is going to progress through three phases: first ridicule, then opposition, and finally acceptance. With vitamin supplements, the jury is still out. You should be aware that there are numerous problems with the studies that are arguing against the value of vitamin supplements. Many of these studies are funded by the pharmaceutical companies that have a strong desire to debunk vitamin supplements so that they can maintain their share of the market. Unfortunately, that is how much of our research system works. Many of the vitamin studies are flawed. Many of the studies are longitudinal and anecdotal, with limited reliability and limited validity. They are based on questionnaires, mailed to thousands of people, with questions like the following sample. Have you been taking any vitamin supplements the past 20 years? Can you remember the specific vitamins, the dose ranges, and the years? Can you remember the illnesses you developed during those periods of your life? I do not know about you, but, even as a physician, I would have difficulty providing accurate answers. Yet, from those studies, researchers will proclaim, to the delight of the company that funded them, that certain vitamin supplements (always oral supplements) offer no benefit whatsoever.

There is an additional fundamental flaw with most studies. Most studies utilize the synthetic vitamins, not natural and whole food-based vitamins. Synthetic vitamins have contaminants that distort findings. It is often the contaminants that create negative results within the study, not the vitamins themselves. So, if you listen to a vitamin study on the evening news, pay close attention. Did they name the company that manufactured the vitamins? Did they clarify whether the vitamins were synthetic or natural? Probably not. Instead, they just highlighted the negative results. You have heard it. Some vitamin was supposed to reduce cancer, and the study showed that the vitamin actually increased cancer. Wrong! It was the synthetic chemicals in the vitamins and the accompanying contaminants that caused the cancer, not the vitamin. My suggestion? You guessed it. Rely on your self-education, not their propaganda.

There's another pervasive problem. Our vitamin studies have focused on a single vitamin supplement, not on a group of vitamin supplements. The human body is a symphony of chemical reactions, orchestrated by the world's greatest computer, your brain. Vitamins work best in concert with each other and a host of coenzymes. There have not been sufficient studies to examine the efficacy of nutritional programs with combinations of natural vitamins. There have been no good studies to clarify a central question: Which combination of natural vitamin supplements might be the most beneficial for your health? Worse, when you examine vitamin studies, they often fail to consider the impact of the other dietary and exercise components that influence everyone's health. Once again, the public is bombarded with misinformation. This country could produce better research studies, but then our government would have to collude less with the pharmaceutical companies; and the pharmaceutical companies would have to spend less money on their profitable advertising and more money on real research. It would be a delight to see these companies shift toward our education, not their profit, but that will not happen any time soon.

Despite my reservations against the majority of vitamin studies, I want to present balanced findings. In my review of the literature, I cannot find consistent evidence that establishes a health benefit from high-dose oral vitamin supplements. However, you should be aware that in the past 20 years, millions of Americans have died from side effects and adverse reactions from pharmaceutical drugs, but only a handful of people have died from supplemental vitamin intake. I believe the risks are greatly exaggerated for vitamin supplements. Nevertheless, here is my recommendation. You are best served by obtaining your vitamins and all your nutrients through a healthy plant-based eating style. Vitamin supplements are not a substitute for a sufficient quantity of vegetables and fruit. However, from my understanding of the better studies, there are some possible advantages with natural vitamin supplements when the supplements are taken as a specific group, accompanied by the vital minerals (calcium, magnesium, potassium, and selenium). Ideally, a vitamin combination would be best if taken intravenously. But who can afford that approach? Just a few of the famous and wealthy. Not us.

If you are going to take oral vitamins, don't rely on a single multivitamin pill. Instead, take a combination of carefully selected vitamins. If you want to follow that approach, consider a broad spectrum of vitamins. Possibly beta-carotene (the precursor for vitamin A), vitamin B6, vitamin B12, folate, vitamin C, and vitamin D3, and vitamin E. Add omega 3 fatty acids. Augment with the semi-essential amino acid L-cysteine, lutein (a carotenoid), and resveratrol (a phenol from plants, especially grapes). However, if you are going to add a specific selection of vitamin supplements to your diet, you are going to need the advice of a nutrition expert. You are not going to want high levels of certain metals like iron, copper, and zinc. Do you have sufficient funds for a good nutritional consultation? Again, for most people, the answer is no. So, wouldn't it be easier to spend your money on locally grown, organic selection of vegetables and fruit? That is still the nutritional approach that I would encourage for you.

Chapter 22

What About Probiotics?

"The important thing is to never stop questioning."
Albert Einstein

Probiotics are live organisms, found in food and juices, which are beneficial for the host organism. For humans, probiotics are believed to improve the amount of healthy bacteria in your intestines. We have around one hundred trillion bacteria in our bodies. Ideally, 85 percent of our bacteria should be the good type while only 15 percent (or less) should be the bad type.

Good bacteria in the intestines improve digestion, helping your cells better absorb nutrients/minerals, better utilize vitamins, and better eliminate the toxins. How important is this process and the role of probiotics? In my review of the literature, I discovered over 200 studies that assert that probiotics successfully decrease the risk (or actually treat) over 170 diseases. As expected, there is a sizable group of experts who claim that probiotics are not that beneficial to your health. So, what should you do? Should you change your diet to take in more probiotics? Should you take any probiotic supplements?

Your body will give you the answer. Do you suffer from daily gastrointestinal problems? How about gas or bloating, constipation or diarrhea, headaches or brief episodes of nausea? Do you need a simple test that is more definitive? Did you watch the *Star Wars* movies? Do you remember the scene where Hans Solo saves Luke Skywalker's life by cutting open the belly of some beast and then stuffing him inside the belly to protect him from the freezing cold? Do you remember his comment? If I remember correctly, Hans Solo said, "And I thought you smelled bad on the outside!" Well, without getting too personal, how do you smell on the inside? If you are attending a friend's party, and if you have to use his or her bathroom for an extended time, do you run an embarrassment risk if someone enters the bathroom too quickly, before the exhaust fan has had time to suck out all of the air? Bottom line? You should smell as good on the inside as you do on the outside. Okay, so that's a bit of an exaggeration. But, seriously, if you have healthy intestinal bacteria, you should smell pretty good.

My observation? If you have any gastrointestinal symptoms (of any type) on a regular basis, your intestines are not very healthy. What causes these problems? Let me repeat some of the factors: too much sugar, chlorinated water, fluoridated water, refined grains, processed foods, agricultural chemicals, agricultural pesticides, and antibiotics (including those given to livestock). All of these elements lead to inflammation (and bad bacteria) in your intestines. Remember that one of the theories of aging is excessive inflammation. The body wears down quicker when it is constantly inflamed. So, what can you do to decrease the inflammation in your intestines that may be damaging your overall health? You can decrease your intake of the above harmful factors and increase your intake of probiotics, found in fermented foods, cultured vegetables, cultured vegetable juices, and probiotic supplements. A list of probiotic foods is too extensive to enumerate, but it includes cabbage, sauerkraut, eggplant, cucumber, squash, onions, and carrots. A list of prebiotic foods (the foods that lead to increased probiotics) is also too extensive to catalog, but it includes some fruits and legumes. Do you need more incentives to educate yourself on probiotics? Some experts believe that probiotics decrease inflammation, decrease physiological stress, improve glucose control, increase the effectiveness of your immune system, and lift your mood. For specific diseases, probiotics are believed to reduce peptic ulcers, gastritis, irritable bowel syndrome, gastroenteritis, lactose intolerance, colon cancer, elevated cholesterol, high blood pressure, dermatitis, acne, allergic rhinitis, and wheat allergies. Probiotics are also believed to help decrease obesity, heart disease, diabetes, and the chronic debilitating illnesses. So, what is my suggestion? If I had to choose between a vitamin supplement regimen and a probiotic supplement regimen, I would select the probiotic supplements. However, instead of taking probiotic supplements, I would still recommend focusing on your diet with your diet incorporating more foods with probiotics. The result? You will feel (and smell?) markedly better.

There is one other crucial point, although this point is not geared to you. Perhaps you can educate your children. There are a number of experts who believe that the health of your intestines directly influences the health of your baby during pregnancy and breast-feeding. In addition, these same experts believe that the health of your child's intestines directly influences their mental development, including the risk of developing certain illnesses like attention deficit disorder and autism. How could there be a connection? During development of the fetus in the womb, the same cells that form the brain are the same cells that form the intestinal system. The two areas, your brain and your gut, are closely linked by the central nervous system with more than a billion neurons. With this close connection, much of your intellectual development is dependent on the state of your intestines. The point? You need to treat your intestines with more respect. Would you bang your head against the wall? Hopefully not. Well, ingesting the wrong food and creating the wrong intestinal environment is equivalent to banging your head against the wall. However, the consequences to your intestines can be far more damaging than any temporary cranial bruise. So, for another habit, start teaching which foods promote health and which foods contribute to disease. Then make certain you walk your talk. And watch your energy and vitality rise to the point where you will be ready to change your life.

Chapter 23

Ready to Try a New Eating Style?

"May all be fed, may all be healed, may all be loved."
John Robbins

So, what are the initial physical health habits for your older years? I am simply following the physician Hippocrates: "Let thy food be thy medicine; and let thy medicine be thy food." Now is the time to focus on your eating style. Throughout your years of work, have you taken the time to think about what would be healthy for breakfast, lunch, or dinner? Have you taken the time to prepare the foods that would be best for your longevity? Have you taken the time to exert control over your nutrition? The answer is no. For too many years, the thing that should have mattered the most (your health) … well, it has been at the mercy of things that have mattered the least (your work). In your golden years you need to shift your priorities. On their death beds people don't wish they had worked harder or longer. They wish they had taken better care of their health. Now is your time. This is your chance. And it's easy. Your eating style will determine if you are going to live in health or die in disease.

My own awareness of the need for good health came early in my adult life, some time in the first years of my marriage and before I developed this resistance to doctor visits. I awoke one morning to a strange mole on my arm and made a prompt appointment with a dermatologist. During the evaluation, the physician expressed alarm at the mole, proclaimed that it could be cancerous, and immediately performed surgery. I left his office with a gaping hole in my upper arm, drove directly to a church, and sneaked my way to a front row pew. After a few prayers, I heard a commotion in the back of the room. Feeling a bit embarrassed (what man prays in the middle of the day in the front pew?), I closed my eyes. One minute turned into ten minutes. More commotion. Many more noises. When the church finally quieted, I opened my eyes. A big mistake. What was set right next to me? A coffin. I took that as a bad sign. I drove home and climbed into bed, suffering from nothing more than worry about my biopsy. Before getting into bed, I arranged a pair of pants, a shirt, underwear, and socks right next to my side of the bed. When my wife arrived home, she glanced at the assembled clothes on the carpet and asked me what in the world was I doing. I explained that if I took a turn for the worse, I could just fall out of bed, crawl into my clothes, and be presentable for the paramedics. Her response? She remarked that if we were going to keep our marriage intact, we were going to need to keep me healthy.

Back then I had a twisted sense of humor, which needed some readjustment. But that day highlighted the importance of health. What about you? Has any health scare brought you to your senses? If not, it's still time to refine your approach. They say that repetition is the mother of skill. So, let us reemphasize the basic health suggestions. You need to remind yourself that the key to improved physical health is not more visits to your physician; the key is prevention, and that is a healthy eating style. Reduce your intake of meat, dairy products, and animal-based protein. Eat more vegetables and fruit (five to ten servings per day). Eat more salads. Increase more plant-based protein. Yes, keep it simple. Have that piece of meat be the smallest item on your plate. Refrain from all those sugars that can populate any meal. Drink more water. Consume fewer sodas. Be aware of the role of vitamins and probiotics. Understand the importance of the health of your intestines. Be cognizant of the crucial role of the healthy intestinal bacteria for your immune system. Believe, with certainty, that you can still achieve the best health of your life, even at an older age. Yes, you can lose weight without a diet. Yes, you can regain energy and improve sleep. Yes, you can change the quality of your life, giving yourself increased vitality and a better chance to redesign your golden years.

As I close our discussion of this topic, let me make one more attempt to make it very simple. When I refer to reducing your meat intake, I mean all meats, not just some meat. For me, the list includes beef, chicken, pork, and lamb, plus processed meats like ham, bacon, salami, hot dogs, and sausages.

Some researchers will tell you that white meat is better than red meat. Other researchers will tell you that baking, roasting, and stir-frying is healthier than grilling and barbecuing. Additional researchers will highlight the health benefits of boiling, steaming, poaching, and stewing. They may be right. But these studies vary too much for my taste. Why hassle with the type of cooking? Instead, I suggest you simply focus on reducing your intake of meat, regardless of the type of cooking. The same approach goes for your dairy products. Make all of dairy portions the smallest portions on your plate. Perhaps even skip some days of any meat and dairy products. Don't focus on what you have given up. Focus on what you have gained. Improved health and a reduced risk of multiple illnesses.

Lastly, do not underestimate the number of illnesses whose risk can be reduced with the eating changes. Breast cancer. Lung cancer. Stomach cancer. Liver cancer. Prostate cancer. Large-bowel cancer. Rectal cancer. Coronary heart diseases. Diabetes. The autoimmune diseases (Graves' disease, rheumatoid arthritis, pernicious anemia, multiple sclerosis, systemic lupus erythemotosus, myasthenia gravis, Addison's disease, etc.). Bone diseases. Kidney disorders. A wide range of vision/eye diseases, including macular degeneration. Cognitive/brain disorders, including some types of dementia. To reduce your chance of all of these illnesses isn't this guide (and its eating-style change) worth the effort? Do what's right for you, not what might be spouted on a commercial. Start reading. Start learning. Start eating healthy. Those are initial habits to incorporate as starting points to prepare yourself for personal change.

Chapter 24

Any Closing Arguments?

It's not how long we live, but also how well we live."
Dean Ornish, MD

As previously mentioned, there are numerous theories of aging. A change of your eating style to vegetables, fruits, and grains addresses every aging theory. For the DNA theory, plant-based foods have been shown to turn off the genes that are most associated with increased disease. Plant-based foods are known to increase telomere repair, which is the repair that protects the length of your chromosomes (and the speed of your aging). For the free radical theory, plant-based food contains antioxidants, which neutralize destructive free radicals, preventing physiological destruction. For the inflammation theory, plant-based food is alkaline while animal-based food is often acidic. Your body needs more of an alkaline state to reduce inflammation. For the mitochondrial theory, plant-based food offers phytochemicals and micronutrients, necessary for activating mitochondria for cellular cleanup. So, in all the theories, plant-based food aligns with the pathways for better health, reduced disease, and slower aging.

I think there is value in reminding everyone that it is equally important to create healthy habits as it is to eliminate unhealthy habits. My sister was fairly good with her eating style, but she had her own Achilles' heel. She loved to drink Coke and Pepsi on a daily basis. That's a lot of sugar. Now, I cannot blame the following events on this one negative habit, but I have my own suspicion. In a two-week period, she went from being able to play tennis with me (and win) to barely able to walk two blocks. What happened? She developed a dental infection; the dental infection seeded to her heart; and she promptly developed a damaged mitral valve in her heart. The surgeons performed open-heart surgery and replaced the damaged valve; and she returned to a good life (except for the click of her new mitral valve). Unfortunately, several years after the heart surgery, she contracted the flu. Unable to keep down her food, she kept throwing up her blood thinner, Coumadin. The result? A blot clot, formed in her heart, lodged in her brain. Her husband, a good man who expected a long marriage with children, returned home from work to find her dead on the kitchen floor. As much as I believe that small advantages can lead to great triumphs, I also believe that small mistakes can lead to huge disasters. Don't underestimate your risks. Commit to a consistency with your eating style.

Many people hesitate, claiming they do not know what to eat. Which vegetables? Which fruits? Which berries? Which seeds? That is a false argument against switching to a healthier eating style. To make it simple, just remember that variety is one of the hallmarks of nature, and it should be one of the hallmarks of your eating style. If you want some specific suggestions, similar to my own daily salad, follow the advice from Dr. Joel Fuhrman, a renowned physician and nutrition expert, who simply recommends the 'gombbs' eating moniker. The foods that are the best antioxidants? Greens (lettuce and vegetables). Onions. Mushrooms. Berries. Beans. Seeds. Which berries? Try blueberries, blackberries, cranberries, raspberries, strawberries, acai berries, and goji berries. Which seeds? Try flax seeds, hemp seeds, pumpkin seeds, and sesame seeds. Need more ingredients for your salad? How about nuts that help prevent disease such as walnuts, peanuts, almonds, or cashews. How about some broccoli, spinach, red bell peppers, brussels sprouts, and tomatoes? Salad can be delicious and far more disease-preventive than any meat or dairy product.

Other people will argue against the higher cost of plant-based food. You have to pay more for 500 calories of broccoli than you have to pay for 500 calories of soda pop or a cheeseburger. They want you to keep buying your groceries at Wal-Mart, which sells 21 percent of all the groceries in this country. Cheap food, but not the healthiest variety. So, yes, you may need to spend more money on your food. That is a cost well worth paying. Let me pose one closing question. In our country, which kills more people? Cigarettes or meat? Some of you may think the question is absurd. It is still worth a debate. There are massive differences between the two products. Cigarettes are harmful from the first inhalation. Animal-based foods are harmful when they reach too high a percentage of your diet. Remember to keep your animal-based protein below 10 percent of your diet. More importantly, view the reduction of animal-based food as only part of the equation. With the decreased intake of meat and dairy products, you are increasing plant-based, healthy foods. You are also reducing the intake of processed foods, sugars, sodas, and all of the other junk food. Again, it will be more expensive to purchase that broccoli. For your golden years, your focus should not be on the cost. Your focus should be on physical health. You want to be able to embrace a life that is worth living. You want to be sufficiently healthy and energetic to be ready to change your life. With this new eating style, you will be primed for the upcoming changes. However, before we discuss those issues, there is another component to improving your current physical health. One step at a time, right? Remember those plateaus? Be patient.

STEP 3

Reshaping Your Physical Activity

"To live is to keep moving."
Jerry Seinfeld

Chapter 25

Appreciate How We're Built

"My idea of exercise is a good brisk sit."
Joan Rivers

After a change in your daily diet, what's your next challenge? You guessed it. A change in your exercise routine. To place it into perspective, let's pause to reconsider the evolution of our species. Homo sapiens emerged on this planet around 10,000 years ago, and they were forced to compete with Neanderthals for survival. Neanderthals had been on this planet for 200,000 years.

The Neanderthals were stronger, tougher, and perhaps smarter. At the beginning of the competition with us they even had bigger brains. They were proficient at making weapons, ready to bring down their game with an onslaught of spears. Homo sapiens were not as muscular; they were smaller and thinner; and their bones were easier to break. If you were a betting anthropologist, the safe wager would have been on the Neanderthals. But there was one factor that was not overtly apparent, a factor that tipped the survival scales in our favor. Homo sapiens, with two anatomical changes (the Achilles tendon and the nuchal ligament), were built to move.

The Achilles tendon, which was missing from our closest DNA match (the common chimp), connected our calves to our heels. The nuchal ligament, which was also new to evolution, attached our skull to our spine. Consequently, during our competition with the Neanderthals, homo sapiens were more athletic, able to run and keep their heads stable while running. There were more evolutionary game changers. With our upright posture, we were able to breathe better than other mammals. While running, all other mammals, except us, took a single breath with each step. Picture a gazelle darting across the desert or a rabbit jumping through bushes. One breath for each leap. Homo sapiens, however, were able to vary the breaths to match the body's needs. Just as important, we developed sweat glands with the ability to cool our bodies. With these physical advances, we became better athletes and superior long distance runners. While the Neanderthals cornered their prey and attacked the animals with spears, we could run across the African savannahs for long stretches of time, chasing our meals until they dropped dead from hyperthermia. While running, we could cool our bodies in the scorching African heat. Our targets could not. They'd reach a point where they would collapse from their internal heat, dead on the spot.

There was a subsequent evolutionary benefit that came from our long distance running. Our hunting was usually a shell game. If we were chasing some animal, that animal would often double back, joining the herd or pack, trying to blend in with the others. The early homo sapiens had to learn how to identify a single animal in a herd or pack, separate that animal from the pack, and then force that animal back into another long distance run. That task required improved cognitive skills with better visualization, more abstract thinking, and expanded foresight with predictive skills. The evolutionary progression? The more we ran, the more our brains grew larger. Our skull and our brain developed faster than that of any other creature on our planet, secondary to our athletic advantages. Those advantages saved our species; and the athletic ability to run (or just to exercise) is equally important to you. There is a saying that we don't stop exercising because we get old; we get old because we stop exercising. For many of us, we need to explore our exercise options, especially as we feel more physically limited.

Now, before we examine the benefits of running (and exercise in general), some reader is going to point out the obvious. Homo sapiens, at the dawn of our evolution, survived because we were better able to kill animals. Ha! There goes the nonsense of changing our dietary habit. Meat was crucial for our survival! True, but partially inaccurate. Homo sapiens, in our struggle for survival, viewed meat as a special feast. But it was not their standard fare. Early homo sapiens existed mostly on roots and fruit with a plant-based protein eating style. Prior to the hunt, even on the African savannahs, the early homo sapiens were carbo-loading. We survived because of the dual combination of a plant-based eating style and exercise. It's my opinion that if you want to survive and prosper in your older years, you need to return to these two fundamentals: an improved plant-based eating style and some type of daily exercise. Older age is not the time for a brisk sit. It's a time for balanced physical activity to regain your physical vitality.

Chapter 26

Is There Beauty In Our Feet?

"Discovery is the ability to be puzzled by simple things."
Noam Chomsky

I realize that many of you do not want to run. You can relax. I am going to offer some alternatives for you. However, to provide educational information, I want to briefly discuss some additional features that relate to the athletic nature of our bodies. Leonardo da Vinci considered the human foot as a work of art. Despite its beauty and superficial simplicity (did you know that there are 52 bones in your two feet?), the foot has become pro-gressively problematic for most of us. Many of us suffer from corns, bunions, hammertoes, fallen arches, and flat feet. Running may be beyond your capability. Runners suffer multiple problems. Around 60-80 percent of all runners suffer annual injuries. They have problems with their Achilles; they have knee difficulties; or they have plantar fasciitis, inflammation of the connective tissue on the bottom of the foot. Do you know one reason for these problems? Shoes. Mankind has not been the same since we started wearing shoes.

Earlier in this book, when I discussed the need for a dietary change, I highlighted the deficiencies in our health care industry and the forces within that industry that were working against you. Well, I am going to do it again. Only this time, I am going to highlight some concerns with shoe companies. With long-distance runners, there is a long-standing joke. If you want to double your injuries, just double the price of your running shoes. The shoe companies will tell you something different, but they are more interested in profit and less interested in your health. Shoe companies will tell you they have constructed this wonderful shoe to absorb the pressure on your feet. But is that really so good? With shoes and the extra cushion, your muscles shrivel, your tendons stiffen, your arch (the greatest weight bearing design in mammals) drops, and your connective tissues lose some elasticity. So, what is the solution? For exercise in your golden years, buy cheap shoes. Or exercise barefoot, at least if you have an area of smooth grass or sand.

At a minimum, do not underestimate your natural athletic ability or your ability to move. Are you aware of the ultra long-distance races like the Old Dominion (100 miles), the Rocky Raccoon (100 miles), or the Leadville Trail (100 miles)? You might want to read Christopher McDougall's *Born To Run*. Each of those races is the equivalent of four full marathons, back-to-back-to-back-to-back, with the winner taking 14 hours to complete the tortuous trail. Have you heard of the near mythical Tarahumara tribe, often called the Running People, living in the Copper Canyons of Sierra Madres in Mexico? They are difficult to find and impossible to pry loose from their native canyons, but one of their champions once ran from New York to Detroit, a distance of 435 miles. They are known for their ability to run ultra long distances, but they are also known for the smiles on their faces as they cross the finish line. They believe that running does not just make you healthier; it makes you a better person. Their tribal society reflects the results of that belief. Not only are there fewer illnesses like heart disease, cancer, and diabetes, there are also fewer social problems. There is essentially minimal crime, corruption, and domestic violence. They are an egalitarian society with much respect for the women of their tribe. Perhaps, as we work to get into better physical shape, exercise will help all of us regain a better, more appreciative perspective on life and each other. If we are going to change and make our lives better, that is not a bad starting point.

Think that perspective is a bit of a reach? I could offer a long list of athletes who contributed to history. Did you know that Abraham Lincoln was excellent in foot races in his youth? Did you know that Nelson Mandela was a good cross-country runner? When he was incarcerated for decades, Mandela ran seven miles (in place) in his cell every day. From my perspective, this connection brings us back to a prior point. If you want more, you need to become more. Some type of daily exercise is part of the program that is beneficial if you are trying to become a better person. It will not only lead you to better health; it will give you a chance to think and reflect. Exercise will give you time to develop the habits that we will cover in the next step on mental clarity. With the new habits, remember: the sum of the whole is greater than the individual parts. A puzzle looks much better when it is fully assembled. With this survivor kit, you need to realign yourself. Exercise will start you toward the right path.

One final point. As a physician, I am actually against long-distance running, even if you are one of the individuals who excel in that arena. Marathon runners, at the end of a long race, show decreased heart function and elevated cardiac enzymes. Both of these are markers for heart attacks. MRIs in long-distance runners often reveal scar tissue in the cardiac muscle. And, in fact, if you look at the group of elite long-distance runners, you will periodically find the runner who dies at an early age (30s or 40s) because of an acute, unexpected cardiac problem, which probably developed from the long-distance running. So, I have passed along this information primarily for educational interest. For most of us entering our older years, running will not be the best form of exercise. We will want to select the right type of exercise, the one that best suits our needs. For some people, that will mean walking or swimming or participating in some type of organized gym exercise. But, whatever the form of exercise, acknowledge the need to maintain your physical health, and acknowledge that movement helps to sustain life. I know, I know. My guide's primary focus is not to sustain your life; it is to change your life so you can live, love, and make a difference. But trust me. Those changes will be so much easier (and enjoyable) when you are fit and healthy.

Chapter 27

When Did You Last Touch The Earth?

"I like the idea of bringing it down to earth."
Randy Newman

Speaking of running (or exercising) barefoot, are you aware of the concept of grounding? There are some experts, like Clinton Ober, who call it 'earthing.' The concept is simple but actually of some importance. To start, let me ask: Are you aware that humans currently touch the earth less than any other species?

Are you aware, with the advent of shoes, that we have progressively less contact with the earth? If you ask the average American adult, "When did you last touch the earth?", can you guess their answer? A couple of minutes? An hour? But what truly counts as contact with the earth? Walking barefoot on the dirt or sand. Gardening with your hands. Climbing a tree. And swimming in the ocean. Skin to earth? That counts. But walking/running on asphalt or concrete, or sitting/standing in your office or house? That does not count. Why is that significant? Because there is the belief that grounding with direct skin to earth contact is valuable for your physical health.

Let me briefly examine the theory of free radical damage. Free radicals are a natural by-product of your body's physiology when it detoxifies certain chemicals, or degrades toxins, or fights various types of inflammation. Some experts believe that the rate of aging is a direct reflection of your production of free radicals, unless you have an ample source of electrons to capture those free radicals. If those free radicals are not captured (bound together with an electron), they cause damage to your cells and your DNA. They also disrupt vital chemical processes, leading to even worse inflammation, and causing, as their most obvious landmark, chronic pain. The free radicals exist only for a nanosecond (a tiny fraction of a second), but their damage can last a lifetime. Your options for combating free radical aging are relatively straightforward. Reduce your chemicals, toxins, and inflammation. Eat plenty of antioxidants. And hope you have an ample supply of electrons in your body to quickly absorb (and neutralize) those free radicals before they can cause damage and increase your discomfort.

Now, where can your body obtain an ample supply of electrons? From the earth! It's easy to think of your body as having a continuous flow of life-sustaining biochemical interactions, but your body also has a continuous flow of electrical interactions of equal importance. That is why the earth is crucial for your health. The earth's surface is negatively charged. In fact, the earth can be viewed as a six sextillion (six followed by 21 zeroes) metric ton battery. The earth's negative charge comes from solar radiation, the earth's molten core, and lightning strikes (5,000 per minute across the entire planet). Whenever your skin touches the earth, there is an instantaneous flow of electrons into your body. The soles of your feet, probably to your surprise, contain a dense network of nerve endings (1,300 nerve endings per square inch). In addition, since water helps conduction, your feet have more sweat glands than any part of your body except your head and hands. So, unbeknownst to Leonardo da Vinci, your feet are more than just works of art; they are designed for the absorption of healthy electrons.

At this point you may have already guessed our problem. For most of our evolution, we have walked barefoot on the planet, absorbing those electrons. In the 1960s there was the advent of sneakers, and 90 percent of the sneakers were made with rubber souls. Rubber does not conduct electrons. That means that humans have become further insulated from the earth. A bit ironic, isn't it? Humans have been on the planet for only 0.01 percent of earth's existence, but we have created more destruction than any other species. Yet, we have the least direct contact with the planet. Could that just be a coincidence? Regardless, the solution, at least for our health, is readily apparent. We are electron deficient and we need more direct contact with the earth. To obtain sufficient electron restoration, most experts recommend at least 30 minutes of direct contract with the earth on a daily basis. So, whatever your form of exercise, try something that allows some skin to earth contact. If that is not possible, you might consider purchasing items (a foot pad for the desk or a special sheet for the bed) that allows for grounding and increases the flow of electrons into your body.

What are the health benefits of grounding? With electrons counteracting free radicals, a person should achieve less inflammation, less genetic errors, faster healing, a reduction of pain, and a slower rate of aging. Studies have shown that rats, which are grounded, are healthier and live longer than rats that are not grounded. Studies document that grounding improves allergies, arthritis, asthma, heart disease, diabetes, intestinal disorders, lupus, multiple sclerosis, psoriasis, eczema, chronic pain, and aging. Other studies have proclaimed that grounding has a benefit in reducing stress and anxiety. The research on grounding is new (with much work yet to be done), but the general concept, a return to nature, has been around for decades with much common sense. So, when you select a course of exercise (regardless of the specific type), why not develop the habit of incorporating more direct contact with the earth?

By now, you can probably guess my own approach. When I read the research on grounding, I began to sit outside on our front lawn each afternoon. I would carry out a chair, slip off my shoes, and sit with my bare feet touching the grass. My neighbors, no doubt, thought I was crazy. In fact, my next-door neighbor was convinced that I was lowering the value of his house. His house had been on the market, taking forever to sell. Every time a family came to see his house, I always seemed to be stationed in our front yard, sitting barefoot like a mannequin. Even visiting kids, crunched in the back seat of the realtor's car, gave me weird stares. Finally, feeling a bit responsible (their house's price was steadily dropping), I stopped sitting in our front yard. Instead, I purchased a special bed sheet for grounding. At that point, I had a lingering hip discomfort from my years of running. It was chronic, not acute, and a rather permanent fixture in my anatomy. What was causing it? Who knows? I am the guy who tries not to see a physician, right? My own guess? Chronic inflammation around the hip from the years of running. Well, you know what? After two months of nightly grounding, my pain disappeared. Completely. First time in years. Now, one anecdote does not constitute a research finding. Nor does the similar disappearance of my wife's chronic pain, also around the two-month period. Grounding? I cannot attest that it confers improved health, but I think it is worth a try. Besides, being more down to earth has always been good, yes?

Chapter 28

A Little High Intensity Exercise?

"We are underexercised as a nation."
John F. Kennedy

Dr. Kenneth Cooper, the Air Force physician who helped train the astronauts to improve their health, wrote a book, *Aerobics*, in 1968 that revitalized running and walking in America. Dr. Cooper developed a standard test for assessing cardiovascular health: How far could you run in 12 minutes? He also advocated 10,000 steps a day of walking for maintaining adequate physical health. Many

Americans view Dr. Cooper as the modern father of aerobic exercise, but most Americans do not know that Dr. Cooper wrote 30 additional books, that he progressed from aerobics to other types of exercise, and that he eventually focused on physical exercises that developed the body's musculature, not just the cardiovascular system. Dr. Cooper became an advocate of maintaining strength, flexibility, and vitality as you age, and his work led others to explore the value of high intensity exercise.

As we grow older, we start losing muscle mass. Your bone density is directly related to your muscle mass. If you want to decrease your risk for falls and fractures, you need, even if you have never picked up a barbell in your life, to incorporate some type of a high intensity exercise with something that involves either weights or mechanical force against resistance. This type of physical exercise is not complicated and is not difficult to incorporate. There are hundreds of videos on the Internet, some of them designed for older individuals. In its simplest form, you need to find something heavy like a barbell. You need to watch a video with instructions for exercise movements for your core muscles or attend a gym with weight training equipment with resistance against muscle movements. You need limited time, just 20 minutes, three times per week (or less) because the key for high intensity exercise is a short burst of exercise with a prolonged time (at least 48 hours) for recovery. Sound doable?

Aerobic exercises, like long-distance running or walking, work by improving the condition of your heart and blood vessels. High intensity exercise works by building up your muscle. With running and walking, you are recruiting some of your muscle fibers. With high intensity exercise, you are recruiting a wider spectrum of your muscle fibers. Why is that important? Because when you employ a wider group of your muscle fibers, you are better able to create greater muscle growth; and when you employ a wider group of your muscle fibers, you are able to improve your muscles' ability to store glycogen (glucose). Let's make this simple. When you ingest sugar, would you like it deposited in your muscles or your fat cells? High intensity exercise will improve your physical strength, protecting you against the fragile nature of old age; and high intensity exercise will also protect you from obesity, creating additional space (in your expanded muscles) to store your glucose.

When you examine morbidly obese people, their muscles have atrophied. When they eat, the sugar is deposited in fat storage, not muscle storage. Which is harder for the body to burn? The sugar within your muscles or the sugar within your fat cells? The sugar in your fat cells is harder to burn. So, the fat person gets hungry more quickly than the muscular person. That's why some people get fatter and fatter and fatter, remaining hungry all the time. You cannot let this happen in your older years. You cannot afford to only run or walk for exercise. Yes, those exercises will help with your cardiovascular fitness and protect you from a host of diseases. But the protection that comes from aerobic exercise is just one type of protection. If you add a regular pattern of high intensity exercise to your aerobic exercise, you will be gaining additional health protection. You will be improving the quality of your health and further reducing your risk of illnesses.

People feel overwhelmed by the multitude of high intensity exercise options. Well, don't do everything. Don't try to be perfect. Several times a week, in a period of brief nonstop action, exercise your arms and legs with weights or muscle presses against a resistance. Exercise your abdomen and back, strengthening and building those muscles. Many experts recommend repetitive muscle movements in eight cycles (overhead presses or bicep curls or leg presses); other experts recommend the same muscle movements in extreme slow motion with only several cycles. The goal for high intensity exercise is simple. You want to work a broad group of your larger muscles to the point of fatigue where you do not want to push yourself through another cycle. If you utilize this high intensity exercise, you will see a gradual physical transformation of your body. Your body will show more muscle mass. Your bones will grow stronger. You will feel an increased level of strength. You will look younger. You will live longer. And it will take only 20 minutes (maximum) three times a week. Worth it? Absolutely.

Now, do I engage in high-intensity exercise? Yes. But I will admit that I prefer aerobic exercise. As someone who played soccer in high school and college, I can still hear my coach yelling, "Run, Courter, run!" Since those early days, I have grown to love running. But as I reach my older years, the running has dropped to more walking; and my activities have moved from the neighborhood to the indoor treadmill. At the head of the treadmill, I have positioned a series of weights. I will complete my 30-60 minutes on the treadmill on a daily basis and then I will perform a series of high intensity exercises two or three times a week. I complete a series of sit-ups (which, I am told, are not as valuable as other exercises), but I will add leg lifts and leg scissors at the end of my sit-up routine. Then I will perform some regular push-ups and knee push-ups; and then I will pick up the weights, lifting them through a series of repetitions. Which type of exercise is easier? Aerobic exercise. However, if we want to maintain our muscle mass and provide our body with the best chance to fight some of the chronic diseases, we all need to push ourselves to add a few minutes of the high intensity exercises. It is not the easiest path, but it is a path worth pursuing. That statement was accurate in the 1960s; it is equally accurate today, especially for those of us who are older. Besides, who cares about your age? We care more about your health and vitality.

Chapter 29

A Possible Exercise Program for You

"Walking is the best possible exercise."
Thomas Jefferson

Let's summarize my suggestions on exercise. You need to resume exercising in your golden years, making some exercises daily, others weekly. For those who may not have been exercising at all, I suggest starting with 30 minutes of daily walking. If you follow just the walking recommendation, you will improve your physical health and longevity. Walking strengthens your heart and your circulatory system. With 30 minutes of daily walking, you will be reducing the risk of heart disease, stroke, and diabetes by around 50 percent. A 30-minute walk lowers your blood pressure for the next 24 hours. For women, you will be reducing the risk of breast cancer and colon cancer. For men, you will be reducing the risk of prostate cancer. You will be reducing the risk of gall stone surgery and hip fractures. Your longevity statistics will rise. Again, I want you to have more than longevity. I want you to have an improved quality of life, but keep in mind that walking is just one part of your program.

There are many additional effects from the 30 minutes of daily walking. It reduces the risk of colds and shortens a cold when it develops. Many older people catch a cold, develop pneumonia, and spiral into a medical crisis, landing in the hospital. Walking can reduce your weight. Studies show that 30 minutes of walking is more beneficial to your physical health than losing 20 pounds. At the same time, walking, by itself, should result in a loss of weight of around 11 to 18 pounds over the first year. Just from walking, you will be losing weight, improving your immune system, and gaining some stamina for countering any age-related decrease in energy. Walking has been shown to reduce the risk of cognitive impairments, even the risk of dementia, including Alzheimer's. Current studies report that 50 percent of Americans will have dementia by age 85. With walking, your morbidity statistics (frequency of episodes of poor health and physical illness) will decrease as much as your mortality statistics.

These health improvements from walking will be further increased if you can develop the habit of periodic running, even if it is just for short distances. Humans are remarkable in that they can run through most of their life. Older long distance runners, individuals well in their 60s, can compete against young runners in their 20s. I realize that many older individuals will balk at resuming running. That's why I have accented walking and the health benefits from walking; and that's why I have equally emphasized the advantages of high intensity exercise. Many of you will not have access to a gym, but most of you will have access to Internet sites that offer routines for home exercises. A set of barbells is inexpensive. You should not perform these high intensity exercises daily. So, they will not substitute for your other activities and other habits. Instead, they will supplement those other habits, offering greater health.

There are also many other alternatives to running and walking. I have a friend, a nurse, who started teaching zumba dancing in her older years. She lost weight; she became more athletic; and she improved her health, reducing her risks for multiple illnesses. You need to follow her lead. Find a group of activities that promote different types of exercise and bring intensity to at least some parts of your exercise program. It can't be passive; it has to be active. If you are worried about the risks of a medical crisis while exercising (specifically, if you are worried about reaching too fast a pulse and encountering cardiac problems), you should remember the basic rule. While exercising, if you can still converse with your partner (or even with yourself), you are doing fine. When you hit the point where you can't comfortably talk to someone while exercising, then stop and start at a slower pace. Be safe, but be active.

Your goal should be to establish a habit of multiple exercises. You do not want to sit on the sofa watching more TV. That passive existence, although fun for the sports fanatic, weakens your heart, your muscles, and your bones. There is truth in that old Bob Dylan line that if you are not busy living, you are busy dying. I hope you choose to live with daily aerobic exercise and periods of high intensity exercise. You should remember the comment of how rapidly science is changing. That applies to the science of exercise. During your older years, there will be new exercise routines and new exercise machines. Keep educating yourself on your many options for improving your physical health. The key is finding a group of exercises, which impact all parts of your body and work best for you. The best health of your life is one of your starting-point goals. The other, even more important, goals will follow.

Chapter 30

Concerned About Your Weight?

"Don't dig your grave with your own knife and fork."
English Proverb

If you follow the eating style and exercise recommendations of my guide, you should lose 10 percent or more of your current weight over the first six months. Around 80 percent of your weight loss should come from your eating style changes, and 20 percent should come from your exercise changes. If you are one of the 66 percent of Americans who are overweight or one of 33 percent of Americans who are obese, you need to know your status. Weight, by itself, can be deceiving. A better test is the size of your waist. For men, if the size of your waist is above 37 inches, you are overweight; and if it's over 40 inches, you are likely obese. For women, if the size of your waist is over 31 inches, you are overweight; and if it's over 34 inches, you are likely obese. Why is the size of your waist a better indicator than your weight? Because the size of your waist reflects the amount of visceral fat that covers your internal organs; and this visceral fat is directly associated with your risk for heart disease and the chronic illnesses. You must lose that excess visceral fat.

How do you reduce your visceral fat? The key is not calorie restriction. The average Chinese worker eats more calories than the average American worker, but the Chinese people have limited obesity with a reduced incidence of cancer, heart disease, and the other debilitating diseases. The key for weight reduction is the quality of your eating style, not just quantity of your calories. In addition to the eating style change from animal-based protein to plant-based protein, you need to reduce your total amount of daily sugar and fat to less than 25 grams of sugar per day (if you are at a reasonable weight) and less than 15 grams of sugar per day (if you are overweight or obese). There are many more ways, besides counting calories or sugar intake, to lose weight. High stress creates hormonal imbalances that lead to fat storage. Reducing your stress leads to weight loss. Increasing your sleep, without any eating style changes, can also lead to weight loss. Hopefully, you get the point. A healthy eating style with a healthy exercise program is what you need, not some popular diet with calorie restriction. So, do yourself a favor. Do not purchase any diet book.

There is another way to lose weight, which I alluded to earlier, by sipping hot water. In countries where that is a tradition, there is lower weight and higher longevity. Why is it not promoted? Who can make a profit? There is no product to sell. There is no diet book to write. Sipping hot water can be explained in one paragraph. Fill your thermos with boiled water (find a source of water that tastes good at high temperatures) on a daily basis. Pour a half inch of hot water into your cup every half hour and sip it within four to five minutes. Repeat this process throughout the day. I have employed this habit on multiple occasions. Each time, over a period of four to six weeks, I typically lose around five percent of my body weight, simply by just sipping hot water. How does it work? Let me explain one more time. Run cold water over a dirty dish and notice how much of the caked food is washed clean. Only part of it. Now run hot water over the same dirty dish and observe how almost all of the caked food is washed clean. Hot water helps clean the cells of the stomach and intestines. The hot water improves digestive efficiency, just the opposite of that ice-cold soda. An improved digestive efficiency will lower your weight by itself. It's actually that simple.

Now I do not expect many of you to develop this habit. Who wants to boil water, deposit it into a thermos, and carry that thermos around all day? Not many. So, why did I mention it? Because I wanted to set up an alternative: hot tea. We have all eaten at Japanese and Chinese restaurants, two populations with lower weights and very limited obesity. What do both countries serve with meals? What do they often drink between meals? Hot tea. Forget the daily can of Coke or Pepsi. Ignore the habit of reaching for some soda. Skip the energy drink with all of its sugar. Instead, switch to the habit of drinking hot tea throughout the day. Hydration will give you energy. And your weight? With the new habits of an improved eating style, an expanded exercise program, and a change in your liquid consumption, your weight will reach its appropriate level. Just give it some time. You do not need to aim for a specific weight. In fact, forget about your weight. Just develop the right habits, as these habits will lead you toward improved health and an appropriate weight. Now, are you ready to move past these fundamentals? Okay. But I want to make one final point on your health.

Chapter 31

Brain Imaging Has Some Warnings

"Life itself is the proper binge."
Julia Child

Your brain may be the most complex object known to science. Although it only weighs three pounds, it contains 1.1 trillion brain cells and one hundred million gray-matter neurons. Each of those neurons typically has 5,000 connections with other neurons, creating over 500 trillion synapses; and each of those neurons fires around 10-50 times per second, sometimes faster. Those neuron signals cross your brain, transporting information, in less that a tenth of a second. For those people with mathematic skills, that translates into an unfathomable number of possible brain states (10 to the millionth power) with a quadrillion neural signals with each breath. So, why am I mentioning these facts at this point? Because your weight is a larger threat to your brain than to your body. I still do not want you to focus on achieving a specific weight. But be aware that excessive weight reduces the effectiveness of your brain with decreased learning, decreased memory, and increased risk of dementia.

Medicine has many brain imaging tools for evaluating your brain. Many of these brain imaging tools simply take photos of your brain's structure. However, some tools (like SPECT, single photon emission computed tomography) examine much more than basic structure; these tools examine the brain's blood flow and activity patterns. Studies show that a person's increasing weight leads to smaller brains and a decrease in the brain activity. An overweight person will typically have 4 percent less brain tissue; and an obese person will typically have 8 percent less brain tissue. Worse, as your brain's gray matter density atrophies, your blood flow becomes slower. The result? Your memory, your attention, and your general cognitive skills are not as sharp as they were when you were leaner and healthier. How can this brain deterioration happen? Fat cells produce compounds (cyto-kines) that cause inflammation. Since the brain, although 2 per-cent of your body weight, consumes 20 percent of your calories, it receives a disproportionate percentage of those inflamma-tory contaminants; and the inflammatory contaminants create destruction within your brain cells and their neurons. In short, your fat cells will make you feel progressively stupid.

There is good news. The brain was once viewed as static, but that perspective has long since been discarded. The brain is pliable; and its deterioration is reversible. Better yet, many of the habits in this guide have been shown to improve brain vol-ume and brain activity. A healthy eating style plays a vital role in repairing brain function. For example, foods with omega-3 fatty acids promote brain activity. The best sources for omega-3 fatty acids? Green leafy vegetables, walnuts, avocados, and salmon. Vitamin D has been shown to help clear the brain of beta amy-loid, an abnormal protein that clogs the brain system, leading to dementia. Sunlight is a great source of vitamin D. All types of exercise have been shown to stimulate the production of the neurotransmitters in the brain, including norepinephrine, serotonin, and dopamine. Increased neurotransmitter production helps increase neuronal activity; and neuron activity helps restore function and expand volume. So, what is my message? Don't be preoccupied with reaching a certain weight. But know that your excess weight is dangerous for your body and your mind. Know that excess weight does not have to be attacked through some artificial diet. Know that a lifelong healthy eating style, coupled with exercise, is the best solution for reaching your appropriate weight, regaining your physical health, and restoring higher cognitive functioning. Remember that this advice comes from a series of medical tests and brain imaging scans, not from any societal expectation.

So, do not underestimate the importance of these initial habits for your eating style and your exercise program. For many of our health experts, these changes represent the end point. They are alarmed by our national health statistics, horrified by our rising chronic illnesses, worried about our rapid aging rate, and focused on their approaches to better health and increased longevity. But this perspective is where my own approach is different. I want the improvements in your physical health to be the starting point for changing the rest of your life. How valuable is living longer if your life is still miserable? I do not want you to regain your health just to pour more hours into your work. I do not want you to walk faster on the conveyor belt of your career. No, I want you to step off that conveyor belt feeling physically great. I want you to be able to look around at the world's debris, inspect your personal challenges, and then progress through this guide to redesigning your life. I want you to progress from a narrow focus on work and money to a broader focus on the areas in your health that will be far more meaningful.

STEP 4

Sharpening Your Mental Focus

"Clarity affords focus."
Thomas Leonard

Chapter 32

Let's Look at Our Cognitive Styles

"No one is going to listen to you until you listen to yourself."
Marianne Williamson

Have you ever watched the British TV show *Doc Martin?* Set in a small seaside village, the male doctor is distant, analytical, and problem solving. As a contrast, there is a female teacher who is friendly, caring, and giving. Of course, as with most TV shows, there is a love interest, with one party (the female teacher) very interested and the other party (the doctor) rather resistant. When the two characters, sitting in the back of a car, have their first kiss, the doctor does not respond with a rush of enthusiasm or even a positive remark. Instead, he tries to diagnose her possible gastrointestinal difficulties from the taste of their first kiss. You can guess the teacher's reaction. First, she covers her mouth, worried about her breath. Then, after listening to his quick differential diagnosis, she slides out of the back seat and slams the door. His problem solving style of thinking? It just doesn't work in relationships. Now, I do not know if you can recall your first kiss with your spouse. I can. I remember thinking, as soon as our lips had touched, "My God, am I in trouble!" And, trust me, I was not viewing it as a problem.

So, what is my point? For all of us, there are two main cognitive (thinking) styles: a reactive mode (which searches for problems and works to correct the problems) and a responsive mode (which is more focused on relaxation and happiness). For our survival, reactive thinking has been crucial, alerting humans to life-threatening situations. But in today's world, does that reactive style of thinking help or hurt? Excluding the periodic natural disaster, the reactive style of thinking has become less helpful and more problematic. Yet, it persists in all of us, often making our lives worse, not better. Doc Martin's response to the kiss was an example of reactive thinking. The teacher's response to the kiss was an example of responsive thinking. Now, which style of thinking had a better chance of leading the couple towards connection and happiness? More importantly, which style of thinking has a better chance of leading you to increased happiness? And to a much better future?

For the nervous system, there is a saying that neurons that fire together, wire together. With your thinking style, it is much the same. Once a certain thinking style is ingrained (often through professional training or years at the office), it becomes far too permanent. Unfortunately, some people (like Doc Martin) have only one style of thinking, the reactive mode. You can argue that it is necessary for your profession, but it can be disastrous for your marriage. As you progress through your golden years, it can be destructive to almost every aspect of your life, even your health. The reactive mood, reflecting the sympathetic nervous system, leads to surges of negative hormones with decreases in the efficiency of your immune system and an increased risk of disease. With the reactive thinking mode, you may be primed for spotting something wrong, but you are also primed for disease and cancer. Doc Martin should have known better, yes?

So, what is the solution? You need to change the wiring of your brain and your ingrained pattern of thinking. Evolution has refined the brain's wiring over the years. Brains have progressed from reptilian to mammalian to human. Behaviors associated with those brains have expanded from avoiding pain to obtaining rewards to attaching to others. Obviously, you want the latter. Unfortunately, you do not have 200 million years to rewire your current thinking style. You only have a few decades. But it is doable. You just need to set a new default mode for your new thinking: the responsive mode. This is one of the goals of this step. I am going to help you leave behind the reactive mood, and I am going to help you better establish the responsive mode. Even your kissing will be more enjoyable. How do you succeed in this endeavor? You have already taken an important step. In Alcoholics Anonymous, they teach its members that the brain is a dangerous neighborhood and that you should "never go there alone." I would frame the issue differently. There are many obstacles that can obstruct your path toward happiness; just don't let your mind (and your reactive style of thinking) be one of them.

Can you guess the action that will be necessary for this part of your transformation? It's simple. You need to start listening to yourself. Your success in achieving mental clarity (and obtaining the benefits from this change) will depend on your understanding of your current style of thinking, your identification of the negative features that constitute your current style of thinking, and the development of habits to change your current style of thinking. It's similar to the Buddhist path: know the mind, shape the mind, and free the mind. However, in my experience, you have to undertake a dual task to achieve this goal. As you clear away parts of your current thinking style that can be problematic, you need to replace those components with a new thinking style that will lead to a better life. Again, as with so many features in your life, this transition demands the incorporation of specific daily habits. This new group of mental habits will help you through this mental transition so that you will be better able to tackle the future additional changes. Ask Doc Martin. If you have watched the TV show, he had to change his thinking before he could change himself. And if you have not watched Doc Martin, try a little kissing with less thinking. Doesn't that make you feel even better? Now, that could be your future.

Chapter 33

The Value of Positive Thinking

"If someone talked to you the way you talk to yourself,
you would have kicked them out of your life long ago."
Carla Gordon

All physicians like to highlight the mind-body connection. For my guide, I wanted to start by first offering some new habits to improve your physical health. I am now shifting my focus to habits for improving your thinking. For your golden years, you need to be functioning well in both spheres. The first mental habit that I want you to consider is basic. Many of you are familiar with the advice. But most of you still do not translate your awareness into action. I want you to observe and improve the quality of your internal dialogue, switching from a negative focus to a more positive focus. I am not offering a new spin for self-affirmations. I am not suggesting Pollyanna thinking. On the contrary, I am asking you to prepare for your older years by shifting your mental focus. Your golden years will require your best cognitive skills. As an initial step toward this goal, I want you to rewire your internal negative/positive balance. Can you improve your internal dialogue? For almost all of us, the answer is yes.

There is the mistaken belief that success in any endeavor starts with a series of external triumphs. Wrong. Success starts with internal triumphs. Discounting the initial simplicity of this habit, there is another fundamental truth. We live life from the inside out. There are plenty of well-known statements that carry validity. The quality of your life starts with the quality of your thinking. What you think about is what you become. The more you think about anything, the greater chance it has of becoming true. As you think, so shall you be. All of these statements underscore one simple message. Positive thinking is one of the keys for an enjoyable life. As you head toward your older years, think about what you want. Do not waste your valuable time thinking about what you do not want. People become too distracted by their daily problems, too distracted to focus on what really matters for their future. So, take control of your internal dialogue, making it less negative, more positive, and more focused on your desired future.

Studies on internal dialogue estimate that the average person has an ongoing, internal dialogue of around 150 to 300 words per minute or around 45,000 to 60,000 thoughts per day. Most people cannot remain mentally silent for more than 11 seconds. Unfortunately, the same studies show that 90 percent of today's thoughts are almost exactly the same as yesterday's thoughts. We are very repetitive creatures. Worse, these studies underscore that 90 percent of your internal dialogue is a mixture of negative thinking and worry. Studies show that 40 percent of worry focuses on things that never will happen; 30 percent of worry focuses on things that are over and can't be changed; 12 percent of worry focuses on unfounded fears of future situations; and 10 percent of worry focuses on irrelevant issues. That means that 8 percent of your worry is genuine and realistic. Therefore, with

92 percent of your worry useless, how productive (or engaged with others) do you think you are going to be? How happy do you think you are going to feel? How much time will you have left to think about how you are going to redesign your life? And if you do not think about that challenge, how will you make the necessary changes? You won't.

If you do not believe your style of thinking has a tremendous impact on the quality of your life, consider Nelson Mandela. Here is a man who was incarcerated for decades in South Africa. There were plenty of potential dark places inside his mind. But if you read his biography or autobiography, the man was able to avoid those dark places. He could have focused on those negative areas and become progressively angry, bitter. Instead, he was able to develop a style of disciplined, positive thinking. He was able to focus his attention on what he wanted for himself and his country, not on what he did not want. He was able to think about future positive developments, giving them time to grow toward fruition. When he was released from prison, he had remade himself into a better person and he had reshaped his final years, and it started from his disciplined, positive internal dialogue and improved mental clarity. Mandela was not an exception. A number of prisoners of war report the same experience. Their captivity forced them to change their thinking. You need to do the same. As a first step, delete the problem solving focus. Then drop the unnecessary worry and negative thinking. Simple? Not really. Like a sentry, you are going to have to guard against the natural, negative bias of reactive thinking. You are going to have to fight against your original wiring. Yes, you are going to have to work to establish a new style of thinking if you really want to change yourself and your life.

Chapter 34

Ready for Escape From Incarceration?

"The best thing you can give yourself is the gift of possibility."
Paul Newman

The Count of Monte Cristo, written by Alexandre Dumas, was published in 1844 and is considered a literary classic. The novel tells the tale of Edmond Dantes who was unfairly incarcerated with a sentence of life imprisonment. During years of incarceration and torture, he was befriended by another prisoner, a 'mad' priest, who secretly provided him with an extensive education, plus the location of a secret treasure on Monte Cristo. When the 'mad' priest died and his body bag was tossed from the steep cliff to the sea, Edmond Dantes escaped by replacing the priest's body with his own, surviving the fall and then swimming to another island. He found the treasure, changed his identity from Edmond Dantes to The Count of Monte Cristo, and started a quest for revenge. But the novel showcases his transformation from anger to compassion, from reactive thinking to responsive thinking, and from negative thinking to positive thinking. Like Edmond Dantes, you need much more than wealth; you need to let go of the pull of your prior negative thinking style.

Think of your golden years as a release from incarceration. Yes, you may still be shackled with employment. No, you will not have any sudden, secret wealth. But it is a chance to gain a different education. It is a chance to garner a different type of wealth. With the instructions in this guide, your older years could provide you with a chance to rewire your thinking and reawaken your mind. Do you want to waste that opportunity? Do you want to slide into further imprisonment? Unlike Edmond Dantes, there does not need to be a life-threatening gambit. You do not need to jump off a cliff. But you must want to grow into a better person. For Edmond Dantes, his escape did not come until after fourteen years of incarceration. In your case, you may have been incarcerated in your job and/or career for an even longer period of time. But the change can come just as quickly as Edmond Dantes's escape. Just read the suggestions and incorporate these new habits; and open yourself to some new possibilities.

You know your next challenge. After deleting your negative, problem solving thinking and your worries, you need to let go of any focus on prior mistakes. By the time we reach our older years, we have all made mistakes. We have created many situations we deeply regret. Most of us have experienced moments we would love to erase. You cannot erase those memories. But you do not have to ruminate over your mistakes. If some of those old memories pop into your mind, try not to dwell on them. I have a friend who claims that thinking makes you stupid. For many people that viewpoint carries some validity. Their negative thinking, their constant useless worry, and their focus on the past disrupts their life, ruining their chances for a good future. Now is your time to change your style of thinking. For your golden years, focus on replacing negative thoughts with positive thoughts. Catch yourself when you are worrying about something you cannot control, something you cannot change. Catch yourself when thinking about something negative or someone negative. Direct your thoughts toward something or someone positive, something you want in your life (and in your golden years). If you can establish this positive mental habit, you will have taken a step toward changing your life. And if I am correct that you live life from the inside out, your mental change will dramatically improve your external life. So, add this mental habit to your new eating style and exercise habits and notice how it sets you free.

Do you know how elephants are kept tied to such a small wooden stake? They are initially held with a large metal stake, buried deep in the ground. When young, they try to pull free of the tether that holds them to the stake, but they cannot break the firm ground. As they grow larger and larger, they don't try to pull against the tether, thinking it would be wasted effort. They fail to notice that the metal stake has been replaced with a small wooden stake. They fail to realize that they could now easily break free and roam the land. They remained trapped not by the stake, but by their old style of thinking. You cannot allow yourself to fall into the same trap. Imagine your old style of thinking as a small wooden peg, holding you back but ready to be discarded. Believe you can move beyond it. A good life, where you can live, love, and make a difference, awaits you. It just takes opening your eyes and seeing how you can change, and then making certain that you create the best mental habits to complete that change.

Chapter 35

Try These Litmus Tests

"Don't go backwards. You've already been there."
Ray Charles

Do you have doubts about the value of shifting your thinking style? If yes, I want you to take several litmus tests. Let's clarify your current mental state. For the next 24 hours, catch yourself every time you have a negative thought or any useless worry. Catch yourself every time you silently complain to yourself or ruminate about something or someone that you do not want in your life. If you can successfully stop yourself with these negative thoughts and useless worry, the result will be a new silence. That new silence is a wonderful starting point for beginning to think in more positive terms. It is the perfect platform for contemplating how to redesign your golden years. The greater the silence, the greater your new free time; and the greater your free time, the greater the opportunity to focus on the core issues that will be addressed in this guide. You want a new, fresh start, right? Then you must spend more time thinking about your future, and less time ruminating about your past.

To prepare for the next habit, how about another litmus test? How is your daily vocabulary? Do you ever listen to yourself talk? Do you think you use more negative words than positive words? Give yourself a short time period, perhaps five minutes, to write down all the positive words you can remember. Then give yourself, back to back, the same time period to write down all the negative words you can recall. Which list is longer? Which list is far easier to complete? If you are like most people, your list of negative words will come quickly; and your list of negative words will be far longer than the list of positive words. What does that tell you? Your external dialogue and your daily conversations may not be much better than your internal dialogue. Both of these dialogues may be far more negative than you realize. If you have not appreciated how disastrous that style can be for your happiness, this step will help you change your mind and your focus.

I suggest an additional litmus test. Read my full guide. Then repeat the above litmus tests after you have incorporated the new habits that fit your own needs. I predict you will be pleased with the results. When I started to work on this guide, I checked my own negative thinking. It was not pretty. I found myself focusing too much on current worries and past mistakes. Let me give you one example. When I was in the eighth grade, I killed a man on the golf course. I hit the longest drive of my life (up to that point); I watched with disbelief as the golf ball carried farther and farther down the fairway; and then I realized, too late, that the ball was heading directly toward an old man in the foursome ahead of us. I screamed "fore." The man jerked around; the ball landed smack beside his feet (missing him by inches); and he collapsed on the spot, right to the fairway grass. As one of his golfing buddies ran for the clubhouse and his other golfing cohorts struggled to keep him alive (he had apparently suffered a heart attack), they told me to just play through to the next hole. I remember hitting a four iron with a slight draw, carrying the water, and landing it right next to the pin for my first birdie on that hole. Did I feel any joy? No. By the time I replaced my flagstick on that hole, the man was dead.

We all have negative moments and negative experiences that seem to have a life of their own. We all have repetitive worries that plague our paths. These thoughts seem to intrude into our consciousness at the strangest moments. With this new habit, I was able to better control the intrusions of my worries, my negative thoughts, even that troubling memory. That event, so long ago, did not change the direction of my life, but it still created a sense of regret and remorse, feelings that can last a lifetime. Regrets are one thing; negative thoughts are another. For this habit, I want you to focus on deleting negative thoughts and useless worry, replacing them with positive thoughts. In my case, by the time I had finished writing this collection of new habits, my mind rarely wandered back to that day on the golf course. I was thinking less of the past, less of any problems, and less of any current worries. Instead, I was focusing more of my thoughts on positive things such as my hopes and dreams for my future. And it worked. More of the things I wanted began to appear in my life. In addition, it created more space for better thoughts and better feelings. Love needs some room to breathe, yes?

Chapter 36

Do You Hear Your Conversations?

"Observe all men; thyself most."
Benjamin Franklin

From the previous litmus tests, you can probably guess this next habit. Once again, we are starting small. I want you to take the same approach from your internal dialogue and apply it to your external dialogue, your conversations. Now I am not going to ask you to become sesquipedalian. Your vocabulary, at this stage of life, is part of who you are. But your vocabulary is a relevant topic. There are over 500,000 words in the English dictionary. The best writers in history have used the most words. Shakespeare used around 24,000 words with 5,000 words used just once. Most people use 2,000 to 3,000 words on a regular basis. Most people's daily vocabulary drops to just 500 words. In those 500 words, there are typically three times as many negative words as positive words. That is not very different from the ratio in the English dictionary. But it is a ratio that needs to change, because vocabulary, positive words versus negative words, is one of the best predictors of future happiness.

Your own vocabulary has been shaped by your career, your coworkers, your family, and your friends. It's even shaped by your gender. Women say 9,000 to 12,000 words per day while men say 3,000 to 4,000 words per day. Regardless of gender, your vocabulary is not really yours; it is part of your group. When you confine a group of people into one work environment, what happens? Their daily vocabularies begin to blend. Their usage of negative words also begins to blend. Think about it. What do many people discuss at work? Repetitive complaints. The discussions are often focused on the problems for that day. Everyone needs to vent from time to time, but too many people focus on the negatives at work. The "One Minute Manager" is not prevalent. Too many people scream foul at the obstacles at work. Too many people discuss those employees they dislike, not those employees they respect. They discuss all the things that are wrong in the office, and then they wonder why their work environment is not getting any better. Where does that leave you? It leaves you living with their vocabulary and their negative external dialogue.

Helen Keller, the first deaf, blind person to earn a bachelor of arts degree and the young girl who was immortalized in the play and movie *The Miracle Worker*, was once asked: Which was worse, blindness or deafness? When presented with a hypothetical choice of having one of the two conditions, most people profess that blindness must be worse. Helen Keller strongly disagreed with that hypothetical assertion. She proclaimed that deafness was worse. She highlighted the power of the word and the power of communication. From her perspective, your voice is the foundation of your independence, the springboard for your future. Her voice may have come through her sign language, but it still gave her the force to reshape her life and move forward to a new, brighter future as a famous author, political activist, and lecturer.

For your golden years, you need to take back your vocabulary and your external dialogue to make it your own. Listen to your conversations. Ask yourself: What did you just say? Then try to use more positive words than negative words. Think about it. Connect a negative vocabulary to an equally negative external dialogue and what does the combination yield? You have people who use negative language to complain about the things they do not want in their lives. If the things you do not want suddenly appear in your life, should you be surprised? No, especially if that is what you have been discussing. The truth may be painful. You helped bring them into your life simply by focusing on them. As the saying goes, you do not achieve success; you attract success. You attract whatever you discuss. Now, are you willing to change the focus for your conversations to something more positive?

Let me share another personal example, although an example from a few years ago. When my daughter Skyler turned sixteen and was able to drive, I had these repetitive negative thoughts that focused on her driving. What if something went wrong with some part of the car and she was stranded? Worse, what if she had an accident? Well, in less than a year, she had totaled the car. I remember her call that day and I can still easily visualize the air bag burns on her arms when I picked her up. It's one of those chilling moments when you realize how much you care for someone. We both cried a little on our drive back home. The crunched car no longer mattered. But, years later, knowing what I now know, I will ask myself: Did all of my worrying (and negative thoughts) increase the chance for that accident? The question may sound stupid, but there are studies that show that negative thinking can increase the chance of a negative result. So, today? Every time I have a worry about one of my two daughters, I delete the thought. I want them to be happy, and that's where I steer all of my thoughts.

So, here is my simple recommendation. Know thyself, and be aware of your own conversations, internal and external. On a daily basis, think about the good things in your life. If there are not a sufficient number of good things, then think about the good things you want in your future life. Or the good things you want in the lives of the people you love. Apply the same approach to your external dialogue. Try to talk about something you want. Try to talk about something others want. If you can follow those suggestions, I believe you will be improving the odds for your future happiness. At a minimum, at least be aware of the power of your conversations, the importance of the ratio of positive words to negative words, and the impact of your daily conversations on your future. They are creating the daily environment for your life, and potentially the climate for your upcoming years. With such a potential massive payoff, it is well worth the effort to be aware, and then take some control of yourself. Without this level of self-control, how will you be able to really change and grow?

Chapter 37

Another Starting Line

"Life is a series of commas, not periods."
Matthew McConaughey

These two habits, your internal and external dialogue, do more than clarify your mind and your daily conversations. These two habits reshape your attitude. At this point in your life, you do not need more aptitude; you need the right attitude. The right attitude leads to the right behavior. For a clarification of the right behaviors, you are going to have to wait for the other components of this guide. But you cannot work on the upcoming suggestions if your mental slate, your mind and daily conversations, is so cluttered with debris from your current life, or your past life, that there is simply no free time for positive thoughts or the development of new habits. These first two habits will create the mental space for your future changes, and a better chance for meaningful changes. With these first two habits, you can, like Helen Keller, break through and find a new voice to start building a new life.

There are studies of people that measure their daily mood. If you score a person's mood from -10 to +10, most people go through life hovering around a daily mood score of 0 to 2. Ask yourself: Do you want to go through your golden years idling in neutral? No, you want to reach a higher number. To reach a higher state, you have to "take in the good," at least that's how experts explain the process. With your positive focus, try to focus on something good, but not just for an instant. Try to focus on it, appreciate it, and savor it. Unlike Doc Martin, savor that kiss. Watch that sunset. Take a glance at the evening stars. Those moments rewire your responsive mood of thinking and reset your parasympathetic nervous system. That creates an internal environment that amplifies your mood, your attitude, and your degree of personal satisfaction. Just as important, it sets the stage for the learning of these habits. How well do you learn when feeling anxious? How well do you perform when worried? Think of the learning that Helen Keller achieved once she broke free of her prior wiring. With these new mental habits, you will be hotwired, ready to learn and grow.

So, make certain you solidify these two habits. Work on them daily. Initially, it will require effort to observe (and control) your internal and external dialogue. But with time, this initial effort will become a habit that requires no effort at all. So, at this point, what am I expecting? I am expecting you to develop the habit of catching negative thoughts, deleting negative thoughts, and switching to more positive thoughts, with your internal dialogue shifting toward the things you want in your golden years. I am expecting you to develop the habit of monitoring your daily conversation, improving your vocabulary (positive words, not five syllable words) and upgrading the content of your remarks. I am expecting improvement in your style of thinking and the focus of your conversations. With these changes, I am expecting you to develop a clearer mind (and a better attitude) that is ready to learn and incorporate new habits. There are many challenges that lie ahead, challenges that must be met to successfully redesign your golden years. At least, with improved mental clarity, you will be free to make these changes.

This perspective is where I may differ from other proponents of positive thinking or positive conversations. These two habits, internal dialogue and external dialogue, are preached by many others in the self-help field. My comments do not represent anything new or fresh. But many proponents view these habits as another end point. I view these two habits as just another starting point. Yes, I support the long-term benefit of these two mental habits. But I am hoping for the short-term benefit. In the subsequent steps, starting with this next step, I have material for you to consider with new habits. My suggestions will not have much success if your mind is not positive and focused, and if your mood is not steady and upbeat. My recommendations will not have much success if your negative conversations remain focused on the wrong issues. So, if you are going to move forward through a series of commas (or phases) and incorporate these mental habits, you will be ready to give my guide a real chance to change your life.

Chapter 38

The Need for a Life Review

"Don't let yesterday use up too much of today."
Will Rogers

For mental clarity, is there anything else you need to do to clear your mind? The answer is yes; and my suggestion may surprise you. You may know Socrates's line, "Know thyself because an unexamined life is not worth living." Right now, as you incorporate those mental habits, take time to pause and reflect; take time to evaluate your important memories. I know, I know. The two approaches seem contradictory. They are not. Yes, I want you to delete random negative thoughts and useless worry. Yes, I want you to push aside conversations with a negative focus. But I do not want you to push aside your past or your strongest, most important memories *yet*. Instead, I want you to gain a better understanding of the meaning within those memories, positive or negative. Why is this knowledge so important? You cannot change your past, but you can better appreciate your past. From my perspective, an improved appreciation of your past will make it easier for you to change your future.

There is the mistaken belief that we obtain wisdom through experience. In truth, wisdom comes from reflection on your experience. Your life constantly moves forward, but you can only make sense of your life by looking backward. No, I do not want you to take this approach over a long period. I want you to take this approach for the short-term (while you screen your thoughts and memories). For most of us, there are certain events that have shaped our lives. However, it is our interpretation of those events that shape who we become. Most importantly, you have to ask yourself: Is your interpretation accurate? Or have you distorted certain memories? Have you only examined the superficial events but not the deeper issues? With any life-changing event, there are often thoughts and feelings that remain alive and powerful for years. Some of these events may never have been examined. Now is the time to correct that mistake, reaching a new interpretation of those events, and a new appreciation of yourself. Why am I making this suggestion? Because I want you to let go of prior faulty self-assessments. I don't want you to let those prior, distorted perceptions define you. At this point, a review of your life can lead you to a better acceptance of the prior events, a more compassionate acceptance of yourself, and better mental clarity for your future.

With a deeper understanding of past events you will be more able to re-author your life story. Clarify who you were at the time of those prior events, who you currently are (through your reflections and learning), and who you can become in the future. With this insight, you can more easily move away from negative ruminations and free yourself from the intrusive pull of your old negative memories. You can also free yourself of the old habits that have risen from those events. Just remember: those habits were reflective of the specific circumstances, not reflective of you, and certainly not reflective of who you want to become.

Forgive yourself for prior setbacks. By reviewing your memories and rewriting your life story, you can undo associated bad habits. You can move past disappointments and unfinished business. You can clean your mental slate to an even greater degree, reaching a higher level of mental clarity.

Here is my suggestion. First, you need to suspend judgment of yourself or the specific events. Second, you need to ask yourself: What four to six events transformed you so that you were never the same? What four to six events forged your personality and made you who you are today? These events could be positive, but for many people those events were negative. Typically, these events were associated with intense emotions with either 'aha' moments or 'ouch' moments. As you recall these events, do not just delete them. Study them. Analyze them. A Japanese poet once observed: "My barn burned down. Now I can see the moon." So, your challenge is straightforward. What can you learn, before you start the habit of deleting these negative thoughts, from your most difficult memories? With better understanding, what can you now see that you could not previously see? If you can harvest your life story and gain a better understanding of these events, you can better disconnect yourself from those difficult events, negative thoughts, and useless worry. That is your larger challenge: complete a life review that propels you toward better mental clarity. Understand the life forces that might be driving your negative thoughts. Understand the 'why' (why you are the way you are) before starting to work on the 'how' (how to change into a better person).

Now, let me add one more point. With this suggestion, I am not recommending therapy as part of this task. I believe that you can complete this process on your own, simply by pausing to reflect. You may find this hard to believe, but I have a bias against therapy unless it's to treat a specific illness. After my medical internship, I completed a psychiatric residency. But I was more interested in using the psychiatric expertise to progress into public health and health care management. When I was in the second year of my psychiatric residency, the head of the program gave each resident the names of five psychiatrists with the suggestion to experience therapy. Do you know what I did? I called each of those psychiatrists at midnight. Days later, when I encountered the head of the psychiatric department, he asked me: "How did those calls go?" I responded, "Great," without ever mentioning that I had bypassed that directive. And you thought I was joking when I stated that I try my best not to see physicians? For you, I am not arguing against therapy for some troubling symptoms. However, for this life review process, try it on your own. Review. Learn. Without taking up a great deal of time. Socrates and Will Rogers are both correct. It is important to know yourself, but you do not want to let yesterday use up today. Complete the review and then move forward, with a sense of freedom for your new life.

Chapter 39

My Confession

"It is never too late in fiction or life to revise."
Nancy Thayer

For many people, if you take the time to review your life story, you can discover the underlying myth about yourself. Let me give you an example of my own life story. When I was in the fourth grade, my family moved from Southern California to Pittsburgh, Pennsylvania. Up to that move, I had always been an outgoing, active participant with the 19 neighborhood kids who lived on my block. With the move, I suddenly had no kids on my block. Instant isolation. And it got worse, not better. I moved to a different city in both the fifth grade and the sixth grade, from Pittsburgh to Louisville to Chicago. By the time of my last move, I was racing home after school, hiding the "For Sale" sign before other children would notice it. For me, as a young kid, my personality changed over three years of moving from an outgoing boy to a quiet, more reserved, isolated kid. And you know what? That style of behavior, that withdrawal into myself, lasted for decades. But was it really my nature? Or was it simply a habit born of those specific geographic moves?

When I asked my mother to describe my personality in my childhood years before those moves, she simply laughed at my nickname, "Buffalo Bill." Apparently, as a toddler, I was constantly running naked down the streets, wanting to play with other children. Now, knowing this fact, you may feel relieved that I was not living on your street. But my natural personality was to engage, not isolate. So, what happened when I reviewed my own life story? I realized that my habitual pattern of isolation did not feel right to me. I was able to break through my distorted view of myself and let go of the disempowering parts. I was able to let go of my earlier faulty conclusions. So, with this new insight, and with less effort than I would have imagined, those memories began to fade. Better yet, I was able to change my habit of isolation into a habit of engagement with a more outgoing nature and more willingness to make new friends. For me, why was that so important? Because, as you reach your golden years, you do not want solo aging. That leads to decay. You want to be involved with others. You will be happier. Suddenly, after my own life review, my future looked much brighter.

So, what about you? Are there events that you may have misinterpreted? Are there some memories that have caused years of discomfort? Are there some old habits, created from those prior events, which have become ingrained but do not reflect the real person beneath your exterior? Some memories are like family skeletons. It is best to bring them out of the darkness and into the light. Examine them. Understand them. Then let them go. With a review of your memories and an understanding of the forces behind those memories, you will be able to reach a new level of understanding and an improved piece of mind. And with awareness, you can revise. You can lose old negative habits, gain new positive habits, and become a better person. As the saying goes, you do not want to live on the litter of your life; you want to rise above the debris of your past. You want to live in the present, free of prior restraints.

So, that is why I would encourage you to combine the new mental habits with this new life review. If you are going to pay increased attention to your thoughts, why not try some multi-tasking that is so prominent with your children? As you develop the habit of deleting negative thoughts and changing conversations, take notice of your memories and improve your understanding of your life story. You will be seeing with new eyes. If you can accomplish this task, you will notice a decrease in the number of intrusive thoughts/memories. You will feel less of a pull toward the past, and you will experience more of a push toward the future. Your thinking will be sharper and clearer, less cluttered with negative memories. Your mental clarity will create space for new hopes, aspirations, and dreams. Embrace these elements. They will play a key role in your golden years. Please do not underestimate the power of this mental change; and remember that it is never too late to revise. If you do not complete some type of life review, you may sail into your golden years wanting to change but with an anchor tied to your stern, dragging in the depth below, slowing your progress. With that type of weight, it will be harder to move forward and much harder to change yourself and your life.

Chapter 40

No Life Review?
Why Not?

"Anything in life that we don't accept will make trouble for us
until we make peace with it."
Shakti Gawain

For most of my life, my father was my "best buddy." We spent hours watching sports on TV and played innumerable rounds of golf. For me, it was sad to watch him develop dementia, slowing losing the better parts of himself. He became progressively angry, erupting into fits of rage. He would recognize me, but fail to recognize my mother. As these incidents increased in frequency, they increased in intensity. At one point, he was driving my mother over to my house, claiming that he did not want to sleep with an unknown woman. He was worried what she might ask him to do (which was a bit awkward); and he was worried that his parents (who had been dead for a godzillion years) would walk in while he was doing something that he should not be doing. So, how does all of this relate to a life review? Or the lack of a life review? As just highlighted in the previous step, if there are skeletons, it is best to bring them into the light. Because if they remain buried, they can fester and explode, ripping at the fabric of your life.

With these episodes, I would drive them back to their house and then sit both of them down, explaining to my father, over and over again, that my mother was his wife. This fact horrified him. He kept saying, "But I don't know her. How do I know if I even like her?" In truth, he loved her, and they had enjoyed 60 years of a great marriage. But during these episodes, as he tried to understand his confusion, the truth was only slowly revealed. He felt some buried resentment because of something that had never been disclosed. My mother, at the start of my father's senior year of college, had become pregnant. Love is love: it happens. His parents had been livid. So, the two of them had eloped to a town close to his college and they had been married in the fall. My father's mistake was not his love and passion. My mother was beautiful. Who could blame him? His mistake was hiding this secret (my parents never celebrated their anniversary on the correct date) and never clarifying his view of this event. A part of him must have believed that my mother's pregnancy and their marriage had negatively changed his life. Instead of following his dream and heading into coaching football (he was the captain of his collegiate football team), he must have felt forced to switch toward a business career so that he could support the unexpected family.

Now, you may ask: What good could have come from a life review? For all of his life, my father had offered the same refrain. Forget the past. Focus on the future. He had followed that perspective by rarely discussing any of his prior athletic triumphs or his earlier years, especially his time in college. In one way, that approach was successful. He became good at deleting negative thoughts until he slid toward dementia. If I could have rewound time, I would have stopped him as he reached his own golden years and directed him to complete a life review. If he had completed that task, he might have gained a new, different perspective on that earlier incident. My father fell passionately in love with my mother when they met; and he loved her throughout their years together. It was not that he did not like my mother; he did not like that one incident. With a life review, he could have seen that the mistake was really the act of love, two people connecting with passion. Is that so bad? Is that ever a mistake? The world needs more love, not less love. If the event could have been reviewed, my dad might have been able to release his buried anger and realize the positives. Yes, he disappointed his parents. Yes, his life course took an immediate different arc. But it was an arc with much joy. Truly, they loved each other. They made a great couple. In his subsequent family, there was much joy. In business, he was successful. In this new arc of his life, he created many friends. If you look at his life from a comprehensive perspective, my mother's pregnancy wasn't a misstep at all. In fact, the only negative was the unresolved anger that erupted in his dementia.

Now, why have I shared this story? Because it repeats the need to combine your habits. You will make progress with the improvement of your cognitive style and the improvement of your external dialogue. But those improvements need to be placed into the right context. What is the right context? It is pausing to review your life, gaining a new appreciation of yourself and your past missteps. When you have those "ouch" moments, your view of yourself and your predicament may be too one-sided and far too emotional. If you can go back and reflect on those incidents, you can see how you were unfair to so harshly judge yourself and others. You cannot correct a misstep, but you can gain a new understanding of the misstep. With just a little effort, you can see yourself in a more positive, forgiving manner. You can also see, and appreciate, the real you who survived the incident. Remember: self-acceptance is crucial for growth. A life review, when combined with the other habits in this step, will lead you to greater mental clarity and greater peace of mind. And you will need both the mental clarity and the peace of mind to be really free for change. So, don't neglect the life review. Give yourself better mental clarity. Give yourself some peace. Make your life better. And who knows? You just might laugh at those incidents and shift all of your focus to your future.

Chapter 41

You're Now Rewired to Grow

"How people treat you is their karma; how you react is yours."
Wayne Dyer

Everyone knows that when you have a brain injury it impacts the quality of your thinking. A concussion can leave you confused for several days. Dementia can rob you of recent memory. But most people do not realize that the quality of thinking can actually change the function and structure of your brain. Can you guess my next point? Your new mental habits and your new style of thinking will dramatically improve the function and structure of your brain. There are studies that verify the lifelong neuro-plasticity of your brain. Negative thinking and negative rumination change your brain waves, decrease the use of oxygen and glucose, and interrupt the flow of your neurochemicals. Positive thoughts and positive conversations sculpt your brain toward a higher level of function. Those mental processes increase blood flow, improve nutrient absorption, and even alter gene expression. So, this new mental clarity is not something superficial; it is tangible and organic, and very beneficial.

Want another revelation? This impact is long-term, not short-term. As previously mentioned, you have around 1.1 trillion brain cells. However, 10,000 brain cells die each and every day. For most of us, that translates to a five percent loss of brain function by the time we reach 65. That explains why we lose our train of thought and why some names become more difficult to retrieve. But did you know that your style of thinking impacts the speed of your cognitive decline? I do not need to mention the obvious, but positive mental clarity with its corresponding increased blood flow and better transport of nutrients leads to a smaller drop in cognitive decline. So, the message is the same. Your thinking style is crucial on so many different levels, especially as you hit your older years. Still unconvinced? Picture your mind as a muscle. If you lift weights, you can increase the size of a specific muscle; and if you can increase the size of that muscle, you can improve its strength and increase its level of activity. Your brain is the same. Do you want to nourish it with positive thoughts and positive conversations? Or do you want it to decline at an even faster pace with negative thoughts and negative conversations?

As for the life review, there are additional unforeseen benefits. You will change more than your mental clarity. You will change your emotional state. Again, the change comes through changes to brain function and brain structure, and temporary changes often lead to permanent changes. Consistent positive thinking increases the thickness of a part of your brain called the insula. This increasing thickness leads to more empathy and greater compassion. With a productive life review, where you can appreciate and accept your history, anger can disappear. Guilt and shame, two emotions of limited benefit, can be vanquished. Depression can shift toward happiness. That is why, when reviewing your life story, you cannot let yourself be cemented to old beliefs. Your old memories and emotions can be reconfigured into something more positive with far more understanding and compassion. Reduce the tendency to judge yourself, compare yourself, or criticize yourself. Learn to forgive yourself (for those negative experiences) and become better able to accept yourself and any prior flaws. You need to be on your team, supporting yourself. Think about it. Good people tend to be happy people; and happy people tend to be good people. A life review, coupled with the right mental habits, should create a clear path for you to become a better (and happier) person.

So, here is my hope for this next part of my survivor kit. With improved physical health, improved mental clarity, a better understanding of your history, more acceptance of yourself, and a greater sense of compassion for yourself, you should be primed to move forward and ready to grow into a better person. Better able to live freely. Better able to love. Better able to make a difference. The habits discussed in the earlier steps may not yet be ingrained, and the life review may not be fully completed, but hopefully you have been able to progressively improve your focus on your future, free from the shackles of old habits. You will be better able to incorporate my suggestions with a new sense of freedom. So, consider these first four steps as just the foundation. Your real future, how you design your golden years and how you change yourself and your life, can now be addressed in the remaining steps. Finally, after pouring the foundation, you can start building a life of value, joy, and meaning. And it will be based on your karma, not on someone else's karma.

STEP 5

Creating a New Direction for Your Life

"The purpose of life is a life of purpose."
Robert Bryne

Chapter 42

Have You Buried Your Dreams?

"Dream ... it gives the heavens something to work with."
Trish Whynot

The Make-A-Wish Foundation was founded in the United States with the goal of granting a wish to child, ages two and a half to eighteen, who was dying from a life-threatening medical condition. This organization has spread around the world, currently offering programs in 47 countries. We have all witnessed the result as some child has been transformed from pain and suffering to moments of disbelief, exhilaration, and joy. For some children, it has been a meeting with a famous personality. For other children, it has been a vacation to some fantasy site. For all the children, it has been the realization of a dream. But dreams are not just important to children. Dreams are vital to each one of us at every age. Too often, dreams are tossed aside, left behind as we meet the demands of our lives. Remind yourself: when you lose the capacity to dream, you lose the capacity to grow. Now is the time to establish a renewed commitment to your dreams. Now is the time to reconnect with the possibilities within your life.

Most people, progressing into their older years, proclaim it is too late to go after their dreams. They cite a litany of excuses. They do not have sufficient time or money. They do not possess the necessary skills. There are too many real-life obstacles. The truth? It is never too late to awaken your dreams. You are never too old to create your own miracles. Now, there is always someone in your life who will tell you that you cannot achieve your dream. A family member. A coworker. A neighbor. But they are not the problem. You, and the doubter and critic within you, are the primary problem. So, what should you do? Ignore the reality of your challenge? Banish the doubter and critic? Just the opposite. Talk to the doubter and critic that reside within you. Listen to their inner voices. But you do not need to believe their content. The doubter and critic are internal bullies from your past, often comparing your worst to someone else's best. In a way they reflect the world. Isn't every commercial, which sells something, telling you that you are not enough? That, to be okay, you must purchase their product? With every single lie, there is a corresponding truth. Yes, you are enough. You just need to develop a tougher skin and a softer heart that will offer kindness, compassion, and renewed support to yourself to follow your dreams.

A dream resides in your imagination. The doubts, the self-criticism, and the subsequent limiting beliefs also reside in your imagination. Be aware of your limiting beliefs. Do you think you are not good enough? Do you think you don't deserve the happiness? Do you think your dream is just not possible? Your negative beliefs can be replaced by positive beliefs. You can choose new beliefs. You can replace the voice of a coworker or a neighbor. You can counter the inner voices of your doubter and critic with the emergence of your new wisdom with a vision of your future.

Remember the outcome of the life review process with better clarity of your past and the establishment of new self-assessment? Take the same approach with the doubter and the critic. Go ahead and listen to them, remembering how people beat up themselves. But just listen, and then move past their false arguments. Move beyond their habit of linking your future to your past. Don't let them fool you into focusing on mistakes or failures. Failing at something does not mean you are a failure. We all make mistakes. We all fail. Many times. Instead, focus on what you have learned. Isn't your central task to shed the old behaviors, old beliefs, and old habits and establish new behaviors, new beliefs, and new habits? What does it take? Practice. And when you practice, don't be overly realistic. Don't get bogged down thinking about strategies. Give your dreams a chance to flourish with sufficient time to grow.

Over the course of my life, I have had an enduring dream of writing. In college, I wrote a novella, which was not published. After my psychiatric residency and my trip to Spain, I wrote a novel, which was not published. During my years of working in public health administration, I wrote, with a fellow writer named Dr. Joseph Hullett, four scripts, which never made it to the big screen. The closest we ever came? Edward Asner, who was a very successful actor and (at the time) the head of the Screen Actors Guild, loved one of our screenplays, The Pledge. He called the telephone number on our script, which was the telephone number to Joe Hullett's home. His wife answered. Asner introduced himself, "This is Mr. Edward Asner. And I am calling to speak to either Dr. Courter or Dr. Hullett." Joe's wife, not catching the name, asked, "Who are you representing?" He responded with a degree of annoyance, "Ed Asner." She responded, "Yes, Mr. Asner, but who are you representing?" Well, you can imagine how that conversation went straight south! But should I look at all of my writing attempts and count the failures? No, I should only look at the process. Did those writing attempts offer me joy? Were they part of my underlying dream? Yes. That is all that matters.

Now, at this point, what do you think I am going to suggest? Negate your doubts and self-criticism? Yes. Reduce your negative self-talk? Yes. Move from a breakdown to a breakthrough? Yes. Push through confusion toward clarity? Yes. But I like the phrase: "the speed of going slow." For me, that phrase accents the importance of moving slowly with small steps. Right now,

I do not want you to list your dreams. Instead, I want you to pause, as you did with the life review, and consider the upcoming issues. If you are going to build something of value (and your dreams have tremendous value for improving your life), it is crucial to first lay the foundation for those dreams. That will take some inner reflection and some personal conversations. So, over the next several chapters, see where our discussions lead you. Once we have further clarified this next component, then we will progress toward your dreams and hopefully uncover the unifying forces to make those dreams come true. Those dreams may just awaken a new vitality that will change your life and those people around you.

Chapter 43

Any Forgotten Talents Or Passions?

"Your talent is God's gift to you.
What you do with it is your gift back to God."
Leo Buscaglia

Let's start by examining one feature of your life. Studies show that 95 percent of people are in the wrong job. For the majority of people, the job became available when they became available. Voila, there was their career. For much of their lives, those

95 percent of people have lived in quiet desperation. Only five percent of people love their jobs. How did that happen? Because only five percent of people have followed their talents. Only five percent of people have followed their passions. How about you? Now that you are primed to redesign your golden years, are you in the wrong job? The wrong career? If your answer is "yes," do you want to remain part of the 95 percent who are not utilizing their innate talents, who are not following their passions? People who utilize their talents and follow their passions are the individuals who are doing what they love. They have become the people they truly want to be. In your golden years, shouldn't you be doing what you love? Shouldn't you be the person you most want to be?

Some people will attest that they have no specific talents and no clear passions. What do you do if you are one of those people? Let me explain my own philosophical perspective. I believe each person has a special, unique talent. I believe each person has a special way of expressing that talent. I believe each person's goal should be to find, nurture, and share that talent with others. It does not have to be a world-changing talent; it can be a talent, small or large, that provides joy to you. However, by finding and sharing your talent, it ignites your (all-too-often-buried) passions. In your golden years, you need to rediscover your talents and let them spark your passions. But what happens if you cannot clarify any talents? Studies show that many individuals uncover their talents between the ages of seven and fourteen. If you were currently uncertain as to your talents and passions, I would recommend reviewing those specific years from seven to fourteen, remembering what activities led to your greatest level of joy. Now, ask yourself: Could some of those enjoyable earlier activities reflect hidden talents and buried passions? Could some of those earlier activities become part of your golden years?

In the search for your talents and passions, you need to remember that you don't have to be great in any of those activities. These activities only have to provide you with joy, not with achievement. Besides, in these activities, do not compare yourself to others. Don't try to be better than someone else. Try to be the best you can be. There's an overriding truth to remember. It is called the 80:20 principle, and it can be applied to many different areas of your life. The reality is simple: 80 percent of your happiness typically comes from 20 percent of your activities. You need to clarify what activities, which 20 percent of your activities, give you 80 percent of your joy. In most cases, those activities reflect your talents and passions. Expand those activities so they fill more of your life. The process of rediscovering your talents and then unleashing your buried passions is a key avenue toward improving the quality of your life. Again, you want your golden years to be filled with those activities that give you the most joy. Expanding your talents and strengthening your passions: that is another challenge, but a challenge can be met when clarifying your life purpose.

As for me, in those formative years from seven to fourteen years, I loved sports, except, of course, on the day I killed that older man on the golf course. I also found a passion for writing. In one of my classes, we were assigned a homework project to write a short story. To my surprise, the class liked it. Now, that was not any great triumph. But I enjoyed the process. So, from those two activities, playing sports and writing, what can I bring into my older years? From my interest in sports, there is a clear progression to an interest in remaining fit to staying healthy. From the interest in writing, there is another easy progression for trying to share my interest in health (and other areas of life) through my writing. Again, does it matter if the process pleases only me? Does it matter if my writing does not lead to the best-seller list? No. What counts is linking your earlier talents and passions to activities that you can do now in your older years so you reactivate some of your buried dreams.

Some people are still likely to draw a blank or find nothing from their earlier years that can be brought forward into their older years. A talent? A passion? But I have no talent! My passions: they must have long since died! To those people, I would expand the question. Over your lifetime, what activities have been easiest to learn and easiest to do? Are there activities in which you have excelled? Typically, a person's talents lie within those activities where they excel, where they can feel good about themselves. The same results hold true for your passions. When do you feel most exhilarated? Most alive? Now, what happens if you find nothing, no earlier talent or passion, which can be brought into your golden years? I would encourage you to search harder, and for a longer period, as everyone (I believe) has hidden talents and buried passions. Unfortunately, some talents and passions are just not that visible. Some of them are buried pretty deep. Some of them are calcified. So, if you cannot find any specific talents or any passion, well … I would tell you that result is perfectly acceptable for now. There are other paths, which we will explore. These upcoming paths will hopefully help resurrect those talents and passions, and, of course, resurrect renewed vitality for living, loving, and making a difference.

Chapter 44

We All Need to Find More Meaning

"It's not uncommon for people to spend their whole life waiting to start living."
Eckart Tolle

For many older people, life becomes meaningless. In your older years, life can become frustrating. The result can be depression and/or anger, with the anger directed at others or even the world. There is a more disturbing truth. The majority of people are not that helpful. They seem focused on themselves and their challenges, leaving you in their wake. In the beginning of my program, I highlighted the spectrum of your many life challenges. In truth, all of us have many of the same challenges. What can we do? We can incorporate the new key habits. There may be limited options for changing your employment, but that does not mean there cannot be major changes in your work, or the search for more meaning (large or small) in your life. Large does not (necessarily) refer to size. Large could refer to its depth. Small can be a wonderful destination. Life cannot be a quest for more money; it has to be a quest for meaning, finding the real you (and the things that matter to you).

Where do we find meaning in our lives? Typically, we find meaning when we combine our talents and our passions. Many of you are stuck in a work position that does not use your talents or your passions. There may not be an opportunity to combine these components with your work. In today's world, that is an unfortunate reality. So, what can you do? Find a secondary career? Or perhaps search for activities outside of your work? That means you have to switch your priorities. Work can no longer be supreme. Yes, you have to pay the bills. No, you cannot retire. So acknowledge that your current work is not going to fulfill any dream. You know my opinion. I do not think the word 'workaholic' fits into anyone's golden years, unless you are one of those rare individuals, the five percent of people, who are working in a job that is already aligned with your talents and passions. For most of us, that's not the formula for our employment. So, starting now, you need to de-prioritize work and direct yourself toward the areas of your life that offer much more meaning. Find ways to utilize your talents and passions outside of the office, and that shift will lead you toward finding more meaning.

I do not pretend this transition is easy. For starters, your work and your many challenges may have already drained you dry. That is why you need to consider all the suggestions. If you are going to make the move to a new career or create more time for searching for new talents and new passions, you may need to accept the reality of simply having less. That is not so bad. That reality forces you to focus on quality, not quantity. It forces you to focus on things of substance. It forces you to make the most of the things you currently have in your life. It also forces you to reexamine our discussion of the 80:20 principle. It may force you, after many years of looking the other way, to shift your focus back to that all-so-important 20 percent of activities. Within that 20 percent of activities, there are often overlooked areas that offer more meaning. If you can refocus on those things that matter, you do not need more. You just need to add more things of meaning to your life. With renewed physical health and improved mental clarity, now is the perfect time to make that life change.

There is something else to keep in mind. In today's world, success is too often defined through money. You need to change your definition of success, especially with the growing financial inequity. Create a new definition of success and apply it to those individuals who combine talent and passion, finding meaning, not financial reward. There are more important rewards than wealth. If you can combine talent and passion, you have an opportunity to create something meaningful, something that will change the quality of your life and your family's life. This shift can arouse initial anxiety and some depression. Why? Because the search often reveals the shortcomings in your current life; how your current work has derailed other pursuits; how your job has interfered with your family; and how, as previously stated, the things that matter the most, well ... they have been displaced by the things that matter the least. Hopefully, you will realize the hidden cost of the current, narrow financial definition of success. I am not a fan of regret or remorse. I am a fan of hope and action. If you can create a new, different definition of success, you can create a new direction for your life; and if you can create a new direction for yourself, you can still create something far more meaningful than a higher paycheck. So, how can you start this process? It starts with a personal mission and a new life purpose. It's time to start changing and start living.

Chapter 45

Clarifying Your Life Mission/Purpose

"The minute you choose to do what you really want to do; it's a different kind of life."

Buckminster Fuller

You have probably been exposed to mission statements from companies. From my experience, those mission statements usually have minimal value. However, for some companies, and for some people, mission statements can be life changing. Jeffrey

Knight, my friend who was discussed at the start of the book, was traveling from Boston to Los Angeles, ready to jump-start his career at the age of 26. He wandered into a small speck of a restaurant, named Good Earth, which seated 18 customers in an old bankrupt building in Reno, Nevada. But its owner, William Galt, offered a mission statement about changing the dietary habits of the world. That mission statement resonated with my friend. He met the passionate owner, offered to work for free (at least at the start), and helped transform the single restaurant into a chain that was feeding ten million people in less than three years. That is the power of a well-crafted mission statement. It can shift your life toward a new, brighter future.

In my younger days, when I was lecturing, I would encourage the audience members to develop their own personal mission statement, encapsulating how they were going to add more meaning to their lives. I now take a different approach. For some people, mission statements feel too work-related. So, at this point, I want to offer a choice. Either develop a personal mission statement or develop a new purpose for your life. Frame the challenge in whatever words feel most comfortable. Just answer two basic questions. Who do you want to be? And what direction do you want for your life? Now, at this point, you need to make an important distinction. It's one of the cornerstones of my belief system. I do not want you to list your personal mission or new life purpose as an external goal. Just the opposite. I want you to ignore the pull of listing any external accomplishment or external reward. Remember my belief that you live life from the inside out. In keeping with that simple perspective (which hopefully permeates through each step), I want you to address your personal mission and life purpose as something internal, not external. Your personal mission and life purpose should clarify your desired internal mental state. It should clarify, more than anything, what type of person you want to become.

Let me explain. For decades, most of you have been struggling toward external goals. Those external goals may have been work-related or home/family-related. At this point, let's just take one example: employment. What have you sought? A promotion? A higher paycheck? A greater ability to provide (financially) for your family? And what has been the result of your constant labor? Have you achieved your external dreams and goals? For most people, the answer is no. They may have made some progress, but they have paid a high price. They have endured chronic stress, with the negative consequences of reduced health, reduced time with the family, and reduced happiness. Why have these people endured such hardship? Because of the mistaken belief that external rewards will lead to greater happiness. Well, it doesn't work that way. Even when the lucky ones achieve their work dreams/goals with some remarkable accomplishment, their resultant joy is usually short-lived. They promptly move on to the next external goal and the next cycle of stress. For your golden years, I do not want you to struggle with daily stress. So, what is my solution? I want you to direct your primary focus away from the external rewards. I want you to direct your focus to your internal mental state and your feelings. In my opinion, that is where success truly resides.

Let me share another of my own experiences. At one point in my career, I was asked to provide weekend coverage at one local hospital. For me, it meant additional income. So, for several months, I tried it. On Saturday and Sunday mornings, I would head out the front door around 7 a.m. and return home around 3 p.m. But I was miserable. I did not want to be the husband or father who just paid the bills. I wanted to be the husband and father who was there, an active member of the family. Bottom line? I did not want to feel wealthy; I wanted to feel happy. For me, my happiness came from loving, giving, and being supportive. So, the real me was like that kid running naked down the street to play with others. The real me was someone who felt good when he was engaged with others. Once I realized the source of my happiness, once I realized that the weekend work was not aligned with the real me, I promptly quit. Instantly, I was poorer. Instantly, I was happier. But when you find the real you and identify who you want to be, the choice is easy.

As an initial exercise, I want to suggest the following self-examination. For your personal mission and your new life purpose, what type of person do you want to be? Do you want to be happy and joyful? Do you want to be loving and compassionate? Do you want to have contentment and peace of mind? Do you want to live with freedom and spontaneity? Do you want to be the person who is comedic, making other people laugh? Do you want to be adventuresome and fun seeking? Which of these inner mental states and personal styles best reflects the real you? Now, you do not have to select just one mental state or one personal characteristic. You could select a unique collage of inner mental states and personal characteristics, deciding that's who you want to be, that's how you want to live your life. Guess what? Do you need external achievement? Do you need more possessions? No. Nothing can stop you from being yourself but yourself. Your success is guaranteed. You just have to redesign yourself and some parts of your life. Your personal mission and life purpose can come alive right now, and you can be that person that you want to be for the rest of your life. All of a sudden, it is 100 percent doable.

I can hear you asking: Is it that easy? The truth? No and yes. It cannot happen with a snap of the fingers. First, you have to clarify who you really want to be. For some people, that process is not that easy. So, pause at this point, and ask yourself a group of fundamental questions. What type of person have you been over these past several years? Is that the same person you want to be for the rest of your life? Then how are the two people different? And what needs to change? And don't say that the starting point is something external. Yes, something external may need to change. But, like with me and my weekend work, the starting point was something internal. I identified how I wanted to feel and I made some changes to make that happen. So, identify who you want to be. Then start changing your world to reflect that person. Think of the reward. No more days where there is a list of activities but no sense of a meaningful purpose. Gone are the days of only empty motion. So, take the time, right now, to clarify your personal mission and your purpose. And what is more powerful than uncovering the real you, the person who makes you feel alive, satisfied, and truly embracing life? It's buried inside you. You just need to find yourself. Once you do, it will help you embrace life and the people around you. And when that happens, you really begin to feel alive. You begin to really live. Regardless of anything external.

Chapter 46

We Need a Different Approach, Yes?

*"The trick is to know who you are
and then do that on purpose."*
Dolly Parton

Need another approach for resurrecting your essential self? Remember the life review and how we looked at the events that most changed your life? This next process falls along the same path. However, I want you to examine the three to five memories where you were most passionate, most excited. Can you remember what you were most passionate about? Can you recall what gave you the greatest sense of meaning, the best internal mental state? Take a close look, not a superficial inspection, at those moments. They may have occurred 30 years ago or 10 years ago. What do they tell you about yourself? What were the moments when you felt the best, the most authentic you? Can you remember and recapture those moments? No, I am not asking you to recreate the past. I am a believer in leaving the past behind, once you have learned from the past. But I am a strong believer in the value of rediscovering your essential self before it is gone, and recommitting yourself to be that person once again.

If someone were to ask me to name the five best days of my life, it would be an easy task: the day of my marriage, the days when I learned that my wife was pregnant (we have two daughters), and the days of their births. Those days are crystal clear. I can remember how great I felt, how alive I felt. I can describe the surroundings in exquisite detail. Now, ask me about my work promotions. I remember very little. How many years was I the associate medical director? I would struggle to give you an accurate number. When was I notified of that promotion? No idea. I can't remember where

I was when I heard the news or even how I felt. So, what does that tell me? It tells me that I feel most alive within the family, not within the workplace. It tells me that my best emotions come from family interactions. It tells me that my best emotions come from loving and caring. That probably seems self-evident. However, it is not. We are all wired differently. Some people really achieve their highest emotions through some other type of activity or some type of adventure. My example is not a value judgment. I use it only to highlight the importance of knowing yourself so you can design your life around your own needs, your own desired emotions.

So, do you have an image of yourself in your best moments? When you felt on top of the world? If yes, then take that portrait and clarify a personal mission and a new life purpose to resurrect that person. Take your desired internal mental state, your personal characteristics that will match the internal mental state, your talents, and your passions, and combine those components to create the new you. Take your time in developing your new purpose. Take your time in clarifying your own destined port. Then, as you head into your golden years, nurture this new clarity. Don't establish a personal mission or a new life purpose and then toss it aside. If your new purpose is to be a loving and compassionate person, try to maintain that internal state each and every day. That does not mean that you will stay on target every moment. What do they say? Airplanes are off target 90 percent of the time? Yet, they still land, for the most part, at the right airport. A personal mission and a life purpose will give you a daily reminder of who you are; when coupling that reminder with the right habits, it will give you the blueprint for staying on your new course.

With a clear personal mission and new life purpose, you will catapult yourself into that five percent of people who are satisfied with their life, who are truly happy and content. You will have bypassed the external circumstances and gone directly to the desired internal mental state. This internal reward will be far more valuable than any additional finances. In fact, with your new life purpose, it is my hope that you move even further away from a financial focus. Remind yourself of the old saying: it is easier to earn a dollar than to make a difference. With a new mission and purpose, you can combine the real you with your talents and your passions; and you can find much greater meaning in your daily activities. So, do it now. Write down a personal mission and a new purpose for your life. Make changes in your future path. Create something meaningful.

I have one additional recommendation. After constructing a personal mission or a life purpose, state it to yourself in the present tense. Do not tell yourself, "I want to be …" or "I want to feel …" as that is not the best approach. Instead, tell yourself, "I am …" (as in "I am loving and compassionate" or "I am kind and considerate"). So, why the present tense? Remember my observation that we tend to manifest what we think about? Or we tend to manifest what we discuss? Those beliefs are still accurate, but when a personal mission and a life purpose are composed in the present tense, they have more power. If you proclaim to be something right now, there is a better chance that, come tomorrow, you will be that something. Think of it as shape shifting. Think it; assert it; and then be it. Bring it into the present, not just the future. Remember: repetition is not without benefits. How do we become good at anything? By practice. Well, it is time for practice; and it is time to be good at being the real you. So, keep repeating your personal mission and your life purpose until they are ingrained in your mind and heart. Make it as strong and consistent as your pulse. Make it the daily driving force for each day of your life. Follow Dolly Parton's advice. Be yourself. Stay on purpose. Let it carry you to new heights.

Chapter 47

A Renewal From the Heart

"If you listen to your heart, you'll remember
who you were all along."
Makena

I'd like to offer one visual image of your life. Picture it as a cone. You are at the bottom of your cone. Your family and loved ones are directly above you. Above them are your friends and close acquaintances. Higher up the cone is your work. At the top of the cone rests the world with its wealth distribution challenges, nation/ethnic conflicts, and worldwide disasters. At this point of your life, you need to move your focus further down your cone, seeking renewal in your heart. I am not suggesting you become selfish and stay at the bottom of the cone. Instead, I am suggesting you find a spot away from the career challenges and global challenges and focus on your personal challenges, redefining yourself, who you want to be, and then sharing the new you with the people you love the most. For many people, this new pursuit will lead to a sense of renewal, helping them remember what is most meaningful. For most of us, the meaning of our lives is found in what we can give to those we love. That's when we can make a difference.

For some people, that directive may not offer an initial solution. They may have already lost their loved ones. They may find themselves alone and discarded, buried at the bottom of the cone. Without loved ones, can you still find renewal? The answer is yes. Just ask the people who have suffered the most. Ask those people who have been victims of ethnic cleansing. Ask the people who have been the victims of terrorism. Ask the people who have lost members of their family to an unspeakable act. Ask the people who have seen how terrible mankind can behave. Talk to the people who have lost everything and everyone. When you read their life stories, there is something remarkable, something that gives you hope for mankind. These people, like the people in the Holocaust who were left with absolutely nothing, often find renewal after their suffering. How? By reconnecting with their heart, then with others. That may sound idealistic. But read the interviews. Read the biographies. These people, when they recover from the external losses, often discover that they are fundamentally loving and compassionate, wanting to give something of value to others. Without a loved one, their pursuit can often lead to an effort to help others better understand the meaning and value of life. Once you have lost what you most cherish, you don't want others to have to shoulder the same level of pain. You want them to appreciate what you have lost and what you have discovered through your own survival and renewal.

So, how about you? Now that you have recaptured the real you, could you share what you have found? Could you create more meaning by sharing more of yourself with your family? Could you find more meaning by helping others? Could you find meaning by helping other people realize that the value of life lies far beyond wealth? Could you, for example, find meaning by helping others become better prepared for their older years? From my perspective, that is what is often forgotten. People, when they know who they truly are (and when they reconnect with their heart), find happiness and peace of mind when they help others, not just themselves. For most of you, I suspect your deepest passions reside in your personal relationships. Your spouse. Your children. Your friends. As you reach your older years, switch your focus to them and their needs, not your needs. Start at the bottom of the cone, find renewal, and reawaken your heart. Then work your way up the cone. Some people can rise higher in the cone than others. People like Mother Teresa rise to the top. They dedicate their lives to helping strangers, anyone in need. Find the level that reflects the real you. Any level is acceptable. But, if you want to create more value in your life, and if you want to maximize your talent, passion, and purpose, you may find the greatest reward in helping others. It's that simple. In fact, once you find yourself, it's easy to see what truly matters. That realization should be a compass for creating more value (and more love) in your golden years.

You now have four new directives. The first directive is to find your talents and develop those talents. The second directive is to clarify your passions and shift your life toward those passions. The third directive is to uncover the real you and develop a new personal mission and a central life purpose. The fourth directive is to delve deeper into your heart and start sharing the real you, first with your loved ones (your family and friends), and then with others. Some people need time with this renewal. It does not have to be a linear progression. If you cannot incorporate your talent into your golden years, try to uncover your lost passions. If your passions remain blocked, and they are often blocked by employment and time commitments, focus on resurrecting the real you and the heart that reflects the real you. If you are still stymied, do not despair. There is no time limit. Give yourself time. Just keep trying and you will triumph. Don't give up. As long as your heart is still beating, there is time for renewal and resurrection.

Chapter 48

Another of My Confessions

*"It is our choices that show us who we truly are,
far more than our abilities."*
J.K. Rowling

Perhaps it is time for another confessional. When I entered my golden years, I was working fifty-plus hours per week. I was the associate medical director of a large health care agency, and I was also working as a physician consultant, offering my opinion on difficult cases across the United States. Was I happy? No. Was

I utilizing my talents? Not all of them. Was I following my passions? No. Was I spending as much time with my wife and two daughters as I wanted? No. Did I feel I was creating something meaningful? No. So, what did I do? I decided to write this program. As previously explained, it was written as much for me as for you. And where did it lead me? To an inventory of possible talents. To a buried passion. To clarity who I was. To a new personal mission and a new life purpose. To a greater focus on my relationships. With these steps, I changed from the inside out. I redesigned myself and my life. I found myself more giving, with a sense of greater satisfaction. Were my golden years better? Immensely.

With the hope that it will help you in your own attempt to redesign your life, let me be more specific about my own transition. I stopped one of my two jobs, losing income but thereby creating more time to reevaluate my life. I worked on improving the quality of my thinking and the focus of my daily conversations. I completed a life review and saw myself in a new light. With improved mental clarity, I rekindled my love to write. It may not have been a great talent, but it was a talent, albeit a minor talent. I clarified my passions. One of them was self-education, especially on health, longevity, and the best habits for an effective life. Over several months, I pored through the literature, adding material to my prior lectures. With the new information, I changed my daily eating style and revamped my exercise routine. To my surprise, I found myself in better shape with a substantial weight loss. I also found myself sleeping better. With renewed energy and a renewed sense of myself, I refocused more time toward my wife, family, and friends. For one of those friends, Jeffrey Knight, my change came too late. For me, that is a personal loss, someone who will never be replaced. But despite that loss, and maybe ignited by that loss, my life has become better and better, just when I was worried that it might be getting worse.

I do not want to deceive you. The process, as previously explained, does not lead to immediate improvement. You have days when you are making progress. You also have days where you hit some headwinds. There are days when you cannot escape the realities of life. I still had the usual stack of bills. Nevertheless, it was wonderful to have time to improve myself. It is wonderful to have time to search for a greater meaning for my life. I found I could focus on less and have more. The increased time at home was priceless. The chance to exercise twice daily was priceless. The extra time for lunch and the movie dates with my wife were priceless. The additional time for my daughters was priceless. The reconnection with neglected friends, especially those who had disappeared for years, was priceless. All of those features guided me to a new definition of success. At this point, I am earning less income but enjoying life so much more. What does that tell all of us? We need to be true to ourselves and our dreams, not to society's financial expectations.

With any change, there are going to be doubts. Can I make this transition to a more focused life? Can I improve my life with less income? Can I create something of greater meaning for myself and others? And am I worthy of this endeavor? Yes, the critic and the doubter. When I started to write this program, I had to address those questions. I had attended an outstanding college, but once graduated, had I done anything of national importance? No. Was I nationally known? No. Despite my initial self-doubts, I still compiled my own group of habits. How did I convince myself to write daily for several straight months? I asked different questions of myself. Did this project reflect the real me? Yes. Was this book something I would enjoy? Yes. Would it add value to my life? Yes. Could it possibly add value to other people's lives? Yes. That was all that mattered. It was the message that counted, not the messenger. All the success and achievement questions were irrelevant. I had found a personal mission and a new life purpose. I felt that I was creating something meaningful. So, with those new answers, my inner critic and doubter grew quieter. My point? To prepare yourself for your own transition, you need to ask yourself the right questions. In fact, asking the right questions is one of the keys to life. Move away from old questions. Move further away from old answers. Assess yourself on your terms, not anyone else's terms. Then make the necessary choices to unleash the driving forces that are buried within.

Chapter 49

Benefits of Written Goals/Intentions

"A good idea is like a lighted match, easily blown out."
Richard Kinder

At Yale University in 1953 they asked the graduating class if they had written goals for the next phase of their life. In that study, three percent of the class had written goals, but 97 percent of the class had no written goals. This study followed this group of graduates for the next two decades. At the end of the two decades, the study reevaluated each person from that graduating class, examining their success in different areas. Surprisingly, the three percent of the graduating class who had written goals had more success than the other 97 percent of their class combined. Through the decades, other studies have re-measured the value of written goals. The Harvard studies in the 1980s produced the same results. Regardless of whether you measure success in business or success in relationships or success in any other area of your life, writing down your goals has been shown to increase the chance of achieving those goals.

You can probably guess what I am going to suggest. But there is a twist. I used to encourage people to write down a group of written goals. But, once again, I noticed that some people link goals too much with work. Since I want you to shift your priorities away from work and income, I want to offer you another choice. I want you to write down goals or *intentions*, whichever word is most comfortable for you. Be aware of several factors. I do not want goals or intentions with narrow, time-limited objectives. I want lifelong goals or intentions that do not have any set end point. These goals and intentions are not the list that you scribble on New Year's Eve. They are not even the items on a bucket list. Again, your goals or intentions can be internal, not external. What type of person do you want to be? How do you want to feel? How do you want to act? What do you want to share? They should be designed to remain as valuable 30 years from now as they are today. So, what exactly am I going to suggest you do? I am going to encourage you to write down a group of goals/intentions that are consistent and reflective of your personal mission and life purpose. I will explain and discuss the goals and intentions in greater detail in the last chapter within this step. For now, think of these goals or intentions as broad based statements that can last a lifetime. Think of these goals or intentions as extensions of your personal mission and life purpose, further clarifying how you can offer value to others across the full spectrum of your daily activities.

I want to return to an old saying: most people have been so busy making a living they have never taken the time to design their lives. Sadly, most people spend more time planning their vacations than planning their life. That's even true for some people in the golden years. Now is the time to solidify your personal mission and life purpose with specific goals or intentions that will enrich your life. There is another saying that you either work for your goals or you work for someone else's goals. You need to be moving toward your dreams, not someone else's dreams. If you have spent your career working for someone else's goals, now is the time to develop your own goals/intentions. Right now, more than any time in your life, you are primed for a new beginning. There is another saying that most people major in minor things while they minor in major things. You need to reposition yourself to go against that grain. At this point in your life, you should focus your energy and your time on the major things that matter most to you, the things that provide the most meaning to your life. The combination of a personal mission and life purpose with a set of goals or intentions is like the combination of improved internal dialogue and external dialogue, or the combination of a plant-based eating style with a broad exercise program. Independently, each component is valuable. But if the forces are linked together? If they are internal, not just external? These habits, linked together, should create a driving, unstoppable force, especially if you take the time to write down your list of goals/intentions. Once written, just don't let them be blown aside by some temporary setback. Let your written goals unleash their power. Just need to stay the course.

Chapter 50

Can You Overcome Your Fears?

"Fear is a pair of handcuffs on your soul."
Faye Dunaway

We are raised to be realists. We are not raised to be dreamers. With the rekindling of your dreams, the development of a new personal mission and a life purpose, and the creation of a list of life-long intentions, there will be a cost. But if there were no cost, what would be the value? You can't expect something for nothing.

In life, if you are willing to pay the cost, you get to keep the purchase. So, what is the cost? For most people, it is increased anxiety and initial fear. Anxiety comes with any significant change. We have already discussed some possible fears. Those fears come from your critic and your doubter. Is your dream possible? Can you find those buried talents and passions? Can you uncover the real you? Can you establish a personal mission and a life purpose that stands apart from your career? Can you create a list of written intentions that extend your purpose and add meaning to your later years? However, there are some additional fears of importance. Those fears must also be addressed.

Two of the more prominent fears are the fear of failure and the fear of having to pay too high a price. As a starting point, let me ask: How are you going to feel if you lose the new you and revert to your old habits? How are you going to feel if you slip back into your old stressful, career focused life? Are these new changes and accompanying anxiety worth the effort? From my perspective, you should try to develop the belief that there is no such thing as the fear of failure. Why? Because failure occurs only when you stop trying. And you are not going to stop trying, right? Think about it. If you have put forth the effort until your last breath, does it matter if you have not reached your destination? No. If you are still trying, you are not failing. Can you adopt that perspective? I also believe that regret far outweighs fear. We live in a world where everyone tells you what to do. It's time to be your own boss and create your own destination. You are the programmer. Delete the old program. Write yourself a new program. When the program is all yours, and not someone else's, your level of excitement and enthusiasm, often gone for much of your life, can help bury any accompanying fears.

What about that fear of paying too high a price? That's why it is so important to have everything aligned. Your talents, your passions, your personal mission, your life purpose, your goals/ intentions: if they reflect the real you, what are you sacrificing? If those areas truly represent the part of your life that gives you the most happiness, you are giving up things of lesser importance for things of greater importance. It's the opposite of sacrificing time with the family for another day at the office. Isn't it about time you sacrificed the things that need to be sacrificed? I had a friend who hated to dust. When you visited her house, there were layers of dust on tabletops. But she loved to read. So, to her, the sacrifice of cleaning made little difference. To others, it would have created an uncomfortable living environment. That is why it is crucial to know who you are and what matters to you, not what matters to others. Again, if you are truly on target, you do not need to worry about the price. Trust me. You will be happy to pay it.

Now, are there other ways to decrease the impact of these fears? All of us have heard the phrase that you fly with eagles and squawk with turkeys. Try to identify the people who will support you. Try to elicit support within your family. Try to select friends who will encourage your new life purpose. If working, try to find cohorts who resonate with your new style and your new direction. Try to find organizations that offer nourishment and compassion. And try to leave behind all those people who would take pleasure in derailing you. Now, how do you reach this point? By sharing your dreams, your purpose, and your new mission. Do not keep it to yourself. Everyone needs a support team. You never climb the mountain alone. So, be brave. Show your new self to the world. Scream your new direction to the people around you. Sometimes you can be shocked at how many people feel just like you. They just have not expressed it. Take the lead. And while taking the lead, bury those exaggerated fears. They are like negative thoughts or useless worry. Just delete and more forward toward your future.

Chapter 51

Clarify Your Goals/Intentions

"Argue for your limitations, and sure enough, they're yours."
Richard Bach

Now what sort of goals or intentions? Well, what's something that ruins most people? It's a lack of balance. I would encourage a list of ten goals or intentions that encompass all the important parts of your life. Your list of goals/intentions need to reestablish the balance within your life. Let me give you some generic examples and then some personal examples. How about goals of feeling physically and emotionally healthy? How about intentions for expressing love to your family? How about goals for creating more time with family and friends? How about intentions on how to help other people become happier? How about the switch to the activities that give you happiness and a sense of meaning? How about intentions to give back to your community? The specifics do not matter. What matters is that you create a new balance for your world. Without balance, the real you will be more difficult to maintain.

For my list of goals/intentions for my golden years, I started with a personal goal of excellent health, a healthy diet, and daily exercise. I progressed toward an intention to increase my love/affection/support for my wife and daughters, plus increased time with my wife and daughters. Then I progressed toward an intention of improved relationships with my friends, some of whom I had neglected over the years of constant work. When forming these goals/intentions, I focused on my desire to share the new me and offer increased support to others. After this central core of goals/intentions, I moved down my hierarchy toward other passions and activities, with continued reading and the pursuit of several hobbies. With each of these goals/intentions, I focused on the internal mental state. What type of person did I need to become? How did I want to act? How did I want to feel? To place these goals in the present tense, I wrote myself a daily reminder: "I feel healthy (eating the right foods and exercising regularly); I feel great focusing on the positive, deleting negative thoughts and useless worries; I feel loving, compassionate, understanding, kind, supportive, and helpful; and I feel proud sharing more of myself with others, trying to make their lives better." Obviously, I will not succeed in every moment. But that statement serves to give me direction; and it helps me stay focused on the desired internal mental state, not just the external action.

At this juncture, we need to acknowledge something. You may need to make some fundamental choices before progressing beyond this point. Many jobs do not offer you much chance for balance. Many companies, good ones and bad ones, are designed to work you to death. Flextime at work is not balance. You may still be working ten-hour days, plus you may still be taking work home with you. You cannot place the quality of your life and your golden years in a company's hands. Stop doing work you hate. If your current job is acceptable, you still need to ask yourself: Can you complete your new your new goals and can you reach your desired internal state with your current employment? Or do you need to reduce your workload or find yourself a new job? Those are difficult but necessary choices that must be addressed as you start the process of redesigning your life and reaching your desired internal mental state.

As you debate these decisions, keep in mind that I am not asking for a major upheaval in your life. I still believe it is the small changes that lead to the greatest triumphs. I am also not fighting for balance squeezed within a single day. I am fighting for balance over a broader time period. Nevertheless, will your current employment allow you to be yourself? Will your boss support more time with your family? Will your company provide you with the space to move toward a new life purpose? Will your current job allow you sufficient room to incorporate these new habits outside of the office? If you do not know the answer to these questions, I would encourage you to try to incorporate these habits while continuing your current employment. However, if you find yourself stymied by your work demands or the inflexibility of your job, I would suggest making a decision to explore other career options and commit yourself to creating an environment for yourself and your family where you can follow your personal mission and life purpose. Don't accept their limitations on your options. There is a better life beyond the office. And that is where you are going to find most of the meaning in your life. That is where you are going to truly live, love, and make a difference.

Chapter 52

Your Reward:
A New Freedom

"The greatest thing you can do is surprise yourself."
Steve Martin

My older daughter, after watching me over my professional years, offered the following observation. She noticed that as I progressed through my career as a physician, I seemed to take certain features of my personality, remove them as you would remove a piece of clothing, and then store them in an invisible bag that I'd carry over my shoulder. Losing some of those original characteristics may have helped me succeed in my career. They may have helped me stay between the lines, better able to do what was required. But the loss of the original characteristics came with a price. In my case, it might have been a reduction in my spontaneity and a reduction in my level of happiness. What about you? What part of yourself have you left behind in the service of your career? Or in the service of raising a household? What innate characteristics can you bring back to life? How can you empty that invisible bag over your shoulder? How can you slip back on some of those old features and old characteristics from the past?

When you align your authentic self to your talents, your passions, your personal mission/life purpose, and your goals/intentions, you will be surprised how easily those buried personality features can escape from that restrictive bag and spring back to life. All the cells in your body may have changed multiple times, but your intrinsic nature and core personality features remain unchanged. Most importantly, if you give them a try, you will realize how much they still suit you. How much they can give you the feelings that you desire. How much they can help you become the person you want to be. So, decalcify yourself. Remove the current job-induced, society-coerced restrictions. Reclaim the good parts of you that have been buried beneath years of work. Rekindle those old personality features that once brought joy to you and to others. Yes, remake yourself by bringing back the old you and then improving the new you with these new habits. Trust me. Childhood may be a great time for personal growth. So too is your current age. This process will lift you toward a higher level of freedom, a level with which you are currently unfamiliar.

So, what are the benefits of this newfound freedom? What are the benefits of regaining your buried characteristics? For starters, you are going to like yourself much more. Other people will also like you more. You will feel freer and you will act freer. You will be better able to spot the positives in your life and better able to absorb their beauty. Freedom of the spirit brings about an attitude change. Do you remember what I preached? This part of your life is all about attitude, not aptitude? It's about the internal, not the external? It's about your ability to focus on what really matters, and it is about embracing the good parts of your life. Do you remember my comments about the reactive mode and the responsive mode? With the above changes, you will be more ensconced in the responsive mode. Do you also remember my comments about the plasticity of the brain and how positive thoughts can affect the physiological and anatomic features of your brain? This new freedom will have the same impact. Infants smile around 400 times a day. Older people? They are lucky to smile 20 times a day. That pattern will change. Your internal mental state will change. Your enthusiasm will rise. Your readiness to learn and grow will rise. Your ability to learn these new habits will improve. What happens when you give a group of people a new sense of freedom? There is an upsurge in happiness. There is more compassion and giving. There is more of a desire to help others. That is what is going to happen to you and your family. Surprise yourself and them. Freedom is wonderful. At any age it leads to a new beginning.

Chapter 53

Is Your Compass Ready to Go?

*"If you don't know where you are going,
you'll end up somewhere else."*

Yogi Berra

You should be able to incorporate the components of this program that fit your needs; and if you incorporate just those components, you should be able to simplify and redirect your life. Hopefully, by this point, you can see the advantage of a healthy diet and exercise, improved mental clarity with a life review, a personal mission with a new life purpose, and goals/intentions, with balance. I hope you can see the benefit of incorporating these items into habits, not passing fancies. I want to repeat my view that 80 percent of the success of your golden years will depend on these new habits. It is also my view that a person's talents, passions, and purpose can be reconfigured into a life course that moves you away from work. Your personal mission and life purpose should be your compass, directing you toward a new destination. You should focus on the compass, not on the clock. In life, you don't need much more than a good compass. See the horizon. See your destination, and like Captain Jack Sparrow, go for it.

If your personal mission/new life purpose is the trunk of a tree, your intentions/goals are the branches. Don't forget that those branches produce fruit. There is an old saying that you can count the seeds in the apple, but you cannot count the apples in the seed. Don't underestimate the potential of unexpected rewards with this combination. Even if you create only ten goals, they will create unforeseen consequences in other facets of your life. Each of those intentions, like a single branch, may sprout other activities, leading to a new awakening. My list of goals has produced unexpected developments and unexpected joys. Surprisingly, they have also offered stability. There's another saying that pebbles, not walls, destroy people. A wall would be an earthquake or a tornado or a natural disaster. A pebble would be a smaller incident. A personal setback. A random insult. With a natural disaster people reevaluate their lives, often developing a new perspective and a new direction for their life. With your personal mission, your life purpose, your list of goals/intentions, and your new you well established, you will not be easily unsettled by either walls or pebbles. In fact, every time you hit one of life's speed bumps, just remind yourself of your personal mission and your life purpose. Remind yourself of your goals and intentions. Remember your destination. It will be much easier to follow your compass and stay on course.

My mother is an example of what can happen to you if you do not develop a life purpose and set of intentions. My mother is smart; she has the best vocabulary of anyone I have ever met; and she is well liked with many friends. However, as she reached her older years, she did not make any attempt to develop a new life purpose or a set of goals. So, when something goes wrong like a break-in into her house, with the theft of some jewelry (the thief even paused to drink the can of Coke in her refrigerator, leaving it empty by the sliding glass door), she loses her footing. For any of us, it would be a setback. But with a compass, you can regroup in a shorter period of time. My mother has a close, lifelong friend who always seems to be helping someone. She volunteers her time at respite centers, providing care to dying patients. When she has her own setbacks, and she has experienced her share of setbacks, she does not show much of a drop of energy or mood. She just keeps going, refocusing on what she enjoys doing, which is helping others. So, if you had to choose, whose path would you like to follow? My mother's path or her friend's path? Sorry, mom, I may love you, but I would recommend following your friend's path, as her life course is so much steadier.

So, at this point, I hope you can stop reading, place in a marker, and close the book. I hope you can spend some time writing down a personal mission, a new life purpose, and a set of ten goals/intentions that reflect the real you. I carry my mission and goals in my pocket. I may not glance at them every day, but I believe in osmosis with the benefit of having them written, almost part of my body. Regardless of where you place your personal mission and new life purpose or where you display your written goals/intentions, they will be crucial. Look at them every few days. Or at least several times per month. Let them remind you of who you are. Let them bring you back from the external to the internal. Let them give you direction. Let them give you stability. Let them help lay the foundation of your new life.

I have one more recommendation. View the initial draft of your personal mission, your life purpose, your goals, and your intention as another starting point. Yes, there are a lot of starting points. That is the freshness of your new life. When you finish reading the entire guide, when you better understand all the suggestions and how they fit together, return to your personal mission, your new life purpose, your goals, and your intentions, and revise and clarify, as needed. Truthfully, while writing this survivor kit my goals changed as I progressed through the nine steps. I gained new insights. I found more balance. Because of my revisions and my own personal changes, I am a better person now than I was when I started writing this guide. My friend who encouraged me to write this book? Maybe he was just trying to give me a compass. Maybe he was trying to make certain that I did not end up on some balcony. Maybe he was just trying to encourage me to become a better person. A more loving person.

STEP 6

Redesigning Your World

"Good enough never is."
Debbi Fields

Chapter 54

Self-Improvement: A Challenge

"When we strive to become better, everything around us becomes better too."
Paulo Coelho

Through this first group of habits, I hope you have noticed the underlying theme of self-improvement and self-reliance. It reflects my earlier assertion that if you want more, you will have to become more. At this point, I want to address self-improvement more directly. From my perspective, it should be your underlying theme. Too many people stop growing when they finish their education. How many people continue to work on self-improvement? Experts claim that the average person only reads one nonfiction book after graduation and that the majority of our population has not been in a bookstore in the past year. Maybe our reading habits will change with our ability to read books online without the printed page. With your older years, you would think it would be the ideal time to kick up your feet and do nothing. But if you truly want to create a meaningful life, your golden years offer one of the best times for a period of personal growth and self-improvement, steered (of course) by your purpose, mission, and goals.

There are numerous advantages from self-improvement, but there is one common denominator. Happiness comes from personal growth. In fact, happiness can come from just the anticipation of personal growth. It is similar to the experience of taking a much needed vacation. A good part of the joy comes from the expectation of the vacation. A good part of the joy comes from the planning of the vacation. A better example occurs on Christmas morning. Can you remember when you were the happiest?

When you awoke on December 25 and first rushed to the Christmas tree and presents? Or when you had finished opening all of your presents? For me, I was happiest running down the stairs from my second floor bedroom and spotting the spread of presents. It was the same for my two daughters. The greatest period of excitement and joy was that first 30 minutes of Christmas when we switched on the Christmas songs and let the two girls divide the presents into four piles. That was the peak moment for them; and it was the peak time for me as a child. And it was all about the joy of anticipation.

During your golden years, it is a wonderful feeling, similar to that excitement at Christmas, when you can feel yourself making changes for self-improvement, when you feel yourself becoming a better person. It's as if you are giving yourself a wonderful present. If you have incorporated our new habits, you have already improved and felt those initial feelings. Your attitude should already be lifting. Your excitement should be growing. Realistically, your journey has just begun. Even with improved health, better mental clarity, and a clearer purpose, your ship has barely left the port. So, as you work through the varied suggestions, I do not want you to focus solely on the destination. I want you to enjoy the actual voyage and relish the small, fundamental changes that are making you a better person. Embrace the positive feelings that come as you anticipate those changes, and the positive feelings that come when you make those changes. Appreciate all the steps of self-improvements. In fact, I want you to appreciate every part of the process. If it helps, sing your own praises. You are worthy of this new journey. You are worthy of bounding down those stairs toward those Christmas presents.

I also want you to remember that self-improvement is independent of finances. Yes, Benjamin Franklin used to encourage people to pour their money into their minds because their improved minds would fill their pockets with gold. Henry Ford, one of the giants who started the American auto industry, reportedly never saved a dollar until his mid forties. Instead, he invested his money in his own personal growth and his own vision. For you, I am not advocating you spend your money; I am advocating you spend your time on improving yourself. Are you fully aware of the potential impact of daily self-improvement? Let's imagine that you have a field of interest, something that you have not had the time to pursue. Do you realize that if you read one hour a day in this field, you would be an authority in three years, a national expert in five years, and an international expert in seven years? Or if you set aside one hour per day to read a short story or a poem or an editorial, you would have the equivalent of a master's in English within three years? I do not want to emphasize any external reward. The goal of self-improvement is not to make you an expert. The goal is not to make you better than anyone else. The goal of self-improvement is internal, not external. The goal of self-improvement is to upgrade your self-esteem, your self-respect, and the level of your personal satisfaction. All of these internal developments are far more valuable than anything the external world can offer.

Chapter 55

Advantage of Long-Term Thinking

"I intend to live forever. So far, so good."
Steven Wright

You may already know about the Chinese bamboo tree. In the first year, there is no growth. In the second year, there is no growth. In the third year, there is no growth. In the fourth year, there is no growth. In the fifth year, there is again no growth. But during the sixth year, there is a short period where the tree grows 80 feet in just six weeks. Now, I am not saying that my guide will take six years. However, I am repeating my admonition to remain patient and develop long-term thinking. I predict that when you realize the rewards of your personal growth, your personal growth will come suddenly, sometimes when you least expect it. I once read a study on how quickly people give up on new endeavors. The question was simple: When you try something new, how many times do you allow yourself to fail before you give up? Do you know the most common answer? Well, prepare yourself once again for the worst. The answer, for most people, was once. That borders on the absurd.

Long-term thinking helps you develop a fresh perspective on obstacles and risks. As they say, obstacles instruct, not obstruct. As we grow older, and seem more brittle, we need to reemphasize those perspectives so we are better able to adjust to any obstacles. You can manage your setbacks, without so much distress, when you shift toward long-term thinking. But what, you ask, about all those short-term risks? The one step forward, two steps back? There is the old adage to fail early, fail often, because that is how you learned in your earlier endeavors. There are studies that highlight how the individual who fails the most is often the one who achieves the most. You are taught that the price for success is a series of failures. The baseball player, who has the most strikeouts, also has the most home runs. The football quarterback, who has the most touchdowns, typically has the most interceptions. No pain, no gain, right? Remember the mental shift that is recommended for your golden years? You are not searching for achievement; you are searching for meaning. You are not searching for something external; you are searching for something internal. That requires a different approach and a shift away from embracing multiple failures.

I encourage you to discard the fail early, fail often philosophy. As you grow older, do you need to experience more mistakes? At your age, is that the best way to learn? I believe you need to learn from observing what goes right, not what goes wrong. If something in my guide feels right to you, then incorporate it into your life. Forgo the experimentation. The change to your internal world does not require all those external trials. You do not need to crash and burn before incorporating a new habit. Feel free to improvise. Go in your own direction. But work with those things that make sense. Make them simple. Make them easy. Let them direct you along a better, more enjoyable path. When you suffer a setback, make it short-lived. Everyone is going to experience setbacks. Everyone is going to fall short from time to time. But reduce those missteps. Make your life easier, not harder. Imagine it longer, not shorter. There is no rush.

If you have any doubt, watch the older professional athletes. The older golfer doesn't always take the 5-wood and try to reach that lengthy par five. The older baseball player doesn't swing as much from his heels. He goes for the crucial single, not the crowd-pleasing home run. The older basketball player doesn't drive as recklessly into the lane. So, go ahead and reduce those missteps. At the same time, remember to keep your long-term focus on the process itself. Embrace it. Remember the pattern of plateau after plateau. As long as you enjoy your progress and don't worry about perfection, the journey of self-improvement, with the incorporation of your personal mission, new life purpose, goals, and intentions, plus the renewal of your talents and passions, will be a delight. You already know many of the secrets. Just focus on the things that matter and the key 20 percent of your activities that provide you with the most joy. But go after those activities without any rushed deadline. It's an adventure to relish. With long-term thinking, it will translate into a far longer (and much more enjoyable) journey than you currently anticipate. And more people will join you on that journey.

Chapter 56

The Last 20 Percent of Effort

"Become the architect of your future."
Robin Sharma

If you asked who was America's most historic president, most responders would reply Abraham Lincoln. Do you know his political history? In 1832, Lincoln lost a race for the Illinois House of Representatives. In 1838, he lost his bid for Speaker of the House of Representatives. In 1855, he lost a bid for the

Senate in a special session of the Illinois legislature. In 1856, he was considered for the position of vice president on the Republican ticket, but he was not selected by the Republican National Committee. In 1858, he lost the Illinois Senate election. Finally, in 1860, Lincoln won the election to be the next president of the United States (in a four-way race). Now, how many of you would have persevered after losing so many elections? What did it take for Abraham Lincoln? It took a long-term perspective. But equally importantly, it was the last 20 percent of his effort that produced 80 percent of his success, his landmark presidency.

Another example is Thomas Edison. You may already know how many attempts were required to create the light bulb. For Thomas Edison, it required well over 2,000 separate experiments. He was once asked how he was able to tolerate so many mistakes. I am paraphrasing, but he explained that each unsuccessful experiment was not a failure. Why? Because it had taught him one more way to *not* make the light bulb filament. Each mistake moved him forward. More than other people, he knew the value of that long-term perspective and the value of the extra effort. You are now older. You too have grown wiser. You can adopt the same perspective. You do not have to embrace the notion of mistake after mistake. As explained, you can now move along a path that does not demand a series of achievements. But it will still be important to accept the long-term perspective and appreciate the need for the continued extra effort, especially the last 20 percent of effort. That last bit of effort will be crucial as you move toward your personal mission, your life purpose, your balanced goals, and your personal growth.

Why is this perspective so crucial? Because success in any endeavor, including redesigning your golden years and improving yourself, usually takes three times longer than expected. Haven't you known someone who is smart and talented, but who has not yet achieved as much success as you might have expected? Failure is not always due to the person's bad luck. Sometimes the failure is due to the fact that the person, no matter how hard he or she may have worked in the beginning, just did not put forth that last 20 percent of effort that would have made all the difference in reaching his or her goals. Too many people give up as the mistakes mount. So, to embrace self-improvement and personal growth, also embrace all aspects of the process. At our age, we should have the wisdom that everything takes time.

One additional recommendation. Even though the emphasis is on the extra effort, do not procrastinate on self-improvement. Don't take forever to incorporate these new habits. Don't prolong writing down your personal mission, your new life purpose, and your goals and intentions. The longer it takes to start something, the less time you have to enjoy the reward. Do you know what will help in the start-up process? Cutting back on other activities. Trimming those other activities. Remember our 80:20 principle and how it applies to different facets of your life? It applies to how 20 percent of your activities lead to 80 percent of your happiness; and it applies to how the last 20 percent of effort leads to 80 percent of your success. Your self-improvement is part of that 20 percent of activities that will lead you toward more happiness. Self-improvement is one of those areas worthy of the additional 20 percent of effort. So don't shortchange yourself with a lack of sustained effort toward a personal mission and life purpose, especially at this stage of your life. Be different. Pledge to yourself to do what it takes, no matter how long it takes. If you can keep this pledge, you will become the architect of your future. Just don't wait too long. You do not want to come alive with your last breath. Let's make it a little earlier.

Chapter 57

My Own Personal Miracle

"The way I see it, if you want the rainbow,
you gotta put up with the rain."
Dolly Parton

It is one thing to believe in the value of your last 20 percent of your effort; it is another thing to live through the experience, witnessing the reward for persistence. In the early years of my marriage, my wife and I patiently waited for her to become pregnant. When it was finally clear that we needed assistance, we sought some infertility specialists. The process was neither quick nor easy. After extensive medical evaluations, there was no identifiable problem. So, we started a seven-year infertility ordeal. My wife received oral fertility medications, then injectable fertility medications, and then in vitro fertilization with no pregnancy. Most of our family and friends encouraged us to give up and adopt a child. As much as I respect those people who adopt a child, we still wanted to try to have our own children. My wife progressed to a laparoscopy, where the physician retrieved three of her eggs. After fertilizing the eggs with my sperm, the three embryos were frozen and stored. We were told the odds were less than 1 percent, but we still persevered and never gave up.

The laboratory eventually thawed the three embryos, inserting them in my wife's uterus. For three weeks we waited for the pregnancy test. It was one of the best days of my life as the results came back positive. We were going to be parents. Remarkably, my first-born daughter was conceived in June and born in July. That is what happens when you have a test tube baby frozen in CryoFreeze for four months. In keeping with the irony of life, our second child was born just 17 months after the birth of our first child, and the second daughter came the old-fashioned way. In fact, if I remember correctly, I took an impulsive, unplanned day off from the office. We must have napped when my eight-month-old daughter, Skyler, napped. Now you know why I am such a fan of life outside the office. For us, it felt like two miracles, especially after waiting so many years. The two births changed our lives forever. For those people who go through the process of a lengthy wait for some positive result, it is difficult to put into words the real value of that last bit of effort. It is also difficult to explain how it changes you, even improves you. We became older parents (than we initially anticipated), but we also became better parents. With each birth, we knew how lucky we were. We knew that our priority was family, not work.

Because of our own struggle and our own reshaped perspective, we were 'there' for both of our children. In their first 20 years, I only missed a couple of days away from home. As a physician who offered a lecture titled "A Prescription For Effective Living," I only accepted speaking engagements where I could talk during the day and be home for dinner. When there were those weekend golf tournaments for physicians, I turned them down, choosing to be home on Saturdays. My wife and I never missed our older daughter's soccer matches or her diving meets; and we attended our younger daughter's piano and singing lessons and her many performances. More importantly, we preached purpose and mission. We encouraged both of our children to follow their dreams. The result? One daughter was a published novelist in high school. The other daughter was an accomplished musician, winning her share of artistic and academic rewards. But the real rewards were not external for our children or for us. The real reward was the loving quality of our family relationship. Without our initial struggle, we might not have been so focused, and so truly blessed, with our family life.

From my biased perspective, our family story illustrates two important points. First, when you persevere and give that extra 20 percent effort (especially when others are telling you to give up), the rewards will often exceed your expectations. And one success leads to another success. One area of personal growth leads to others areas of personal growth. So, have faith in the eventual positive outcome and keep on pushing toward your new life. Second, I am a strong believer that time leads to quality. So, when a goal takes longer, that goal becomes sweeter. For a family, the more time you prioritize for home, the more moments of joy will come your way. Our children (young ladies) still love to get together with us. They will pop in for the weekend. We will meet for a monthly dinner. We still take some short trips together. This year we went to Maui. Beach activities and three shared meals per day. Family time can still be created for any family. It does not have to be Maui. It does not have to cost much money. You just need to make that commitment. You just need to make a sustained effort. And you just need to spend the extra time. The rainbow is worth the rain; and the rainbow is always worth the wait.

Chapter 58

Is Personal Growth So Difficult?

"Nobody cares if you can't dance well.
Just get up and dance."
Martha Graham

By this point, we have already discussed the many areas that should be part of your personal growth. A healthy eating style, an exercise program, the development of mental clarity, and the creation of a personal mission and life purpose with balanced goals should all be part of your personal growth. What other areas are there? Actually, the list is endless. In your quiet moments, you should consider the general areas in which you want to improve. They are probably the same areas you would want for your child. Higher self-esteem? More self-discipline? An increased ability to accept setbacks? A willingness to accept more responsibility? An ability to be directed by your instincts, not directed by someone else's commands? More independence to create your path? A greater appreciation of life? Those are all areas that can be improved during your golden years. And again, they are all internal, with no real external obstacles.

In many ways, your golden years are the perfect bookend to your childhood years. Both of these transitions represent periods when you have the best chance and perhaps the greatest need for growth. The child may grow physically and emotionally; you need to grow toward a higher mental state. Some people say that it is a shame that youth is wasted on the young. Well, some people can take the flip-side perspective and proclaim that it is a shame that the golden years are wasted on the old. Our collective response? Let's not waste our golden years. It is not a time to calcify. It is a time to change and grow. Stop wondering if this new focus will work. Just strive to become a better person. The results will follow. But know why you are doing something. Know your motivation. Ask yourself: Will these internal changes lead you toward a life with more meaning? With your own improvement, will you be adding more value to your life, a family member's life, a friend's life, or a stranger's life? Will you be taking a step toward making your own world better? Personal growth is not an option; it is a necessity for maximizing the joy within your older years.

With personal growth, to elicit your interest, I have emphasized a large list of habits. However, a shorter list is better. That does not mean that you do not need to address the other habits. It just means that you do not need to address all of them. The same holds true for your own personal growth. You do not want to throw away time. For the golden years, time is far more valuable than money. You just need to spend it wisely. First, abandon those activities that are not leading to much happiness. Second, look to replace those activities with the new activities that have a greater chance of improving your happiness. Third, examine your personal features, deciding which areas are most in need of improvement, or which areas, if improved, would lead to the greatest jump in your level of happiness. Your motto should be simple: you want to get the most out of doing the least. Get started. Get going. The most important step is often that first step. Create some momentum. Then keep it going. Believe you can do it. Believe in the long haul and the destination. Then watch yourself and your life transform into something unexpected and ever so satisfying. And, again, it flows from the inside out, and no one can derail you from this transformation but yourself.

Now, what was the area where I felt the need to most improve? What was the area where I wanted to start the process? Remember how I mentioned how my older daughter, Skyler, observed that I seemed to be losing many of my characteristics, and by that remark I think she was referring to my better characteristics. So, I asked myself: What personality features had I lost the most during my years of employment? For me, there was an erosion of spontaneity and witty remarks. I would catch myself, at so many administrative meetings, filtering my thoughts, thinking of something funny to say (a remark that might have started a humorous banter with a fellow colleague), and then blocking that remark. I know, I know. It's not much of a personality change. But, as I worked on improving myself, I decided to unleash some of those previously filtered comments. The result? There was more banter and more fun in my relationships. Small changes can lead to bigger results, remember? For me, that initial small change made a difference in the quality of my life. So, let me ask, what do you want to improve first about yourself? Go for it! And don't worry about what others think. Besides, as Martha Graham observed after this chapter's initial quote, "Great dancers are not great because of their technique; they are great because of their passion." So, create a passion for personal growth! Truly, it is not that difficult.

Chapter 59

Can You Create a New Rudder?

*"Living is like constructing a building;
if you start wrong, you will end up wrong."*
Mary Angelou

With this guide, what issues can prevent you from reaching your health, your mental clarity, your personal mission, your balanced goals, and your personal growth? From my perspective, there are a number of key barriers that can derail you. One of them is a lack of structure in the morning. I know your response. Isn't this exactly what you need to escape? Too much forced structure? Let's take a look at the famous people like actors and artists. When do they derail? They derail in between projects when they have no structure and subsequent poor time management. That's when they allow themselves to drift off course into bad habits, impulsive poor decisions, and disastrous consequences. Without structure and effective time management, there are more mood fluctuations, impulsive behavior, and wrong choices. Everyone would be better served by creating more, not less, structure in their daily routine.

For years, you have probably been getting up Monday through Friday morning, inhaling your breakfast, perusing the headlines, and rushing out the door toward the office or toward some household tasks. If you raised children, you likely spent that first 90 minutes of your day in a blur, dressing and feeding the kids, packing lunches, and driving them to school. For all those years, those first 90 minutes of your day were a daily grind, a track meet to race you into the day's routine. With that type of start, it is amazing that you even made it to work. Or that you successfully raised your kids. You should congratulate yourself. Fortunately, in your golden years, that early morning rush should have slowed. In many cases, you will still be working, but your children should have graduated into their own lives. Remember that commercial, from years ago, that asserted that a certain cereal was the breakfast of champions? Well, how you handle those first 90 minutes of your day (commonly referred to as the rudder of the day) is just as important as what you consume for breakfast.

Use the first 90 minutes of each day to set the tone of your day. Take time for yourself so you can build a positive internal dialogue, create a positive attitude, and establish positive energy. For each person, the new routine will be different. But that is the point. Make it different from what you have been doing for years. Maybe it's a new habit of reading something positive, something uplifting. For some people, it could be more time with their spouse. For other people, it could involve an early morning walk with friends. Whatever the specific activity, it will be to your advantage to create a positive routine, something that places you in the right physical and mental framework. When you hit the mid-morning activities or those later scheduled activities, you do not want to be frazzled or harried. You want to be already progressing along a positive, more relaxed course.

Some people confuse structure with being busy. It can be just the opposite. In fact, I am a fan of productive idleness for this morning period. Haven't some of your best ideas and best moments come during times of idleness? Isn't that when you actually see things more clearly? You are not alone. Didn't Archimedes 'Eureka' moment (a mathematical breakthrough) occur when he was stepping into the bathtub? Didn't Isaac Newton's insight into gravity occur when he was relaxing by an apple tree? There is an old saying that life is too short to be busy. Don't chase money. Do just the opposite. Chase time. Use it wisely. Now, isn't that a better approach for the start of each day? Don't you see how positive morning activities can lead to a steady stream of better days? And can't you see how that habit can subtly shift the course of your life? Besides, how stable is a building if its initial pillars are off-kilter? We all need that solid morning foundation so we can enjoy each and every day.

Want to know an additional advantage? Your baseline physiology is established during the first 90 minutes of the morning. What you eat each morning helps set that baseline. But so do your other activities. By eating a healthy diet and by creating an early morning routine that lifts your mood, your mind and your body will establish a better resistance to stress and a better resistance to disease. Remember my comments about dark-field microscopic photography of your body's internal water and its different crystalline patterns. Your internal cellular chemistry and the structures in your own fluids dramatically change according to your morning. Once set, those baseline structures give you a mental and physiological foundation for the day. In your golden years you can improve your health, your energy, and your resistance against disease (and life's external challenges) simply by improving those initial 90 minutes of your morning. As stated, a positive morning rudder can also offer you a daily primer for your physical health. And physical health, coupled to mental clarity, can lead to everything else. So, for one of your additional challenges for personal growth, establish a morning rudder.

Chapter 60

My Additional Confession

"He who stops being better stops being good."
Oliver Cromwell

In my two decades as a physician in health administration, my mornings were a blur, at least for the first half of my career. I would inhale my breakfast, drop off one of my daughters at school (while my wife dropped off the other daughter), and then I would rush through traffic until I arrived at the office. Of course, once I opened my office computer, there would be fifty-plus emails waiting for a response or some action. Throughout the morning, I would jump from my emails to staff meetings to physician consultations to more emails, or possibly (God forbid) more staff meetings. At work, I had no control. Unfortunately, for many years, I did not pay much attention to the wasted time en route to the office. Halfway though my career, I realized my mistake. I made some changes with a different morning routine on the way to the office. With this new routine, my health and mood improved. With a different morning structure, I was a different person.

For the last half of my career as a physician in health administration, I used my morning commute as my classroom. No, I did not listen to programs that were focused on my work. Instead, I listened to programs that were reflective of my broader interests. I listened to programs on the great world leaders and their wisdom. I listened to programs on spirituality and the world religions. When it came time to write this survivor kit, and when I stopped one of my two jobs to create the necessary time, my first step was to establish another new morning routine. As soon as I awoke, I read something positive. Then I progressed through an early morning exercise program. After a shower and a healthy breakfast, I sat down at the computer, ready to write, feeling refreshed and invigorated. Did that process help this writing? It did not change my limited writing skills, but it helped create a positive creative climate for this writing process. So, regardless of what you do, try to get yourself centered and balanced with a daily, positive routine before you jump into your daily grind of any scheduled activities. Or, better yet, skip your busy schedule and shift your focus to your new passion and mission. Just find the routine that leads you toward the right mental framework and see how much easier it is to maintain that mental clarity once it is established.

Some people rail against any structure, especially in their older years when they are striving for a more spontaneous life. I would argue that structure does not prevent spontaneity. In fact, it establishes the proper attitude to have more spontaneity. I wish I could share a snapshot of my computer room as I write this page. There are a dozen nonfiction books spread beneath my desk and across the carpet. There are eight or nine personal journals, from my decades of listening to audio programs, also scattered across the carpet. In the few open spots of space, there are clumps of three-by-five cards with my scribbling beneath various headings. My wife does not dare enter the room. She considers it a risk for an accident. But let's examine my current computer room in its proper perspective. In my earlier days, before establishing my morning routine, my computer room would have been the epitome of order and neatness. If there were two books on my desk, they would have been stacked and aligned. Now? The books, as mentioned, would be scattered on the floor. My point? To me, the change reflects a shift toward spontaneity, a shift that sprouted from my morning routine. Still uncertain? Then try it yourself. Develop a morning structure or routine and see if it does not improve you and the spontaneity of the rest of your day.

Chapter 61

Shall We Limit Wasted Time?

*"Nothing is worse than wasted time;
it's the one thing you cannot get back."*

Anonymous

Are you aware of how much time we waste? Over the course of an average life an individual spends seven years in the bathroom, five years waiting in line, two years cleaning the house, one year searching for things, eight months opening junk mail, six months sitting at red lights, and 120 hours brushing teeth. But here's the worst part. Studies show that an average American spends four to thirty minutes a day talking with his or her spouse and one to twenty minutes a day talking with his or her children. These statistics reflect a fundamental mistake in our priorities. We are wasting too much of our valuable time. It is all within your control. The responsibility is yours. If you want a better life for your later years, make better use of your valuable time. Reduce your constant busyness. Time management is not just for the office; it is also for your life. Too many people do not realize that fact. You are running out of time. You cannot afford to waste it. At this point in your life, as strange as it sounds, you need effective time management more than ever.

At this point, let me offer a personal observation. Remember when I mentioned that the habits will eventually fit together like pieces of a puzzle. They will enhance each other, improving your life in unexpected ways. Now, do you think I can link our first habit, a change of eating style, with this habit of wasted time? No? Let me give it a try. If you work in any administrative building, you have probably observed what I have noticed. There is always one coworker who heads to the bathroom carrying part of the newspaper or perhaps a magazine. It looks like the person is preparing for an extended stint of reading (and sitting). And what typically happens? Twenty minutes later, the person comes out of the bathroom, much relieved, with half of the reading material finished. Do me a favor. When that person exits from your bathroom at work, ask the person about their eating style. Can you guess what you are going to discover? Those meat eaters? In the bathroom they sit the longest. I guess those cows don't come out without a fight. But the plant-based eaters? They are in and out of the bathroom in a flash. So, appreciate how your new habits will coalesce to improve your life. In this case, you will be healthier and you will have more time!

Other activities? Remember the 80:20 principle: 80 percent of your happiness comes from 20 percent of your activities. You want to maximize activities (usually the ones that occur away from the office) that provide you with the greatest joy. Sometimes those activities can happen by accident. However, there is an advantage in planning many of those activities. At this point in your life, your time should not be squandered. There is the saying that you shouldn't start your day until you have finished your day. If willing to try another litmus test, try writing down a list of your desired activities at the start of each day. As they say, plan your work and work your plan; although, in this case, the word work refers to your life, not to employment. It is the compass-and-clock analogy. Through this guide you are developing a new setting for your compass. Now, you need to be careful with your clock. You need to focus on the important, not the urgent. Let me remind you, once again, of the James Huber saying that the things that matter the most, well, they should not be at the mercy of things that matter the least. In my opinion, your health, your mental clarity, your personal mission, your life purpose, your specific goals, and your personal growth matter the most.

There are some people who claim that real happiness comes from living in the moment, staying in the present. Those people have a tendency to argue against any type of planning that takes away from living in the moment. Let me share my perspective. When you read about the great coaches, they all preach fundamentals. Athletes, when they master the fundamentals, are often quoted as saying that the game actually slows down for them. Do you want time to slow down time during your later years of life? Lord knows time seems to be speeding up as we age, flying past us quicker and quicker. It has been my experience that the right habits slow down time. Yes, it takes effort and time to ingrain these habits. But once incorporated, these habits make life easier, not harder; they make your life more enjoyable, not more problematic; and they make time move slower, not faster. Slowing time? Isn't that what you want for your older years? A series of long peaceful days, filled with meaning, and not disappearing in a rush? Push aside all of that superficial busyness with no free time. With effective time management, you do not need to cram something into every minute of your day. Throw away your watch. I have, and it feels great! You just need to plan, then live, letting your planning save you time so you can enjoy the most of each and every day.

Chapter 62

Our Need for a Second Rudder

"Light tomorrow with today."
Elizabeth Barrett Browning

As previously stated, the hours of your sleep are crucial. Do you remember that you need to get to sleep by 10:30 p.m. for the best rejuvenation? It's part of the natural sleep cycle and circadian rhythm. You sleep in ninety-minute cycles. Around 10:30 p.m. your body's physiology becomes more active. If you are staying up, that extra physiological activity often allows you to stay up even later. But think what you lose. If you are asleep, that increased physiology can be used for cellular repair. Cancer cells can be identified and destroyed. Other cellular mistakes (and the subsequent debris) can be cleansed. As we grow older, we need this physiological repair more than when we were younger. Yes, there will be physiological repair through the night, but the first 90 minutes, when they occur from 10:30 p.m. to midnight, is the most important period for physiological repair. So, you need to develop a routine, a second rudder, to help you establish this pattern.

There are sleep studies that document how the quality of your sleep impacts the quality of your health. Specifically, there are hundreds of genes that are turned on, and turned off, by the quality of your sleep. With a good night's sleep, several hundred genes, which nurture and renew cells, show a higher level of activity. These are the genes that repair protein, counter inflammation, and increase your immune system. With a poor night's sleep, several hundred (different) genes, which induce damage to your cells, seem to awaken. The bad part? These damaging genes are associated with higher rates of high blood pressure, stroke, heart disease, and diabetes. Worse, a poor quality of sleep stimulates cortisol, a stress hormone, and an appetite-stimulating hormone. So, after a poor night sleep, you have missed your opportunity for physiological repair, and you are primed for stress and increased eating. That is not how you want to prepare for the next day. Your tomorrow will be darkened, not lightened.

For many people, falling asleep at the appropriate time is not an easy task. They may climb into bed at 10:30 p.m., but they cannot manage to fall asleep at that hour. The key impediment is often too much late night mental or emotional stimulation. Or too much late night conflict. Sleep medications and/or alcohol are not a solution. Alcohol may help you fall asleep, but it disrupts the natural sleep cycle, reducing physiological repair. The same effect occurs with sleeping medications. The pharmaceutical companies would love to convince you that sleeping medications improve sleep. They may improve the speed at which you fall asleep and they may improve the length of your sleep, but do they improve the depth and physiological repair of your sleep? No. Too often, the sleep medication destroys the natural architecture for sleep and the circadian rhythms, which are needed for activating the right genes. So, you need to create the environment and the nightly routine that allows you sufficient time to decompress and sufficient time to feel relaxed, so you will be able to fall asleep easily, usually within eight to twelve minutes, hopefully before 10:30 p.m. without any medications.

What is the part of the day when your mind is most susceptible to negative influences? It's actually the 90 minutes at the end of the day. Think about it. Don't you hate it when you receive negative news just when you are getting ready for sleep? Researchers completed a study of the successful CEOs in Japan in the 1980s during the time when Japan was so prosperous. What was part of the routine of many CEOs before going to bed? Surprisingly, the most common habit was reading the Bible. The key finding is not the specific religious text. It could be any religious text. They are all valuable. It was the fact that a significant percentage of successful people were reading something positive and something uplifting right before they went to sleep. They were ending their days on a positive note, setting themselves up for an easy transition into sleep and a successful transition into physiological repair.

For you, that means establishing a second rudder each night. In the evening that means not rushing from daylong activities directly to bed. It means taking your time over the last 90 minutes. Again, people must find what routine works best for them. But listening to negative evening news or reading negative evening news is not relaxing. Allowing yourself to be preoccupied with negative events from that day is not relaxing. In the last 90 minutes, you need to regain your balance, center yourself, and relax to the point where you are primed for sleep. More than ever, you just need to set the right emotional climate, and even the right physical climate. Do you like to sleep with the room cold? Do you like to sleep with the window open? Each of us has our favorite thermostats for sleep. Studies show that most people sleep better with lower room temperatures. But each of us has to learn how to set the right mental, emotional, and physical thermostat. For rejuvenation, those steps are important, and those steps constitute the second rudder. So, establish this second rudder, pair it with the morning rudder, and make both of them daily habits.

If you asked my wife, she would claim that I have developed a new idiosyncrasy for every year of marriage. It's a wonder she's stayed with me all these years. My going-to-bed ritual? I love to sleep in a cool room, buried in the bed under the weight of multiple blankets. Even in mild weather, I often turn on the air conditioner. For me, the key is the weight of the blankets. As I get ready for bed, I have two heavy Afghan blankets that I slip between the cover and the bedspread (on my side of the bed). How much weight do I like? Enough to plaster me to the sheets so that I can barely move. Flip flop while I sleep? Not a chance. But here's what my wife does not understand. Taking out the blankets from the cupboard, slipping them into their positions, and rearranging the sheets? It's just one part of my pre-sleep routine. Of course, I also lie down on the floor, stretch my back (rolling my legs from side to side), and relax my spinal area. You get the point. Yes, I can progress through fifteen minutes of rituals to get ready for bed, but that routine relaxes me. Do you know my wife's biggest complaint? And, clearly, she has many! I always fall asleep before she does. So, develop a routine. See if it helps your sleep. If not, at least it will create some lively discussions with your spouse. And those can be fun too. Part of *living*, yes?

Chapter 63

Are You Managing Your Clock?

"I must govern the clock, not be governed by it."
Golda Meir

At this point, you should have a healthy eating style and an exercise program. You should have improved physical health with a reduced need for medical interventions. You should have better mental clarity with a sharper focus toward your future and your golden years. You should have completed a life review with a better understanding and deeper appreciation of your life path. You should have developed a personal mission and a set of balanced goals, moving you away from your career. You should have a plan for personal development and personal growth. You should have better management of your clock. You should have received an infusion of daily structure and time management with the morning rudder and the evening rudder, combined with better management of your day, creating more time for those activities that give you the greatest joy. With these time management skills, you should already feel happier, ready to live longer.

So, what can I add? If you have read personal development literature, many of the experts recommend starting and ending the day with a review of a daily group of positive questions. What are you excited about? What are you grateful for? Who do you love? Who can you help? Some experts encourage everyone to utilize these questions to focus on the core group of positive activities that you want to accomplish. Other experts suggest focusing on some personal questions, thinking about positive options and positive solutions. However, I am against such a formal approach. From my standpoint, those additional questions are not necessary. If you have set up that morning and evening routine, that is more than sufficient for me. The above questions will likely pop into your mind at random times of their own accord. From my perspective, there are just two repetitive points. Try to start and end the day with the correct structure that leads to good physical and mental stability. Think of those morning and evening rudders as course correctors, steering you back toward your desired destination.

Anything else? For those people who are still working, do not let work issues intrude into your time (morning and evening) at home. Do not allow yourself to be scheduled into prolonged hours at the office or sucked into taking work home. Longer work does not always translate into more productivity. It certainly does not translate into greater happiness. More importantly, you read those earlier statistics. Too many people spend an insufficient amount of time communicating with those people whom they love the most, their spouses and children. Even if your children have moved out into their own lives, still create time to communicate with them. Create time to be part of their lives. If you do not establish a routine and manage your clock, you will not create time to increase these crucial connections. You will grow more socially isolated. Your life will be less connected. There will be less meaning and less value. So, follow your new compass and manage your clock. Both are equally important. After all, if you are going to create a new, enriching life, you want to have sufficient time to enjoy it.

STEP 7

Rediscovering Your Spirituality

"If you leave spirituality out of your life, you are a moron."
Eldon Taylor

Chapter 64

Dare to Reevaluate Your Religion?

My religion is very simple. My religion is kindness. "
Dalai Llama

You can probably guess what important area of your life has not been discussed. It's the spiritual part of your life. I left this part of your life as a separate habit because of its importance. It should not be underestimated. When you watch people win an award on a TV broadcast or achieve an accomplishment at a national event, what do they do? Many of them thank God before thanking anyone else. Many of them simply point to the heavens, gesturing with their hands. That common gesture is not incidental. For the majority of successful people, the belief in God is part of the cornerstone to their mission and their goals. From my perspective, the spiritual component should be a central part of your golden years. It should be a separate habit, right there beside physical health, mental clarity, a personal mission, and a list of specific goals. But let me make myself clear. I am differentiating spirituality from your specific religion.

Why the attempt to separate religion and spirituality? We live in a time where ethnic conflict and religious conflict seem paramount. When examining history, I am not certain how many eras have passed without these conflicts. Everyone seems to think his or her ethnic group and religious beliefs are superior to anyone else's. Now I do not mean to offend anyone's religious beliefs. What you believe is your right. But the perspective of one (single) true religion has never resonated with me. Let me take a philosophical perspective. God (or whatever 'force' you believe in) created a world of diversity. Let's look just at humans. We have 3,000-8,000 languages and around 5,000 ethnic groups.

We have 730 established religions with 3,200 different sects. With such variety, do you believe that God would have created just one single religion? Can you say that carries any logic? God creates diversity in every facet of the world, but not in religion? Okay, then, let me ask you one hypothetical question. At some future point in history, when our species explores the universe and encounters another life form, are we (as a race) going to argue that our religion is better than their religion? How do you think that's going to be received? Isn't that perspective a little egocentric? And isn't that bias a poor reflection of the tenets of our collective religions?

For me, there was a personal bias from my early years. Each Sunday my mother would attend the Catholic Church and my father would attend the Episcopal Church. My sister and I would rotate the churches. One day, feeling annoyed at the arrangement, I asked my mother several pointed questions. Weren't you both praying to the same God? If yes, then why did we have to go to separate buildings to pray to the same God? Funny, I don't remember the answer. But there was one comment about how one of them was better than the other. That comment did not make much sense until we started moving from city to city: Pittsburgh, Los Angeles, Pittsburgh, Louisville, Chicago, and Los Angeles. In each of those cities, do you know what, as a child, I heard? I heard how each city was the best. The people were nicer. The school system was better. The environment was richer. By the age of ten to eleven, I learned a common denominator. People always felt that whatever they had, including even their religion, well, that was the best. To my eyes, each city was different, but each city was very similar. Why? Because the people were the same wherever I went. Even as a young child, having attended different churches, I viewed religions in a similar context. You could tell me your religion was the best, but, sorry, I had heard that line much too often.

For the purpose of this brief discussion, let me take a historical approach. First, there were the primal or tribal religions, which provided much needed guidance to our early ancestors as they struggled to survive on this planet. Then, through the course of history, there came the development of the great religions. Scholars view Hinduism and Judaism as two older great religions, and they view Buddhism and Christianity as the adolescent religions that rebelled against the older religions. Weren't these adolescent religions attempting to take the earlier beliefs and transform them for a new generation? Just as an adolescent rebels against his or her parents? From this snapshot, can you acknowledge the evolutionary force that has created a number of great religions? It is the same natural force that has created such diversity across our planet, including the other 700-plus religions. From a perspective of tolerance, I view all of the world's religions as equally valuable. To me, they are colors in the rainbow. The rainbow, and the world, is more beautiful with multiple religions.

My point? Our spectrum of religions does not need to compete with each other. I have always liked Doug Floyd's observation: "You don't get harmony when everyone sings the same note." Like voices in a choir, our religions just need to coexist with each other. You are probably well aware of Gandhi's famous statement: "In heaven there is no religion; there is only God." So, here is my request. Realize that your religion and your spiritual beliefs are an important part of your golden years. Realize that this component will add additional balance to your life. Do not neglect your faith as your grow older. Embrace it. Let it help you through your current challenges. Let it guide your decisions. Many people search for answers at this time of their life. In fact, more people change religions from the age of fifty to seventy-five than any period of their life. Regardless of your religious choice, please be careful to reign in the belief that your religion is the only religion. Try to rise above the perspective that what you have (or what you believe) is always the best. Perhaps try to move toward greater understanding of other people with more appreciation of their different religious views. Remember the underlying principles in many religions. It is more important to be fair than right, and that applies to respecting other people's religious beliefs. It also applies to the Dalai Llama quote at the beginning of this chapter. We all need to show a little more kindness. And with increased kindness, there is greater harmony and greater love.

Chapter 65

Can We Have a Moment of Silence?

"Where do you go to replenish yourself?
Each of us needs a free place."
Gloria Steinem

If you do not believe in God, that is not an impediment for this habit, but it is going to make it more of a challenge. There is the perspective that you are as young as your faith, as old as your doubt. You are as young as your hope, as old as your despair.

There is the belief that what counts is not the wrinkles on your face, but the wrinkles in your soul. As for the existence of God, I would employ the often-used phrase that the absence of evidence is not evidence of absence. I would also remind you that our biggest human dichotomy is not the mind-body dichotomy; it is our mind-body-spirit continuum. Even if your disbelief is entrenched, do not skip this part of the guide. Suspend your disbelief. Bury your resistance. Take a chance and see how much of this material can still be incorporated into your golden years. You may be surprised by the success of your spiritual transformation. I am simply asking you to reconnect with that component.

Set aside your religious convictions or lack of religious convictions. Instead, try to focus on expanding your spiritual component. Let me return to my lifelong friend, Jeffrey Knight. In his fifties, after the death of his wife, he traveled to the Buddhist monastery Wat Pah Nanachat in northeast Thailand. For six months, he lived with the monks, learning practices that had been taught for 2,500 years. He lived in a small hut in the forest, meditated daily, and followed a strict regimen. He had his head, eyebrows, and facial hair shaved. He ate a simple diet of one meal a day. He awoke at 3 a.m.; he had multiple menial tasks;

and he participated in the spiritual teachings. I have a picture of him wearing a dirty T-shirt and shorts, meditating amidst free tigers. He was close enough to touch the tigers. But that experience helped him through that troubled period. He returned from Thailand with a better connection with his spiritual component. Now, you may respond with the observation, "But it didn't work. Years later he still jumped." But from my perspective it did work. It kept him alive; and he returned to the United States in a far better physical, emotional, and spiritual place. He would not have lasted until that late night call if he had not traveled to Wat Pah Nanachat.

I recall listening to a pilot who was shot down on a NATO mission. For six days, he was trapped behind enemy lines while the enemy army kept searching the hillside for his position. For six days, he stayed hidden, moving from bush to bush, burying himself as much as possible. At times, enemy soldiers came within a single foot of his hiding spot. For many, it would have been the nightmare from hell. For him, it was a spiritual retreat. The background chatter in his mind subsided. He became immersed in his own silence; and in that silence he reawakened his own spiritual component. To cultivate your own spirituality, you should try to shut down your own dialogue (internal and external) and cultivate this silence. There is value in this silence. There are some who believe that all of man's troubles stem from man's inability to sit quietly all alone for any significant period of time. Try it. It is not that easy.

My recommendation is simple. Create time for your silence. Create your own place to replenish your spirit. Consider a trial of meditation. Some meditations employ twenty minutes of deep breathing with the 4-7-8 pattern. Four seconds to inhale. Seven seconds to hold your breath. Eight seconds to exhale. Does the time matter? For me, no. Just find your own rhythm. For sounds, some meditations use "ahhhhh" (a sound associated with creation) or "ooommmmh" (a sound associated with gratitude). Again, does it really matter? All roads lead to Rome. There are numerous programs on the Internet. Short meditations. Long meditations. But they all work. They help clear your mind of intrusive thoughts; they help you connect with God; and they reenergize your spirit. Meditation may not be for everyone. If not, you still need to find another activity that offers silence, giving you a chance to reconnect with your spiritual needs. Perhaps a walk in the woods? A respite in the park? An exercise routine? Choose whatever activity gives you the best chance for periods of silence. In these moments of silence, discover a path to renewal. See what secrets you find. Discover what wisdom lies within. Embrace the mystery. If you are agnostic or an atheist, it just may awaken a rethinking of the meaning of life. And regardless of your religious beliefs, it may still help you better appreciate yourself, your relationships, and your life. That is crucial for each one of us.

Chapter 66

Our Need for Deeper Connection

"If you stick to what you know, you sell yourself short."
Carrie Underwood

Let me offer one consequence of resurrecting your spiritual component. A spiritual foundation reasserts how much we are all connected. Radioisotope studies show that when you take a breath, you are breathing in 10 (to the power of 22) atoms. In the course of your life you will have breathed in atoms from every historical figure. You will have breathed in atoms from every species. The atoms, which have circulated through you, have also circulated through the bodies of our great religious leaders. With the wind patterns of the world, when someone exhales, another person inhales. It's a flow of recycled atoms. Walt Whitman used to proclaim: "Every atom belonging to you also belongs to me." He was more accurate than he imagined. We are more connected (physiologically) than we acknowledge. Most individuals set their sights on all of the differences between us. Science, when combined with a spiritual foundation, can actually remind us how connected we are to each other.

So what is the message of this connection? Hopefully, it inspires you to think more about your connection with others and the need to give to others. I am hoping it will inspire you to ask yourself some basic questions. Do you help or hinder? Do you contribute or consume? Do you give or receive? We enter the world with nothing; we leave the world with nothing. You can't take anything to the grave. So life can't be in the getting; it has to be in the giving. This guide asks you to develop new habits so that you can achieve a better life. Superficially, that is a selfish endeavor. This part of the guide attempts to remind you that your golden years should also help others achieve a better life. You need to commit to more than yourself. You need to commit to your family and friends. As they say, it is more valuable to gain the respect of your family than to gain the adulation of the masses. With your mission and your goals, you need to meet your own needs. But, with this expanded focus, your mission should try to meet the needs of the individuals who are most important in your life.

At the same time, it is important to extend your giving to others beyond just your family and friends. I remember a story told by a famous football coach. When he was in college, his parents divorced. When told the news, he decided to head home to see his mother. However, he had no money, no transportation. So he decided to hitch a car ride across the state. Unfortunately, he got stuck in a severe snowstorm. He found himself abandoned by the side of the road on some turnpike for several hours in the middle of the night. Freezing. Standing knee deep in snow. Miles from any safe haven. Finally, a car came along. It was an old couple that was getting off the turnpike in a couple of stops. But after hearing his story they drove several hours beyond their destination, dropping him off at his mother's house. He had no money; he could not repay them for their kindness. When he expressed his regret at his inability to express his full appreciation, they suggested another option. They encouraged him to follow their example. If he had a chance to help someone, he should; and whenever he helped someone, they had just one request: think of us. The old couple knew the value of giving. They knew the value of feeling connected. That is a feeling that you want to incorporate into your life. Otherwise, even with possessions and accomplishments, your life is going to feel empty, with something missing.

So, regardless of your circumstances, start reaching out to others, some close, others more distant. Let me share my own example. It's nothing significant but still representative of the little connections that you can create to add some meaning to your life. Each year, I receive the newsletter from my high school, Lake Forest Academy, in Lake Forest, Illinois; and each year, I scan the graduating class to see if anyone selected my college, Williams College. Two years ago, I found someone who was embarking on my own high school/college path. So, what did I do? I wrote to him as he reached his freshman college dorm, explaining that I had walked the same path. Yes, there was a difference of several decades. But I still offered my perspective on the transition from our high school to our college; and I also offered suggestions for how to make the most of his Williams College career. Well, the young man responded with a kind letter. He was quite an interesting individual with a remarkable skill set, including his own band. We have now established an email relationship. Again, it's nothing that is going to dramatically change the course of his life. But it is another human connection that will hopefully provide some value to him and me. And it is also a cross-generational relationship. Don't think of connecting with only those of your age. Think of connecting to others who are younger, and think of trying to create something meaningful. There are many ways to make a difference, large or small. As with so many parts of this guide, the time to start is now.

Chapter 67

Need to Refocus On Your Friendships

"My friends are my estate."
Emily Dickinson

Many people perceive friendship as something unique to humans. That belief is wrong. Friendship is too valuable to be confined to one species. Monkeys, chimpanzees, baboons, horses, hyenas, elephants, and dolphins create lifelong friendships, and that is only the beginning of the list. Many of these species create friendships early in their life, continue them throughout life, and mourn the death of their friends. Chimpanzees are known to isolate themselves for several months after the death of a lifelong friend. The same reaction occurs with dolphins. After the death of a close friend, the dolphin will swim alone for several months before finally reengaging with the other dolphins, slowly moving to establish new friendships. All of these species, like us, move forward after a loss, eventually forging new relationships. Why? Because whether we like to admit it or not, our survival depends on our friendships. We need each other much more than we often admit.

There are many primatologists, biologists, and anthropologists who have spent decades analyzing friendships within other species. The commonality is striking. In each species, friendship comes down to acts of sharing, acts of sacrifice for another, and acts of grieving with the loss of the companion. In many species, the acts of sharing should teach us a lesson. Research on the friendship between chimpanzees reveals that favors to each other can appear unbalanced for months at a time. However, when tracked over a lifetime, those favors become surprisingly balanced. For chimpanzees, what matters the most is a long-term friendship, not a short-term friendship; and the lifelong friendships are worth the periods of giving without necessarily receiving. In some ways, we have much to learn from many species. They may say that a dog is a man's best friend. In truth, friendship is a man's best companion.

Researchers have studied the physiological benefits of friendships in a number of species. Rhesus monkeys with close friendships show reduced levels of stress hormones and improved health. How do researchers complete these studies? They measure the stress hormones (glucosteroids) from their urine and feces. The stress hormones rise when there is a death of a friend. But those same stress hormones decrease when the monkey finds a new friend. Horses, when they are grooming each other, show slower heart rates. Baboons with close friendships are four times more likely to live until the age of fifteen. The offspring of baboons, when their mothers have close friendships, are far likely to stay alive. Overall, in study after study, there appeared to be a health and longevity benefit for those members of any species that have sustained friendships. From an evolutionary standpoint, friendship is a key factor for survival.

Humans are not any different. With humans, a friendship appears to lower blood pressure, reduce stress hormones, and improve the immune system. How strong is the effect of a close friendship? A lack of a friendship is considered to be a health risk that is equivalent to smoking a pack of cigarettes a day. A lack of a friendship is considered to be a health risk worse than obesity. So, as you enter your golden years, you need to appreciate the value of friendship for your health, your happiness, and your survival. If people are not available, adopt a pet. We need that companionship at any age. In the first three years of my life, my parents lived in a rural setting outside Pittsburgh. I have memories of only one friend, a local dog. He would come down to our house every afternoon; and he and I would play for hours. Every day, a black limo would roll into our not-so-grand driveway. A well-dressed butler would pick up the dog and deposit him in the back seat of the limo, then drive away. It was not until years later that I was told that the dog belonged to the Hunt family of Hunt's ketchup fame. Apparently, they lived about a mile away, but the dog still found me. So, human or animal, rich or poor, it makes no difference. A friend is still a friend, something we all need. And something far more valuable than any other part of your estate.

Chapter 68

Marriage – For Better Or Worse?

"The secret of a happy marriage remains a secret."
Henny Youngman

At one point in my education, I ran across an elderly professor. He was beyond his teaching career, but he loved to gather a group of students and tell them how his experience in World War II helped prepare him for World War III, his marriage. The only difference between the two conflicts? World War II ended.

His World War III was apparently in its fifth decade. Never ending warfare: that was his phrase. The students would laugh, but the divorce statistics for our country are not particularly good. Around 50 percent of our marriages end in divorce. The odds do not get better with multiple attempts. Around 40-50 percent of first marriages end in divorce; around 60-67 percent of second marriages end in divorce; and around 70-73 percent of third marriages end in divorce. Clearly, practice does not make perfect. But these statistics underscore a common theme: our constant need to add a meaningful connection to our life. That need does not go away as we age. For some people, it grows stronger.

There are other statistics that raise some points. Couples with children have a lower rate of divorce than couples without a child. Sociologists hypothesize that childlessness can lead to loneliness. Is that the reason for the increased divorce rate in childless couples? Their loneliness? Maybe that explains why my wife has tolerated all of my idiosyncrasies. We persisted through those six long years of infertility; we were lucky enough to (finally) have two wonderful daughters; and after all of that perseverance and good fortune, anything else is tolerable, right? Actually, there is a more important question to address. With all of our infertility challenges, what kept us going? In truth, it was a desire for a deeper connection with something that extended beyond each other. For childless couples, it is often a connection to an extended family. For other couples, it may be a connection with God. Some of us need to connect with much more than each other; we need to connect with a greater force.

There are numerous books that help people prepare for marriage and educate them on how to succeed in marriage. There are articles describing how to prepare yourself for your partner, how to select the ideal partner, and how to work together to achieve the best possible relationship. To be honest, I have never been a fan of those books. When you fall in love, you fall in love, and usually when you least expect it. When my wife and I were dating, her father took her aside and asked her only two questions about me. Does he respect you? And is he treating you well? When my future wife shared her father's initial concerns, I remember laughing at his questions. Me? I was thinking of the passion, the romance, and the wonder of our intimacy. I was more worried about the lady who lived downstairs beneath my apartment. She caught me in the elevator one day and shared that she and her husband were envious of all of the laughter they heard from my girlfriend and myself. I was just hoping that was all she heard. But 33 years later, my wife's father could not have been wiser. From my experience, a successful couple respects each other, and they treat each other well. Marriage is that simple.

In my three decades of marriage, my wife and I have experienced only a few arguments. I cannot take the credit; it's a shared process. We are just a couple who is not wired for conflict. We are responsive, not reactive. We are not inclined to judge or try to change the other person. The more judgment, the more your reactive mode; and the more your reactive mode, the less time to love, right? But I will repeat Dalai Llama's declaration that his religion was kindness. Every couple needs kindness, understanding, and, most importantly, forgiveness. What do they say about forgiveness? Only the strong forgive? The weak don't? If you are going to become a better person, you need to forgive yourself. If you and your spouse are going to become a better couple, you need to forgive (and accept) each other. Develop the ability to listen. Never underestimate fairness. And never discount your initial commitment. As the traditional wedding vows underscore, didn't you marry for sickness and health? Richer and poorer? Good times and bad days? Those cycles are blips in the course of any successful marriage. What counts is that commitment to each other, especially as you grow older. Appreciate and cherish each other. If you stumble from time to time, just keep trying. As with most endeavors in life, don't give up too early. Too many marriages are lost when they could have been saved.

Chapter 69

How to Avoid Solo Aging

"The only thing worse than being alone is wishing you were."
Carolyn Hax

Studies of solo living (living by yourself) are not encouraging. In America, in 1950, 9 percent of households included just one person. Today, in America, 28 percent of people live alone. In Sweden, it's 47 percent; in Great Britain, it's 34 percent; in Japan, it's 31 percent; in Italy, it's 29 percent; in Canada, it's 27 percent; in Russia, it's 25 percent; and in South Africa, it's 24 percent.

Studies have shown that the number of Americans who felt that they had no one to share personal concerns had tripled over the past couple of decades, currently reaching almost 25 percent of the population. So, many people, as they head into their golden years, are looking at an increased chance of isolation and loneliness. Once you establish a single residence, a person in his or her golden years is more likely to remain in that residential setting than any other demographic except a married couple. You might argue that living alone offers advantages for increased independence and freedom. In truth, loneliness kills more people than cigarettes.

The solo living trends are part of the reason why it is so important to design your golden years. You want your golden years to be the pinnacle of your life, not the lonely years of your life. The evening of your life is not just a continuation of the afternoon of your life. You have to prepare yourself for new challenges and likely losses. You will have pebbles and some earthquakes, including the eventual loss of people whom you have loved. That unfortunate reality places more emphasis on incorporating new habits and new friends; and it places more emphasis on shifting your focus from what you do to a focus on who you are. But there is good news. At this point in your life, people will be far more interested in who you are than what you do. You will be able to spend more time being, less time doing. But who are you? If you want to avoid solo living, that question must be addressed. And, once again, if you want more, you are going to have to be more. At least you are going to have to share more of yourself. For many people, that increased sharing requires some inner work.

So, what does this inner work entail? We have already covered many of the areas; and we will cover more areas in the final chapters. But inner work demands continued personal growth during your golden years. It requires that you view these challenges as opportunities. You can change. You can become someone better. You can find your authentic self, the real you. You can realize what you were meant to be and then be that person. You can live in the present. You can rediscover your values. You can become more compassionate. You can even learn to accept suffering and move beyond it to a new level of gratitude for yourself and others. But these actions are best taken with the support of others, not in a solo living environment. These actions are best done to help others. Your connections and your friendships are crucial. So, as you design your golden years, do not let yourself be isolated and lonely. Think about it. When alone, whom can you defend? Whom can you mentor? Whom can you educate? More importantly, to whom can you give? Make a commitment to create a living environment that gives you the chance for these types of giving.

When my father died, my mother lived by herself in their house. It was lonely. Her efforts to maintain the house grew progressively harder. During the subsequent years, I tried to encourage my mother to move into a retirement home, a nice residential facility where a half dozen of her friends already lived. The facility offered regular meals, plenty of social activities, and a wide range of excursions. My mother tried to convince herself to leave her house, but she couldn't, even though she was miserable. When she finally reached a point of increasing physical weakness, the real estate market had sunk so low that her house did not sell for months and months. She grew discouraged. What was she missing? It was transparent: a connection to other people. A chance to give to others. So, don't let the same inactivity block your happiness. If you find yourself living alone, do something about it. Either take someone into your home or move into another home with others. Or develop a lifestyle that is packed with daily human interactions. Why? Because each of us needs to feel like we are still contributing and still giving. As for my mother, we let her move in with us. It made a difference in the quality of her life and our life. We were each able to give more, not less, to each other. That alone increased the happiness within the family.

Chapter 70

Our Challenge of Giving

"When I give, I give myself."
Walt Whitman

Confucius was a Chinese thinker and social philosopher around 500 BC. His numerous writings were consolidated into a system of philosophy called 'Confucianism.' In these teachings, he championed strong family loyalty, respect for elders, and a series of guidelines for social interaction. These guidelines differentiated the appropriate style of interactions for parents, siblings, children, friends, acquaintances, etc. As different as the social interactions might be, Confucius accented compassion for others and the act of giving to others, from the highest ruler to the lowest peasant. He established the golden rule: "Do not do to others what you do not want done to yourself." His teachings were popular and timeless. Why? Because we all struggle with relationships, wondering how to best conduct ourselves. But beneath Confucius's message there was a strong belief in the importance of love and the value of giving.

Confucius's recommendations are a struggle for many people. Some individuals do not love themselves and have limited capacity for loving others. Others are too self-focused to have sufficient emotional space to love others. Some people have difficulty just with the act of giving. They are unsure to whom to give. They debate how far to extend their giving. They argue how much to give. The act of giving? Sometimes, it seems to occur less and less these days. Giving does not have to be anything of material value. It can be a smile, a compliment, a gesture, or anything that will add joy to another person's life. There is the catchphrase: give back to your community. For some people, that act often translates to a charity donation. I have a suggestion. Giving money is not the best avenue for giving back or connecting to others. How much personal connection comes from writing a check? If you want to give to others, you should give in person. That's far more meaningful. Try volunteering at a hospital. Try volunteering at a shelter or a community service. Through this type of direct personal connection, you are not just giving something to them; you are giving something of yourself.

There is a personal benefit that comes with giving: less social isolation. A spiritual connection and a social connection often go together. There are too many people who stay focused on themselves and their own problems. What is the result? They become progressively isolated, spiritually and socially. I am not advocating that these people, as they age, move to a senior citizen residence, as I am a strong believer in the benefits of cross-generational relationships. Instead, I am advocating more contact with others and more giving to others. You do not want to be the mole in Franz Kafka's "The Burrow." After you create something special (in the mole's case, it was an intricate series of burrows), you do not want to keep it only for yourself. The greatest joy comes when you head out of your burrow and engage the world. The greatest joy comes from sharing, not in hiding. Think of the successful people whose last years were miserable. In most of the cases, they were miserable because they were so isolated. So, when you reach the point where you have rekindled your spiritual component and you are ready to give to others, become more socially active, not less socially active. Embrace others. Embrace their difference. Offer your love. Offer your emotional support. Surprisingly, it will do more than make them feel better. It will also make you feel better.

In my case, I have spent every Saturday morning at my parent's home for over the past decade. In the beginning, it was to help my father pay his bills. With the start of his dementia, he showed more and more anger with each new bill. To help my mother have better control of my father, I wrote all the bills, presenting them quickly for my dad's signature. As he grew worse, I helped with his care; and when he finally died from his dementia, I continued my Saturday visits to help my mother with her mourning and then with her upkeep of the house. But who was the real beneficiary of those weekly visits? My dad? My mother? No, the person who benefitted the most was actually I. It kept me engaged with others. It kept me focused on giving. It reminded me (weekly) that what counts the most in life is contributing, not consuming. Taking care of an older family member can be taxing. It can test your patience. But it also serves as a reminder that as long as we are giving, we are living in the best sense.

Chapter 71

Try Creating Your Own Temple

"Peace comes from within."
Siddhartha Gautama

There is a saying that it is easier to build a temple in your heart than find your heart in a temple. By now it is obvious. For this habit, I am not encouraging you to become more religious; I am encouraging you to become more spiritual. Try to build a temple, a spiritual core, with a feeling of connection in your soul, and try to connect this temple to the act of giving. This spiritual-social component will do more than maintain your connection with people; it will help you appreciate everyone's different roles and different beliefs. It will also provide you with wisdom, giving you guidance. It will give you a peace of mind with the belief that your life is on purpose and the belief that some force is helping you complete your own mission. As earlier highlighted, your golden years are not something you can do on your own. You need connections with something more, and a sense of peace only comes with those connections.

So how do you maintain this feeling of connection with the world, especially at times when there is so much conflict and so many challenges? For many people, it will be through these little personal incidents where you have a chance to connect with someone else and a chance to give to someone else. Try to find the approach that works best for you; and try to make it a habit that you can follow on a daily basis. If you find yourself struggling for the best approach, review your history. In your life, what has worked for you? What are the moments when you have felt most connected to others? Try to find a common thread and then try to duplicate those moments of connection. In an earlier chapter,

I encouraged you to write ten goals that would be aligned with your personal mission. I would suggest that you now add a couple of additional goals to that list. These goals would be focused toward increasing your spiritual component and increasing your connections with others. Remember that there are three items that clog the human soul: negativity, judgment, and lack of balance. Add these habits, spirituality and giving to others, and your soul will never become clogged.

One person's spirituality does not have to equal another person's spirituality, just like one person's religious beliefs do not have to match another person's religious beliefs. Again, they can all coexist. But when you reconnect with your spiritual component, you now have new references for reevaluating your mission and goals. Your progress should be reevaluated as you expand your connection with others. What is the greatest gift in the world? It isn't money; it's love. What is the most expensive indulgence? Hate. With this spiritual resurrection, you have a greater chance of becoming a better person. Your new habits will steer you along the right path. This additional habit will propel you even further. Be the best you can be for others, not just for yourself.

With this process, there is vulnerability. There is uncertainty. To share with others, to love others, requires you to expose your own imperfections. Sometimes there is fear. Sometimes there is shame. It always takes some courage. Remind yourself that no one is perfect. Remind yourself that you are worthy. Remind yourself that vulnerability is the starting point for connecting. It is the starting point for loving. Do you want to be loved? It's easy. There are no external barriers. Like much of this guide, it's all internal. Do you want to be loved? Then just be loving. But to appreciate others, you have to first appreciate yourself. Follow the viewpoint of the spiritual leaders. If we are all connected, and science shows us how connected we are, then God is part of you. That part alone is worth loving. That part alone is worth sharing. So embrace your vulnerability. Embrace the uncertainty. Embrace the mystery. These are the components that make life so meaningful. Your spirituality and connections with people? They are often one and the same, equally valuable and equally satisfying.

Chapter 72

Ah, Serenity: Simple, Yes?

"A mind at peace, a mind centered ...
is stronger than any physical force."
Wayne Dyer

There is a wonderful destination for your journey: serenity. From my vantage point, serenity occurs when you have established an inner peace with a sense of gratitude, affection for others, and a higher level of tranquility. You will know you have reached this destination when you are open and honest with yourself, when you do not feel a need for judgment or blame (for yourself or others), and when you are respectful and loving of others with no need for any sense of control over others. I do not expect you to have reached this destination by this stage of this guide, but I still want to highlight this progression, as it will emerge as you establish the habits for this guide. For many of you, serenity is an abstract concept, not too relevant in today's stressful world. You are wrong. It is achievable. It is worth the wait; and it's important to be aware of its uplifting features.

I have offered the viewpoint that you attract what you think and you attract what you discuss. Some people argue you attract what you are. They might be correct. That is another reason for becoming a better person. The better you are, the better things you attract, and that includes peace of mind and serenity. As you progress along your path, your ability to learn and create should be magnified. You should become better at pushing aside past doubts, prior limitations, and old prejudices. You should begin to see new solutions and new paths for yourself and others. I am not asserting that you will look younger (which seems to be a preoccupation of our society), but I think you will feel younger. I am rather fond of wrinkles, as long as they are external, not internal. They give people character; they tell their life stories. People often have plastic surgery to change what's on the outside because they are not able to change what's on the inside. But what matters the most for your happiness, peace of mind, and serenity is (don't listen to the plastic surgeon) on your inside.

If that perspective is difficult for you to follow, if you find yourself still focused on your physical appearance, I want you to try my approach. Do not look in mirrors. My dad gave me that advice when I was much younger. I do not know if that was a Courter tradition (the family is Dutch and we looked like a group of farmers?) or if I were simply looking especially scraggly that day. But I took his advice and it worked. I developed the habit of looking in the mirror twice a day: when I washed my face in the morning and when I washed my face in the evening. It's amazing how good you can imagine you look when you do not have to see yourself in any reflection. I do not have any experience in the ladies room (I suspect some of you will be relieved to hear that fact), but I have watched many adult men, standing before the bathroom mirror, staring at themselves long after they have finished washing their hands. Personally, if I had been staring at their reflection, I would have ducked for cover. How could they stare so long? Iron grade stomachs? I have no idea. But, if you want my advice, don't waste your time in front of any mirror. Keep repeating the word internal and keep those eyes focused on your character, not your appearance.

Take it a step further. Do not expect serenity to come from external events; it's going to have to come from within you. But there are many things you can do to speed the development of serenity. You can focus more on the beauty of life. You can become more authentic, true to yourself. You can feel more gratitude for the miracles that your body performs, and you can start treating your body as a temple. You can stop focusing on mistakes by yourself and others. You can express more love for yourself and others. You can stop seeing yourself as separate from others and separate from God. You can reduce those imaginary boundaries. The quickest path toward your serenity comes when you bring joy and serenity to someone else. You don't have to change the world. You just need to change your own part of the world. As worry gives way to hope, as conflict diminishes toward cooperation, and as ambition cedes to meaning, serenity will emerge, not overnight, but bit by bit, changing you and your world. And for that development, you do not need any reflection.

Serenity will not mean you are free of stress. Everyone has good days and bad days. You will still have financial challenges, physical ailments, and personal conflicts. But you will have a sense of peace and an associated belief that you can move beyond these problems. You will find yourself returning to your challenges with renewed focus. You will have confidence, despite the obstacles, that you can create a serene life. There is the well known Serenity Prayer: "God grant me the serenity to accept the things I cannot change, the courage to change things I can, and the wisdom to know the difference." Serenity will give you that wisdom. Serenity will give you the strength. With wisdom and strength, you will create a new sense of peace in your life. You need it; and the world needs it. And it is something that you can pass along to others, making their lives better and richer.

Chapter 73

Have You Considered a Memoir?

"Writing teaches us our mysteries."
Marie de l'Incarnation

Do you feel a need to go deeper into your spirituality? If yes, have you ever considered writing a memoir? With a life review, you examine a group of circumstances or events that shaped your character, and then you use the life review to free your character. With a memoir, you explore a larger and broader collection of random memories. You do not need to search for your life changing events. There is no pressure to prioritize any of your memories. If you want, a memoir can be arranged into an autobiography. However, a memoir is more than an autobiography. For most people, a memoir is a search for your soul, not just a review of your history. That's why there's always a focus on your emotions, not just the events. There is value in exploring these emotions because they often lead to a spiritual reawakening. A life review is easy. A memoir is often more difficult. Maybe the soul is deeper than the heart? For a memoir, Walter Wesley Smith once observed: "All you need to do is sit down … and open a vein."

There is a story, which I have first heard, from Wayne Dyer. I may not have all the details (and I may be paraphrasing), but I remember the message. A man lost his car keys and was searching for the keys in the grass around a streetlight. A stranger came along and joined the search, pacing back and forth beneath the streetlight. Finally, the stranger asked: "Is there any chance that you might have lost the keys over there in the grass away from the street light?' The man did not hesitate. He responded, pointing to a darkened area of the grass, far removed from the streetlight: "As a matter of fact, I think I lost the keys right over there."

The stranger was perplexed: "Then why are you looking beneath the streetlight?" The man's response was honest: "Because it is dark over there; and it's light over here." The point of this story? At least from my memory? If you want to retrieve some things, which may have been lost over time, you need to step bravely into the darkness. From the darkness there often comes a light, which is far brighter than the dim glow of some streetlight.

Within this light, there is often something of greater value. The stories that we carry in our head, as we have seen, are superficial visions, covering a deeper emotional reality. The process of writing a memoir involves exploring that darkness to uncover the emotional truth of who you are. Some people ask: "If I do not undergo this exercise, will I ever truly know myself?" The answer is yes. But for some people, there is a pull to know their soul, not just their history. Are you one of those people? You will know if you have completed this guide and still feel that something spiritual is missing. If you feel that something is still missing in the darkness. That something may be a broader understanding and deeper appreciation of your soul, including the depths of your own spirituality. For those people, this process can be a grand adventure. Spiritual beliefs, heretofore unknown, may emerge.

Hidden desires and hidden issues may be drawn into the light. Your values, belief, and hopes may be better understood. Do I recommend this process for everyone? No. But if you are still feeling unsettled or somehow empty, you should be aware that a memoir offers a spiritual path toward greater fulfillment.

Medieval labyrinths were once considered to be paths that could lead someone to their spiritual center. Memoirs are much the same. If you are going to give it a try, follow this approach. As a starting point, let your mind run free. When you hit upon a memory, write down the details of that memory, but focus more on your emotions that are buried within the memory. This task, unlike the process for a life review, is helped by working with someone (like the stranger in the story). There are coaches and classes for writing a memoir. Most of these writers claim that there is a benefit in sharing the story, as you write it, with someone who is nonjudgmental and not critical. Someone who can coach you toward uncovering more emotions and discovering a deeper spirit. These writers claim that memoirs are successful when they help you peel the onion, going deeper into these areas. At some point, when you have a sufficient collection of memories so you can see the underlying theme of this emotional undercurrent, you should also be able to reconnect with your spiritual core.

For many people, writing is a challenge, something that does not come easily. But, again, it comes down to whether you want to explore your own spirituality. For some people, especially as they grow older, there is an urge to clarify that remaining mystery. If you are one of those people, I encourage you to ignore your writing skills. Grammar? Correct spelling? Does any of that really matter? What counts is your own journey, and if your writing speaks to you, not to anyone else. Yes, you may want it to be a legacy. You may want others to read it so you can share your insights. But, as with so many activities in life, focus on the process, not the end point. Focus on exposing those buried emotions. Focus on uncovering the spiritual issues and your spiritual beliefs. Focus on finding your spiritual soul. If you can succeed at that task, your memoir will have served its purpose. Sharing your spiritual soul, for many people, is the best part of leaving a legacy, and another route for making a difference.

Chapter 74

A New Perspective of Death

"Death is the destination we all share.
No one has ever escaped it."
Steve Jobs

You already know that America has 74-77 million baby boomers, born between 1946 and 1964, who are progressing into their golden years. Many countries throughout the world have a similar population bubble for this older generation. Even China is facing a generation crisis, with a massive number of older individuals. As this population ages around the world, there will be a global surge of deaths. This guide is designed to enhance the quality of your older years and extend the number of your golden years. However, as we age, death is something that needs to be faced. Not everyone has the perspective expressed by Steve Jobs, the former CEO of Apple, who claimed death was life's single best invention. Other cultures have a more respectful, deeper appreciation of death. Our American culture? Not so much. But we need to develop a new perspective and apply a new meaning to death. Yes, let's make the most of all of our years. But let's not waste any time fearing the next dimension.

When I was a young medical intern, working my first night of On Call duty, my very first patient arrived, straight from the morgue, with a death certificate. Now, as an inexperienced physician, it did not take me long to return him to the morgue with another death certificate, signed by me. But in the four hours when the patient was under my care, it was a surreal experience. I wanted to gather the medical information, focusing on his recent cancer and his current physical symptoms. He could have cared less about his medical condition (he knew he was near the end of his life); and it was difficult to extract much clinical information. Instead, he wanted to discuss his death experience in the morgue. To my horror, he could remember everything. The morticians cutting open the body next to him. The assistant's name and the details of their forensic conversation. He even recalled their medical terms, which were well beyond his education. But mostly he wanted to discuss the light, the feeling of floating above his body, and the wonderful relief from his chronic pain. He also wanted to share his new perspective on death. For him, it did not look so bad. Not so bad at all.

My patient's account was not atypical. There are innumerable reports of death or near-death experiences. Individuals who seemingly die in surgery, but can later recount all of the conversations of the surgeon. Accident victims who can describe the details of the car crash, the arrival of the police, and the seemingly failed attempts of the paramedics. The person's recall of the sound and smell is often impressive. For many observers, these experiences are near-death episodes, not actual death. However, there are also innumerable reports where the victim returns with new information or even new capacities. There are verified reports of individuals who, when revived, can speak a new language. Latin. Greek. Or when they return, draw a diagram that can be found buried in some religious book, which they have never read. So, what can we surmise from all of these cases? One fundamental truth: our knowledge of death is limited and superficial. Death is, and will always remain, a mystery.

For most people, death represents pain, misery, fear, and loss. Buddhism has a different and valuable view of death. Buddhism offers the belief that death is not the end of life; it is only the end of our current body. Buddhism believes that our spirit survives, that it usually seeks a new body (although heaven and hell are possible places), and that our spirit is permanent. From the Buddhist perspective, where do we go after death? That depends on our karma and how much good we have done throughout our life. There is a benefit with that viewpoint, as it reduces the fear of death. That belief replaces fear with hope of a rebirth for your spirit, the hope for earning additional chances at life, and the hope of progressing toward something better. For the Buddhist, death still involves loss, grief, and mourning, but it also offers a sense of peace. It also encourages each person to prepare for death by behaving in a manner that is good and positive for yourself and others.

Many Christians are not inclined to embrace any of the Buddhist views. For most Christians, it's either heaven or hell.

However, I want to accent the value of increasing your spirituality, not just sticking to your own religion. I want to emphasize the value of increasing your sense of interconnectedness. Since our atoms are recycled, used by generation after generation, part of you will remain in the physical world. With that realization, isn't it easier to imagine that part of you will also remain in the spiritual world? America's spiritual leaders, like Wayne Dyer, have argued that we are spiritual beings living in a physical world. If you listen to their wisdom, your spirit was alive before you were born, alive during your journey through human life, and alive after your death. In truth, none of us knows what comes next. So, it becomes a fair question: Are there beliefs that could make your life easier and your death more comfortable?

With this guide, I want you to live an enriched life with wonderful golden years and an increase of golden moments. I want you to enjoy your life and the people in your life to your final day; and I want your final day to be something that is not feared. But when death comes (and no one lives forever), I want you, at that moment, to embrace death. I want you to have no unfinished business. I would love to have you follow the lead of Steve Jobs. Most people know that his final words were, "oh wow, oh wow, oh wow." I am hoping those words reflected his perspective on the duality of life. I am hoping those words reflected his appreciation of our life and his surprise at what's coming after our life. We would all do well to follow his lead. Regardless of your specific religious beliefs, you are lucky to be alive, and you cannot dispute the fact that your luck may not be ending with your death. Yes, it is a mystery, but it is another mystery to embrace, not fear.

Chapter 75

The Question Never Asked

"Wisdom begins in wonder."
Socrates

There are a number of self-help and spiritual leaders who seem to have discovered serenity. Yet, you will read headlines saying they have been stricken with leukemia or brain cancer or some deadly illness. You may silently wonder about the question that is never asked: Didn't their higher level of consciousness and higher level of serenity offer them any protection against these illnesses? The answer is yes and no. With the mind-body connection, the mind can improve the immune system and your health. With the mind-body-spirit continuum, there can be a further improvement in your resistance against disease. But I want to offer a cautionary warning. Remember the importance of balance. You need to include all of the habits in this guide, which fit your needs, not just habits that spark your interest. What did so many of these spiritual giants neglect for their own health and longevity? Give it some thought. Can you guess?

Many of these individuals have been so focused with their insights into their own spirituality and serenity that they have neglected some health fundamentals. What was missing in their life? In many cases, it was their eating style. Many of these leaders did not follow a plant-based eating style with limited animal-based foods. While they were creating breakthroughs in their spirituality and serenity, their body was still producing errors with random DNA mistakes and the creation of cancer cells. Their heightened immune system may have improved their defense against these cancer cells, but some of these cancer cells likely remained undetected, slowly spreading. At this point, I want to reemphasize the earlier habit of your eating style. Yes, spirituality and serenity are important. Yes, regular exercise is beneficial. But I would attribute 80 percent of your health to your eating style. That arena cannot be neglected. In fact, none of the habits in this guide, at least those habits that fit your needs, should be neglected. You can't focus on one habit while neglecting your other needs. That will not lead to sustained, high-quality golden years.

Why am I making this argument at this point of the guide? Reread the first step. Too many people stop prescriptions before they complete the full bottle of pills. Too many people skip doses and then bemoan to their physician, "How come I am not getting any better? You promised these pills would work!" As a physician, I have asked patients the crucial question: "How many pills have you taken? Hmmm. And how many pills have you skipped?" With this prescription, your challenge is harder. There are habits to learn, not pills to swallow. Despite the broad spectrum of material, I don't believe that this survivor kit is difficult to incorporate. It won't take much time for you to read these chapters. It will just require a commitment. You cannot sit back and passively digest the prescription within this guide. You have to be active, transferring knowledge into action. Sorry, but I would not want it any other way. I want you to be your partner, not just your doctor. I want you, not me, to take the lead in redesigning yourself and your golden years. You are the one who has to step into the darkness. But by participating actively, you will feel worthy of your improved life. Without this sense of worth, you would not be able to enjoy it as much. If you incorporate these new habits and improve your life, you will have earned it.

In the early 1500s, Michelangelo, the famed Italian artist, received a commission to create a new sculpture. That sculpture became "David," one of the masterpieces of the Renaissance. Apparently, it took Michelangelo several years to find the block of stone, several years to carve the block of stone, and several years to sand and polish the block of stone. When asked how he could create such a statue, Michelangelo explained that he envisioned David and then removed, from the block of stone, everything that was not David. This guide is similar. Every person is a potential masterpiece. But remember that we are all an assembly of habits. With this new guide, you must identify those habits that need to be removed, chipping them from your block of stone. Replace the old habits with new, better habits. Remind yourself that you are not trying to sculpt an arm or a leg; instead, you are trying to create a new sculpture of yourself and your life. So, do not focus on just one area, no matter how valuable that one area. Spirituality is an area of the great value. Just do not forget the other many components of this guide. You will need many of them for your golden years.

STEP 8

Lifting and Maintaining Your Mood

"Guard your good mood."
Meryl Streep

Chapter 76

Challenge of Emotional Health

*"One has the sense that a catastrophe has occurred
in the psychic landscape."*
Leonard Cohen

If you were born in the 1960s, your risk for a depressive episode
in your life is greater than if you were born in the 1950s. If you
were born in the 1980s, your risk for a depressive episode in your
life is greater than if you were born in the 1970s. That trend of an

increasing prevalence of a severe depression has continued with each decade right to the present. In fact, the chance of developing a depressive episode has increased tenfold since World War II. The World Health Organization is predicting that depression will afflict more people than any other illness by 2030. Our risk for a severe depression is as high as any country of the world. Studies estimate that half of Americans will suffer from a mental illness during their life. That is not good news for you and your golden years. It creates another challenge for you, a challenge to maintain and improve your emotional health.

There are numerous epidemiological studies on all the psychiatric symptoms, but depression is fairly reflective of the overall pattern. The risk for your depression to go undiagnosed and untreated is worse as you grow older, and severe depression is not a normal part of aging. You will experience more challenges and face more losses, but a severe depression does not have to be part of your emotional landscape. But why are there so many depressions that go undiagnosed in the older population? Studies show that the average visit with a physician lasts seven minutes in our country. Is that enough time for a physician to assess your emotional health? The suicide rates in our older population suggest otherwise. The suicide rate for baby boomers has increased 28 percent in the past decade. Studies show that a significant number of suicides in the older population occur within one month of a person's last visit to a physician's office. That means that the physician and our health care system have once again failed those patients.

Your predicament is double edged. We have already addressed the challenge for good physical health. Well, your emotional health will have a significant impact on your physical health. Studies of depression in the older population demonstrate that it often precedes (or follows) a severe medical illness. A depression in your golden years will increase your chances of developing a serious medical illness. And if you are diagnosed with a heart condition or a cancer or diabetes or a stroke, your chances of sliding into a severe depression increase by 25-50 percent. The mind-body connection? The emotional-physical connection is just as powerful. For your golden years, you must maintain good emotional health. Ideally, it would be wonderful if you could experience a drug-free older age without any need for psychiatric medication. Try to take the same approach to your emotional health that you are hopefully taking with your physical health.

Without stable emotional health, you will struggle to maintain sufficient daily energy to redesign your golden years and you will fail to truly live, love, and make a difference. So, from a physician's perspective, a renewed focus on your emotional health should be your next area for improved habits. As with the other areas in your life, these new habits will not be radical, but they will be crucial.

Chapter 77

Barriers to Emotional Health

*"The more modern a society's way of life,
the higher its rate of depression."*
Stephen Hardi

In an earlier chapter, I encouraged you to question our national

health care system. I encouraged you to question our medical

research programs because of their biased, self-serving fund-

ing sources. I encouraged you to question the bulk of medical information and medical advertisements. I encouraged you to be skeptical of insurance companies and your ability to access adequate physical health care. Well, my assessment of our psychiatric care is not much better. In the United States, in the last decade, the number of Americans taking an antidepressant drug has more than doubled. Today, in the United States, one in ten people are prescribed an antidepressant drug. The statistics go higher if you include all psychotropic medications and sleeping medications. We are the most medicated society in the world. Yet, we are also the most depressed. To me, that means that the solution is not another pill or another doctor visit.

For the mentally ill, one hundred years ago we were drilling holes in the skull to relieve pressure. One hundred years from now, will our current psychiatric medications look like much of an improvement? With the rapid pace of scientific discoveries, I have my doubts. The antidepressants of several decades ago, which can still be prescribed, cost pennies per pill. The newer antidepressants cost dollars per pill. Are they more effective than the older psychiatric medications? I remain unconvinced of any higher efficacy. Too many of the new psychiatric medications cause medical problems that already afflict so many Americans, from weight gain to the development of diabetes. If our psychiatric medications are so effective, why are the rates of depression still rising? Why are there black box warnings of increased suicide risk when you take antidepressant medication? The advertising of antidepressant medications has quadrupled in this past decade. That should tell you the pharmacology companies are making a fortune. But once again, their focus seems to be on their profits, not your health. So, you need to be skeptical of pharmaceutical companies and what they proclaim for the efficacy of their new, more expensive psychiatric medications. Not all advertisements are providing you with the best psychiatric advice.

There is another significant problem: psychiatric medication side effects. In an earlier chapter, I highlighted how the third leading cause of death was physician error. Those mortality statistics include adverse reactions to psychiatric medications. Today's new psychiatric medications cause many of the physical conditions that we don't want. For starters, they increase the risk of weight gain, cardiovascular disease, and diabetes. Just what you don't need when you are already depressed. Can you guess what you also do not need? Sexual dysfunction. Would you like to prevent it? Two steps. First, switch your diet away from animal-based foods. Do you remember how Diesel fuel clogs your blood vessels, which are five millimeters in diameter? The blood vessels to your private parts are only one millimeter in diameter. Those popular little blue pills? For meat and dairy eaters, guess which of your arteries clog first? And those circulation problems impact women, not just men. Second, avoid those psychiatric pills that are known to disrupt sexual function and your ability to enjoy intimacy. Again, it's another area where you have the capacity to take control of your life simply through expanded knowledge. With fewer psychiatric medications and a plant-based eating style, you can return to the land of the living.

Once again, with so many of these issues buried, you cannot always count on a successful rescue from the psychiatric health care system. So, know your risk factors and adjust your life accordingly. The risk for a severe depression is worse if you live in an industrial country than in a nonindustrial country. The risk for a severe depression is worse if you live in the city rather than in the country. The risks with our current lifestyle are undeniable. We were not designed for our postindustrial life. Let me clarify the trend. For 10,000 years, we were acclimated to an agricultural, rural lifestyle. In the early 1800s, 95 percent of our population lived on farms. In the early 1900s, 45 percent of our population lived on farms. In the early 2000s, only 2 percent of our population lives on farms. Worse, most of our population (over 80 percent) now lives in urban cities. That translates to a dramatic lifestyle change over the past century for the average American. According to recent census bureau statistics, we are congregating more, not less, in confined areas, so our lifestyle is progressively more urban. America does not contain the city with the world's highest population density. That honor goes to the Mong Kok district in Hong Kong with 340,000 people per square mile. But many of our major cities are not that far behind, growing denser and denser by the year.

From a physician's evolutionary perspective, we were not designed for such a cemented lifestyle. Instead of manual labor (remember my comments on the advantage of walking barefoot?), we sit in chairs at work and at home with our TVs, computers, and other technological devices. We were not designed to eat industrial agriculture animal-based food with all of its contaminants. We were not designed for the constant overload of information that overwhelms us on a 24/7 schedule. We were not designed for such social congestion, coupled to social isolation. Yes, we have constant contact with others through social media with cell phones, emails, texts, tweets, Facebook, and other technological tools, but do we have more face-to-face contact? Not really. And which type of contact offers you (and your physiology) a healthier boost? A few typed characters on the phone? Or holding hands with someone you love? We were also not designed for such limited spirituality. It's not just a reduction in church attendance (or any religious attendance); it's a reduction in time with nature, a reduction in time with God. Appreciate all of these negative lifestyle influences on your emotional health, so you can understand the challenge to combat these negative factors that corrupt your life. It is your responsibility to overcome these barriers and it is your challenge to incorporate the necessary habits for better emotional health.

Chapter 78

So, Who's Really at Risk?

"Mental illness is so much more complicated than any pill."
Elizabeth Wurtzel

There are some people who will be more at risk for a psychiatric illness. If you have experienced a traumatic event or a series of negative experiences earlier in your life, you will be more susceptible to a psychiatric illness during your later life. Any trauma or negative experience changes the wiring of your brain. You become more sensitive to negative situations, even showing increased reactivity to negative news. You probably know the type of person. Is there something horrific in today's news? That person feels much worse than others. But there is good news for this group of people. As they grow older, they may discover what part of themselves needs to be healed. There are ways to promote that healing and reduce your risk of a mental illness. As previously discussed, with the neuroplasticity of the brain, there are ways to rewire your brain. You will still face the increasing national risk of a psychiatric illness, but you can reduce your own heightened risk for a mental health setback. That part is within your control.

So, how do you change the wiring of your brain and reduce your current high risk for a psychiatric illness? By embracing the good in your life. Positive experiences can negate negative experiences. Positive experiences rewire your brain. Hopefully, with the habits in this guide, there will be more and more positive experiences. Hopefully, there will be fewer negative thoughts and fewer negative experiences. What can you do? Open your eyes. Stumble upon a positive experience or look for a positive experience or create a positive experience. But when you encounter those positive experiences, do not rush through the experience. Let the positive feeling seep into your heart. Savor the positive emotions. Then you need to couple one of those positive moments with one of your negative memories. What? Are you serious? I know it sounds ridiculous, but it works. Here's how. You take a minute to absorb the positive emotions, but you let part of your attention wander back to some distant trauma or negative experience that still plays with your mind/mood. Make certain that the negative experience remains in the background. Make certain that it does not hijack your positive emotions. By pairing them together, the positive with the negative, that resets the wiring in the brain, decreasing the prominence of old neuron pathways. In a way, it's like scratching an old bad-memory CD. Scratch it enough and it will not play. You want to do the same with your bad memories, getting them to a point where they do not carry impact. Their sound is muffled.

For me, I have done that with my golf. For quite awhile after killing that man on the golf course, I was bothered with the image of my drive, the ball landing close to his feet, and his body dropping to the grass. In my younger days, I would tell the story during a golf match, trying to unnerve my opponent. In truth, I probably unnerved myself more than the other golfer. However, when I learned about the above technique, I started to apply it. Whenever I hit a booming drive with the ball traveling further than expected, I would pause to enjoy the ball's flight for several seconds and then, as the ball was landing in the fairway, I would think back to that drive in the eighth grade. I would make an effort to connect my current positive feeling to that old negative image. And you know what? It worked. Over time, my uncomfortable feelings with that ancient image eased. I was actually able to joke about it. Yes, I was the only one in my family who had never scored a hole in one, but how many people had played a 4-iron, just feet from a dead man, for a birdie? I am still sorry that I had not sliced that drive into the rough. But the discomfort has finally disappeared. Now I have self-acceptance and forgiveness.

The message, for this chapter, is that there are antidotes to your past trauma and negative experiences. You can remove some of your pain. You can fill the hole in your heart. You can move from anger to love, from hatred to peace, from greed to happiness, from heartache to forgiveness. How? Start by practicing more gratitude. Don't take life for granted; and don't take yourself for granted. Psychologists have written books on the success of this approach and the resulting transformation. At this point, just realize that it is doable. You can repair yourself by accepting yourself. With better acceptance, you reduce your risk for emotional discomfort. Self-acceptance and self-appreciation may help you steer clear of our health care system. For you, and for anyone with prior trauma, your self-acceptance will level the playing field. So, before we explore the other habits for emotional health, develop the habit of embracing the good within yourself and letting it soak into your heart, and (just as importantly) letting it soak into your brain, rewiring those old negative pathways.

Chapter 79

Be Aware of Our Additional Risks

"Poisons and medicine are oftentimes the same substance."
Peter Latham

If you were to peek into a hospital's psychiatric unit, do you think you would have any difficulty finding a psychiatric patient? Surprisingly, the answer is yes. There are very few pure psychiatric patients. The majority of psychiatric patients (70-90 percent) also have comorbid substance abuse problems. After all, we are the world's greatest importer of cocaine and amphetamine. I read that Americans spend more money on alcohol than our government spends on national defense. Do you want to drive your car late on a Friday or Saturday night? Well, you can expect one in ten drivers to be, legally speaking, driving under the influence. We are not just the most medicated nation; we are the most self-medicated nation. That presents more than a simple driving risk as you enter your older years. If you have abused any substances (alcohol or drugs), acknowledge the long-term consequences. If you are still abusing alcohol or some drug, promptly abstain from that unhealthy habit.

After years of tracking psychiatric patients in emergency rooms and hospitals, I have my own personal belief, although I do not know of any specific studies to support my view that alcohol and substance abuse reduce the effectiveness of most psychiatric medications. I also hold the conviction that the more you stop and start any specific psychiatric medication, the less effective it becomes. So, as you enter your golden years, there is a progressive consequence of decreased efficacy for many of the psychiatric medications if you have previously used them. Unless you have been emotionally healthy for all of your younger years, psychiatric medications are probably going to be less effective as you grow older; and all the psychiatric medication studies are typically done with young adults, in an attempt to make the drugs appear as effective as possible. You wouldn't expect a pharmaceutical company to do less, would you? So, your predicament in your older years? Psychiatric drugs may be of decreasing effectiveness.

That assessment, of course, is my own personal bias. But I have other biases that are even stronger. I think our psychiatric medications are misdirected. Our psychiatric medications impact small changes in the flow of certain neurochemicals in the brain with the hope that these changes will result in changes in your mood. But the neurochemicals are not produced in the brain. Serotonin, one of the chemicals that help regulate mood, is mostly produced in the small intestines. Do any of our psychiatric medications work to improve the small intestine's ecosystem and its natural production of serotonin? No. Do psychiatrists advise their patients on the importance of their eating style and the necessity of the healthy bacteria in the small intestines for the increased production of serotonin? No. Instead, they simply prescribe a pill. And our psychiatric community wonders why we have such a high rate of recidivism. We are focusing on the wrong area of the body without looking at the whole person. I dare you to walk through a psychiatric unit at lunchtime. The food, which the psychiatric patients are consuming, is killing the good bacteria that help produce the neurochemicals that naturally lift mood. In a sense, we are trying to step on the gas while simultaneously slamming on the brakes. No wonder why so many of the patients remain stalled with limited recovery.

We have too many specialists in this country. We have too few physicians who are able to take a broader, more complete view. We have a national debate on whether to expand our health care system to a more universal system. Well, here is the truth. Even if you expand the health care system, if that system is flawed (and remember our current system ranks thirty-seventh in the world), the expanded system may be larger and more encompassing, but it will still deliver poor results. As you enter your golden years, try to depend less, not more, on our health care system. Try to depend less, not more, on psychiatric medications. Be aware of our shortcomings in all of these areas. Hopefully, we will start to make fundamental changes in our health care delivery with emphasis on the whole person and a primary focus on prevention.

Until those changes occur, don't shirk your responsibility of taking care of your own emotional health. There are ways you can improve your daily emotional mood. Think about what you have read in this guide. This is not a quiz, but you should be able to list numerous habits, from this guide, that could effectively lift your daily mood without any psychiatric medications. Make those habits part of your daily life.

Chapter 80

Your Critical Need for Sleep

"When I am sleeping I do a lot of living."
David Johansen

Sleep is one of those areas where you can, and should, take more self-control. When you take a detailed history from a psychiatric patient, what is one of the first, most commonly overlooked markers for the patient's emotional deterioration? It is a change in their natural sleep routine. That often precedes the other symptoms. So, as you enter your older years, redesign your sleep. In some Chinese cultures, the experts recommend going to sleep between 9 p.m. and 9:30 p.m. They preach the viewpoint that an hour of sleep before midnight is equal to two hours of sleep after midnight. That seems more myth than fact. However, as discussed in the chapter on your second rudder, your best physiological repair occurs early in the sleep cycle. That is the time when you achieve the most cell regeneration, the highest hormone production, and the healthiest brain wave activity. Do you want to take advantage of your circadian rhythm and maintain your emotional health? Get to sleep early, not late.

Let me repeat my earlier refrain. As a physician, I was taught that the best time to fall to sleep was between 10 p.m. and 10:30 p.m. If you fall asleep in this time period, your circadian rhythm will kick into gear as you slip into sleep, further activating good physiological repair for the neurochemicals that are important for maintaining your emotional health. Of course, there are people who claim they are night owls. I am not convinced. They are often people who have just fallen into the fast rhythm of today's society. Were there night owls when people had only a candle and its single (one) watt of light? No. But today, with all of the high watt appliances and the excessive light (imagine a room with hundreds of candles), it is easy to stay awake and easier still to convince yourself that you are simply one of the people who were born to be a night owl. Well, here's a warning. You may be squeezing more hours into the day, but I think you run a higher risk that your neurochemicals will not remain well balanced. I think you run a higher risk of subsequent mild depressions.

Do you recall the earlier discussion about the hundreds of genes that are turned on, and turned off, by the quality of your sleep? How, with a good night's sleep, several hundred genes show a heightened level of activity, repairing protein, counter-ing inflammation, and increasing your immune system. Or how, with a poor night's sleep, several hundred (different) genes are activated, leading to increased damage to your cells? Again, there have been more studies on physical health than emotional health. However, it is my belief that the quality of your sleep also impacts those genes that regulate your emotional health. With a good night's sleep, there may be genes that help regulate your emotional stability. With a poor night's sleep, there may be genes that are triggered to create a physiology with an increased risk for mental instability. That is my bias. So, acknowledge your own capacity, simply through sleep (and an appropriate diet), of protecting your own emotional stability. Don't underestimate what you can do to help control your own mood.

Be aware of the other emotional consequences of the quality of your sleep. People who go to sleep late are not as emotionally stable as those people who go to sleep early. People who work variable night shifts are not as emotionally healthy as those people who go to sleep at the same hour each night. In reviewing psychiatric charts, do you have any idea how many patients have been security guards? Or how many patients worked odd (or late) hours? So, to protect your emotional health, how much sleep should you get? Most studies show that people should sleep between six to eight hours for the best the best emotional health. For those people who sleep less than five to six hours, there is an increased risk of psychiatric illness. Many episodes of bipolar disorder and major depression are triggered by interruptions in the sleep cycle. Even if you have no psychiatric illness, how many of us become anxious, depressed, or a little irritable with limited sleep? It is human nature. So, if you want to maintain good emotional health, watch your sleep on a nightly basis.

You may be asking: If too little sleep is unhealthy, could the same be true for excessive sleep? Well, sleep is not like a bank account. You cannot deposit extra sleep on the weekend and expect it to balance the lack of sleep during the week. But there are people who go through periods where they sleep more than eight hours per night. For many of those people, the need for the additional sleep is an indication of an underlying and probably undetected level of inflammation throughout the body. Either medically or psychiatrically, their body is trying to heal. My recommendation? If your body is asking for additional sleep, listen to it. An afternoon nap, ala Spain's daily siesta, is not a bad idea for more physiological repair, as long as the nap is ninety minutes (one sleep cycle). And do not worry if you are one of those people who consistently need more sleep. Albert Einstein was renowned for sleeping ten hours a night, and his brain and his mood were just fine. A hundred years ago? Most people slept closer to nine hours a night. Again, listen to your body. Be kind to your body. Give it sufficient sleep. For your emotional (and physical) health, that is a habit that you cannot neglect.

Chapter 81

Try an Emotional Litmus Test

"Chart your own course and live life on your own terms."
Michelle Obama

How is your daily mood? Do you accept responsibility for your mood? Or do you blame others? You have probably heard of this analogy. If you cut open an orange with a knife, if you pound the orange with a hammer, if you run over that orange with a truck, what comes out? Orange juice. What matters are not the various stimuli: the knife, the hammer, and the vehicle. What matters is the quality of the orange juice. The analogy applies to your emotions. What matters is not what happens around you. What matters is the quality of your own emotional response. What's inside of you matters, not what's on the outside. Throughout life we run into people who are knives or hammers or trucks. Learn how to navigate around those people. Take control over your mood and lift your daily emotions. You cannot go through your older years in a sour mood, agitated by setbacks. Sorry, but your sour mood will kill you. The destructive physiology of a depressed mood will lead to a physical illness sooner or later.

For some people, lifting your daily mood is not that easy. You will need to do more than randomly catch yourself in a down mood. You will need to upgrade your mood on a daily basis. The habits, discussed in this book, will be a good starting point. Have you been using them? That is the real litmus test. The right eating style and an exercise program will improve your emotional health, reducing triggers for a negative mood. A positive internal and external dialogue will improve your mood. A personal mission with goals will improve your attitude with a sense of a worthwhile purpose. The process of personal development, knowing that you are becoming a better person, creates its own level of anticipation and joy. The daily structure, with the morning and evening rudders, combined with effective time management, will increase the likelihood that your activities will further improve your mood. A spiritual component will improve your mood by decreasing your sense of social isolation and improving your feelings of connection with others. So, in my opinion, all of these habits will start you in the right direction. But again, ask yourself: Have you started utilizing these habits? That is a necessity, especially since you will need to depend on yourself, not on the disease care system, for maintenance of your mood.

Many people, when feeling depressed, will place the responsibility of their getting better on their doctor or their therapist or their counselor. We have already discussed the limitations of psychiatric medications. What about therapy? Yes, it works. Yes, it can help. But it too has limitations. In many types of counseling, the therapist is going to direct you to focus on your past problems. The therapist is going to have you discuss your feelings of low self-esteem or insecurity or sense of isolation. The therapist will want to break down your defenses so you can get in touch with your negative emotions. Once you have reached that emotional level, the therapist will try to help you gain insight into your prior pathology so you can begin the process of rebuilding some better behaviors. But many therapists miss the larger picture of your full life story. If you do not complete that life story, your history may remain a mystery with a persistent, inaccurate interpretation of your most important life events. My suggestion? Before you commit to therapy, try a life review (on your own) and ascertain what you can learn through your own inner work. See how much you can repair yourself without having to pay someone for the same service.

Some therapists, especially those involved in counseling for substance abuse issues, will direct you to place your trust in God, accepting your own powerlessness. Personally, I have never believed the best solution is feeling less empowered. I believe the best solution is feeling more empowered, which comes with reengagement in life with the right habits. After reading this guide, you probably do not have any difficulty guessing my bias. I believe in encouraging people to rely on their own self-interventions, not someone else's treatment. That does not mean I support isolation. For substance abuse patients, a sponsor is often crucial. Attending AA meetings is often crucial. But you need friends who provide support. A friend or a therapist? I would first choose a friend. A family member or a therapist? I would first choose the family member. So, for your emotional litmus test, ask yourself: Are you engaged in life? Are you engaged with others? Do you have a close personal friend whom you can trust? A family member who supports you? If the answers to these questions are repeatedly yes, then your task is to ask that person (or people) to help you with these habits. And, if you are lucky, maybe your friends will follow your lead and try to develop the same habits. Now, if you do not have those types of people in your life, that's when I would search for a therapist to help guide you on the path toward improved emotional health.

Chapter 82

The Miracle of Your Body

"What the world needs is healing and regeneration."
Joel S. Goldsmith

For the Federal Drug Administration to approve a pharmaceutical drug, the new drug has to be compared with a placebo, an inert compound with no intrinsic biological properties. Yet, placebos are 30 percent effective with no side effects. What happens when a doctor gives you a placebo? The doctor tells you that you are being prescribed a painkiller and gives you an inert compound. With the doctor's directive, your body produces an opiate that is stronger than any heroin. If the doctor gives you a placebo for ulcers, your body produces an H2 receptor blocker that interferes with the secretion of the hydrochloric acid. In both situations your body produces a curative molecule that is far superior to anything that the pharmaceutical companies can produce. So, yes, there are alternatives to prescribed psychiatric medications. Ideally, you want your own body to produce these drugs, not the pharmaceutical company.

Do you remember what Norman Cousins, the famous political journalist, did when he fell seriously ill? When he was ill in the hospital, he set up a living arrangement allowing him to watch comedies all day. It was disruptive to the other patients, so the facility moved him to a hotel where he had daily nursing care, plus his endless supply of comedy films. For Norman Cousins, laughter was the best medicine. He knew his laughter would change his neurochemistry and improve his immune system. His own approach saved his life. Norman Cousins' recovery was not an exception. There are numerous examples of people healing themselves through behaviors that change their internal chemistry. There are numerous examples of other nonmedical, nontraditional interventions leading to recovery. Spiritual heal-ers are often successful. Studies even show that prayer can be beneficial. What is the underlying message within all of these atypical interventions? An appreciation of your body and a belief that your body has the power to heal itself, especially when it receives appropriate support.

At this point, I want to highlight the multitude of new treat-ments for depression, treatments that are not based on psychiat-ric medications. As explained, science is always progressing with new solutions. There are new antidepressant interventions with vagal nerve stimulation, transmagnetic stimulation therapy, and low energy neurofeedback (where electromagnetic fields stimu-late brain activity and restore brain flexibility). There is the use of hyperbaric oxygen chambers. I do not want to belabor all of these options. But it is useful to step back and appreciate the possibilities. It is also important to realize how little we know of our brain function. I have already mentioned that the brain has 1.1 trillion brain cells, one hundred billion neurons, and 5,000 possible connections for each neuron. The complexity of interactions, with many occurring instantaneously, are beyond our imagination, just as the extent of our universe is beyond our imagination. Our current psychiatric medications focus on four to six neurotransmitters. Well, there are probably 20-30 neurotransmitters involved in the regulation of your mood, plus hundreds of specific genes. My point? Trust your body. Trust in the miracle of your body. Try to develop a new, higher regard for how your body can heal without additional psychiatric medications. Try to nurture the faith that your body can, as it often does with placebo medication, create the necessary neurochemical changes to improve your emotional health. Yes, have faith in yourself.

At the same time, try to maintain the belief that your brain can change its wiring. There is one type of intervention called tapping. It's incredibly simple. To reduce your physiological stress, you run through a series of tapping sequences (your finger tapping on your skin five to seven times), progressing from spots on the side of your hand to between your eyebrows to other spots under your eyes, under your nose, under your mouth, on your collarbone, under your arm, and the top of your head, while repeating phrases to acknowledge your stress, release your stress, and accept yourself. It may sound a bit superficial, but these taps likely interrupt the current state of your nervous system; these taps likely redirect your own focus of your nervous system; and these taps likely change the feeling of your body, hopefully reducing stress, eliminating pain, etc. I cannot vouch for this intervention's success. My own message is more nonspecific, but important. Your body has the inner tools to heal itself. You just need to utilize them. Don't underestimate your potential for self-healing. Don't overestimate the effectiveness of an outside drug or compound. It's your orange juice. Own it. Make it. Just the way you like it, without any outside interference.

Chapter 83

Don't Muffle the Power of Sound

*"There's no such thing as a wrong note
as long as you're singing."*
Pete Seeger

There is no known culture, now or in mankind's history, which lacked some type of music. Some of the world's oldest artifacts are musical instruments. Music was not properly notated until the last 200 years; and music was not recorded until the last 100 years. Today we are in a unique historical period. The average American listens to music around five hours a day. You cannot escape it. The grocery store. The car. The elevator. With the Internet, we have access to more music than any generation. In fact, almost every recorded song in history is available for free. From my perspective, music is part of our culture and part of our identity. It offers another pathway for emotional well-being. Indian sages chant mantras for healing. Tibetan monks ring singing bowls. Many African communities drum for healing. The most powerful tool in a sound healer's repertoire? It is the human voice, which has its own power to heal.

Sound is more than auditory; it is somatic. Place a pitcher of water next to a boom box and watch the water vibrate. Since our bodies are 70 percent water, we also vibrate to the sounds of our environment. For those individuals who are living in a loud, chaotic urban setting, those frequencies can cause agitation. For those people who manage a trip to nature, the sounds of a chirping bird or a wandering creek can elicit relaxation. The same comparison applies to internal sounds, our own positive or negative thoughts. The bottom line is unchanged. Sound has a tremendous but often under-appreciated impact on our bodies and our emotional health. Its role as an alternative medicine is expanding. Sound healing practices are being employed with stress management, addiction recovery, injury rehabilitation, and other medical conditions. But, by now, you know me. I am not recommending you dive into music therapy. Instead, I am encouraging you to consider how to incorporate music into your own healing process.

There have been an extensive number of studies on the architecture of sound and the natural frequencies within the human body. Some researchers have proclaimed that certain diseases have their own particular resonance and they can be cured with specific frequencies of sound. Other researchers have explored cell sonics with the belief that cells vibrate and sing with different frequencies depending on their level of health or disease. The Chinese have long held the conviction that certain sounds activate specific organs. From their perspective, if you want to improve the health of a certain organ, you need to create the appropriate sounds, and those sounds can be vocalized by you. Your own sounds vibrate through your body, sometimes calming a distressed cell, sometimes repairing a certain organ, and sometimes, if the sound is toxic, releasing chemicals that cause further damage. Some of these researchers claim that sound will be the medicine of the future, noninvasive and healing.

What is my point? You probably already know what sounds work for you. What upbeat energetic sounds help you when you are depressed or sluggish? What classical or down tempo sounds help you when you are stressed and anxious? If you are going to be exposed to music five hours each day, you might as well take control of some of the sound waves that permeate each of your cells. Once again, it is similar to your effort to delete negative thoughts and negative dialogue and your effort to increase positive thoughts and enriching conversations. Try to decrease the 'white noise' in your life. Try to increase the sounds that bring you pleasure and relaxation. Let the emotionally uplifting type of music sift through your home. Try to sing along with the music that resonates the most with your soul. Who cares if you hit the right note? The vibration of the song will still ring through each cell of your body, changing the vibration within your body. Give it a chance. You might be surprised by the healing power of your voice.

If singing is not part of your repertoire, explore other music options. Hang wind chimes if that soothes your soul. Build a fountain if you like the sound of running water. Do whatever works for you. Because the correct sounds in your environment may likely reduce your stress, improve your mood, boost your immune system, and increase your sense of well-being. As always, this change only requires initial awareness and then the development of a new habit. As for me, I wrote every single page of this book to a background of music. I was like one of those automated, glass cage figures that move only when you deposit the correct number of coins. When the music stopped, I stopped. Now some of you may have wished for a power outage, but there was none. When one CD was finished, I just slipped in the next group of songs. Most of the CDs were sound tracks from favorite movies. Other CDs came from my favorite, easy listening artists like Enya or my own daughter Austen. Or other piano collections. Sorry, but no hip-hop, at least not while writing. But, for me, music is a powerful force. It lifts my spirits at times of frustration. It helps me through difficult, personal passages. It even helped me at times of indecision with the writing of this guide: "You're thinking of sharing that story? Just to make a point? Come on, the story is going to make you look ridiculous. Oh well, no one's ever going to read it but a few close friends!" So, I encourage you to embrace the role of music in helping to maintain your mood and guide you through life. Even with my mother, when I used to visit on Saturdays, that was one thing that she was always doing right. There was always music, from the earlier eras of her life, playing in the family room, lifting her spirits. See, even in her nineties, she was still insightful.

Chapter 84

There's a Time for Grieving

*"Grieving is a journey that teaches us
how to love in a new way."*
Tom Attig

There is the saying that there are only two certain things in life: death and taxes. For those of us who reach the older years, you can add a third truth. There will be a time for grieving. If you live long enough, you will lose a loved one: a parent, a spouse, a sibling, a friend, or even worse, a child. With these losses, there is an overwhelming array of feelings with shock, sadness, anger, remorse and (sometimes) guilt. But the flood of emotions is only part of your challenge. With any bereavement, there is an increased risk for mortality and morbidity. In the six months after the death of a loved one, you have an increased risk of dying. You have an increased risk for hypertension, cardiac problems, diabetes, and cancer. Through the grieving process, you face higher rates of physical illness, physician visits, medication use, and hospitalization. You also face a higher risk for psychiatric illness and suicide. So, when you hit any period of loss, you need to be aware of the grieving process and how to get through it.

There are many books written about the process of bereavement. Some experts list the five stages of denial, anger, bargaining, depression, and acceptance, similar to the stages of dying. In my own experience, each person grieves differently and each person grieves for different lengths of time. You should be aware that the depth and length of your grieving is not a reflection of the quality of your relationship with the person who has died. In some situations, the cleaner the relationship, the shorter the length of grieving; and the more conflicted the relationship, the longer the grieving. A person, who has experienced a wonderful marriage and then lost that spouse, may actually grieve for a shorter time than a person who has experienced a more turbulent marriage. Relationships are labyrinths. Once inside, the path to emotional independence may not be so clear. Even when you have worked your way through your grief, returning to some form of normal life, don't expect the loss to ever disappear.

So, what should you know? People tend to work harder to avoid a loss than recover from a loss. Appreciate the grieving process that you will need to complete. You are going to have to face more than a flood of emotions. You are going to have to deal with a host of associated complications, starting with reduced functioning, social withdrawal, and a resistance to rejoin the outside world. You are going to face a roller coaster, where intense feelings can erupt at any time. Anniversaries, holidays, and milestones are typical triggers, but anything, a certain smell, a familiar meal, just the sight of another couple, can be an unexpected trigger. I am not recommending that you delete your thoughts or your feelings during this process. The grieving process is a time when you must allow yourself to feel the pain, when you must force yourself to express your feelings. To overcome your loss, you must face the loss, release the loss, and, at some point, try to replace the loss. And replace does not mean forget.

How do you replace a devastating loss? The best antidote for grief is love. If you are going to reflect on your past with the loved one, focus on the positive moments, not the negative moments. For the present, focus on the ways that you can pay a positive tribute to that person by expressing more love toward those people who he or she loved. For the future, direct your activities toward building on that love, offering emotional support for others. If you can move toward rekindling your ability to love, you can move toward happiness and peace of mind. You can also move toward personal growth. A time of grieving can be extremely challenging (for many people, it can be the worst period of their lives), but it also can be a time of positive change. Remember: what's the best way to feel that you are loved? To be loving. Love the memory of the person who has died. Love the people who remain in your life. Love life itself, because it's what gets you through each day. Love, as they say, is a type of gratitude. Be grateful for the gift of life. Be grateful for what you have already enjoyed. Be grateful for even this very moment. There are billions of dead people, lying in their coffins, who would trade spots with you in a heartbeat. Love and gratitude: they are what open the next door. They lead you to a better life for yourself and others. So, don't wait for life to be good to you. Instead, be good to life (and to the people in your life).

Chapter 85

A Better Path to Emotional Health

"There are no regrets in life, just lessons."
Jennifer Anniston

What is the best sign of good mental health? It is not a smile. Or

the ability to laugh. It is your ability to live in the present, not the

past. It is your ability to let go of past mistakes and past regrets. It

is the ability to look at them as lessons, not regrets. At this point

in your life, especially as you become older with a longer history of mistakes and regrets, you need to forgive yourself for any prior mistakes. Research shows that 75 percent of all decisions are wrong. The key is not to make the right decision; the key is to make the decision right, to eventually make any decision work in your favor. Despite all of our best efforts, many decisions turn into mistakes. Who among us does not have regrets for those mistakes? To consolidate the habits for improved emotional health, you want a fresh emotional start, unchained from the past, actively living in the present, and ready to embrace your new future.

Try to switch from a focus on doing to an appreciation for being. With this shift, do more than forgive yourself for your mistakes. Try to forgive others. For much of your life, you have been fighting to be right. You have seen that battle at the office. One person thinks he or she is right; another person thinks he or she is right; and the argument lasts for hours, days, even weeks. At this age, focus on how to be fair, not right. And that applies to how you treat yourself and others. Life may not be fair, but you can be fair. How do you make this transition? By pushing yourself toward more understanding and less judgment. Negativity, especially when aligned with a pattern of constantly judging others, undercuts any emotional foundation. At this time in your life, when you need that high emotional level and the health benefits that it offers, just stop judging yourself and others. Accept yourself as who you are, which should be easier when you have become your authentic self, and when you are not just meeting someone else's expectations. At the same time, accept others for who they are, with their imperfections. If you can make that shift toward more acceptance and gratitude, your mood will lift. Your internal physiology will self-correct toward a healthier climate. Your health, emotional and physical, will improve.

Acceptance has its own transformational magic. With increased acceptance toward yourself and others, you will gain more understanding (first, strive to understand, then strive to be understood), more patience, more empathy, more open-mindedness, and more balance. You will find yourself moving away from prejudice and hate. You will find yourself moving toward joy and love. This crucial transition can lead to an improved attitude and an improved mood. Together, these traits can create a greater peace of mind. With a greater peace of mind, there is a higher level of focus on those things that matter the most. For your golden years, you will need to maintain a peace of mind. You will need to maintain a steady balance. The key is not repeated interventions to improve your mood through some psychiatric treatment; the key is your daily effort, maintaining your emotional level, preventing any depression. Again, all of these actions, especially when they become daily habits, are crucial to your emotional health and your ability to handle life's challenges.

What's the best antidepressant? It's not psychiatric medication. It's not therapy. It's not some new treatment intervention. It's kindness to yourself. Kindness to others. Those are the experiences that will lift your mood and change your health. Why have I left emotional health toward the end? Because I know the challenges you will have to face. I know the grieving you will have to endure. Growing older is not easy for anyone. Never was, never will be. So, to survive and prosper in your later years, you will need a sustained mood and a positive attitude. The higher your mood, the better your life. The best part of this equation? No one is in charge of your happiness but you. Your mood, like your internal dialogue and external dialogue, is controllable. Unfortunately, you may have become so busy and so distracted, that you have forgotten your own level of control. Now is the time to take the material from this chapter and the other habits and utilize that control for a better mood and a better life for yourself and for others.

STEP 9

Redefining Your Legacy

"As you go through life, no matter what you do, or how you do it, you leave a little footprint and that is your legacy."

Jan Brewer

Chapter 86

What Is Your Legacy?

"Children are our legacy. Our responsibility.
They are our destiny and we are theirs."
Dick Benedict

There is a psychiatric term, dysthymia, which refers to a chronic depression. For some people in their older years, there is scattered activity without the habits in this guide and a subsequent sense of emptiness. For some people, it reaches a chronic level of emptiness that progresses into a baseline depression; and for many people, they cannot identity the reason for this sense of emptiness. If you see a psychiatrist with this complaint, you will likely receive an antidepressant medication. If you see a therapist for this complaint, get ready for months of weekly counseling sessions. Unfortunately, both of those treatment interventions will likely miss their mark. In my experience, many of these people have failed to start the most important work of their lives, work that is far more important than their earlier professional career. They have neglected to give much thought to a simple question: How best do they want to be remembered? And what can they do, before it is too late, to create a satisfying legacy?

For people of wealth, this process often entails a charitable donation, leaving something in their name. For the rest of us, this process will have to involve something different, and hopefully something better. I recommend something far more personal. Ask yourself (again): Who are you? What is your authentic self? What are your core values? Whom have you influenced? Whom do you want to influence? What can you give to others? To whom do you want to give? To whom do you want to connect? A family member? Your children? A relative? A specific person in your life? God? These questions serve several purposes. They allow you to distance yourself from your achievement-oriented adulthood. They allow you to face your mortality. They coach you toward your unfinished business. There is a belief that if you deny your mortality, you are already dead. However, if you can accept and embrace your mortality, you are liberated. Taking time to consider your legacy, and then shifting your focus to creating your legacy, is emotionally lifting and gratifying, and it is a great antidepressant.

So what happens when you are not leaving some material legacy? Just give of yourself while still alive. Honor people. Give them compliments and support. Give them your love. Bridge any remaining differences between yourself and your loved ones. Share your wisdom and your perspective of life. Become a model for how to appreciate life. Become a model for your values. Become a model for giving. Help others learn that life's real reward comes from helping others. In short, as you move toward your final years, become a better teacher, guiding your loved ones through their lives and helping them gain a better understanding of what is truly important. A life well lived: that is something you can help define. For many people, this new insight and these new acts can be the missing piece that changes the emptiness of their life into a sense of fulfillment.

After all, what could be a better legacy than changing the life of someone you love? Changing their appreciation of life or changing their definition of success, shifting their activity from receiving to giving? Helping others learn to judge themselves on their standards, not society's standards? Or what could be more rewarding than showing your loved ones how to face death with courage? With faith and hope? Sometimes it is valuable to give others something that they will need for tomorrow, not today. You may be physically gone when that tomorrow arrives, but you will be in their hearts, and your gift will live well beyond your own life. It will help them at their time of need. Isn't that what we all want? To give something that lasts past our last breath? That was certainly part of the driving force behind this guide. I may have failed to hit all of my own targets, but that type of legacy is doable; and that type of legacy can be emotionally rewarding. So much more fulfilling than gaining more for yourself. There is also a hidden advantage: once you have discovered what you need to do for your legacy, it allows you to get busy helping others with the same challenge. So help your family and friends leave their own legacy. Help them complete their life paths with happiness, not emptiness.

Chapter 87

Another Legacy: Self-Education

"In order to learn one must change one's mind."
Orson Scott Card

One of the underlying themes of this guide is self-education. Each of us needs to move beyond the education we received in our youth. With America's wealth, you would think we should be the most educated population in the world. Not true. When you examine the percentage of the population that has received a post-secondary level of education, Canada has the highest level at 50 percent. Israel is second at 45 percent; Japan is third at 40 percent. America lags far behind. Where does our country excel? Prisons. America has five percent of the world's population but 25 percent of the world's incarcerated population. In our country, we have 2.2 million people behind bars. China ranks second with 1.5 million people incarcerated; and Russia ranks third with 870,000 people incarcerated. What does that tell you? Americans have room for improvement. My personal belief? If we, as a nation, are going to progress toward societal improvement, the responsibility falls with each of us for self-education (well after our formal education) and constant self-improvement.

We are all aware of the rising cost of institution-based education. In America, the most elite colleges claim that it costs them 60,000 dollars per year to educate a single student. At the same time, we have a rising number of individuals with student loans. The amount of student loans in a single year recently rose above one hundred billion dollars. America's total loan cost now reaches above one trillion dollars. For that enormous cost and burden, you would think we have the world's best education system. Once again, we are not even close. Study after study has revealed our educational achievement gap, stretching from kindergarten through college. Our children and young adults in the urban centers do not have the same educational opportunity as those in wealthier suburbs. Ethnicity, race, and socioeconomic factors derail any chance for a significant portion of our population. Programs like "No Child Left Behind" and "Race To The Top" have produced nominal improvement. Overall, our formal educational system from preschool to our graduate programs still does not warrant a passing grade.

Some of you may be fans of Ray Bradbury, one of the most celebrated American authors of this past century. He specialized in fantasy and horror stories, best represented by *Fahrenheit 451*. In 2007, he won a Pulitzer citation for his 500 published works. But most importantly, he never had a formal education beyond high school. Instead, once he had graduated from high school, he spent all of his time, hour after hour/day after day, at the local library, educating himself. He followed his own passions, learning about Greek and Roman mythology, studying the universe, and examining human behavior, and then he translated that knowledge into his numerous stories. So, what is my point? Formal education may be the path for some individuals, but it does not have to be the path for all of us. In fact, we now have the great equalizer for education: the Internet. You do not need a great teacher. You just have to be a great learner. When I graduated from high school, our principal gave our commencement speech. He had one hope. He didn't care what we had learned in our four years of high school; instead, he only hoped that we had "learned how to learn."

For your final progression toward changing your life, that would be another habit, continued self-education. Hopefully, you have received a broad education through this book. But consider this book as the initial steps for your self-education, not the closing steps, with the self-education directed toward self-improvement. When I was in college, did any professor discuss the benefits of certain habits? Did any teacher even mention the possible advantage of writing down your goals? Did any professor discuss living with passion and purpose? For most of us, formal education is overrated. Grades are overrated. What counts is how much you learn about life, not how you do on some standardized test. Do you know one of the things that I respect the most about my younger daughter? Not that she was Phi Beta Kappa, but that she progressed through four years of college without ever looking up a single grade for any course. She focused strictly on learning.

What really counts is how much you learn, not the grade you achieve. And what really counts is what you learn outside, not inside, the classroom, and what you learn on your own. With this guide as a stepping-stone, search the Internet for topics that capture your interest. Follow your passions. Chase those dreams. Let self-education guide you along the path toward the better life and the better you. Be both the teacher and the student. Build a life of expanding knowledge and wisdom. Remember Eleanor Roosevelt's quote: "Never mistake knowledge for wisdom. One helps you make a living; the other helps you make a life." Let your expanding wisdom help you make a difference and propel you forward (one foot at a time) toward your legacy. Equally importantly, make certain that you share your wisdom, not just your knowledge, so that others can realize an equal opportunity for creating their own footprints.

Chapter 88

Letting Go – To Find Diamonds?

"When I let go of what I am, I become what I might be."
Lao Tzu

What's the next stepping-stone for completing this guide? Perhaps you already know how they capture rhesus monkeys in Indonesian. They find a coconut, carve out an opening at the top, and clean the coconut, creating a hollow core that can be filled with rice or peanuts. The coconut is staked to the ground. The monkey finds the coconut, reaches its hand into the coconut, and grabs a handful of goodies. But when it attempts to extract its clenched fist with all of those goodies, the larger fist cannot slip out through the narrow opening. With many monkeys, they will not let go of the goodies. They will not release the rice or peanuts. They stand trapped, waiting to be caught by some local native. My question is simple. What rice or peanuts are you holding? What is it that you cannot let go of? For some people, it will be a fantasy of riches or material possessions. For other people, it may be a lifetime of bad habits. To move forward toward expanded wisdom and greater happiness, you must often let go of something.

When my father died, my mother was left living alone in their house. It was one of the most difficult crises of her life. As explained before, she repeatedly resisted a move out of their house. Why? As she explained on more than one occasion, she could not give up her possessions: her clothes, her jewelry, and her books. Happiness is defined by each person. There should be no judgment with any definition. However, regardless of your definition of happiness (or bias against living in a senior-citizen retirement facility), my mother was like that monkey. She was trapped because she would not release her fist of goodies.

Freedom awaited my mother. A better life awaited my mother. Inaction led nowhere. In addition, my mother never developed any new habits. No new personal mission. No new life purpose. No personal development. No attempt at increased spirituality. The result? Her golden years grew miserable. She deserved more. Sadly, it took years before she could release her fist, let go of her beloved goodies, and make the move into our house. No, it did not offer any fancy view of the ocean. But it offered a much better view of life. And a better way of living.

Have you ever listened to Russell Conwell's sermon "Acres of Diamonds"? It is the well-known story of Ali Hafed, a Persian farmer who lived near the River Indus. This man lived around the time that diamonds were discovered. If a man could find diamonds, he could become instantly wealthy. So Ali Hafed sold his farm, left his wife and family, and undertook a search for diamonds. For several years, he probed through Asia, Europe, and Africa. Finally, broke and destitute, he drowned himself in Barcelona. A year after his suicide, the man who had purchased Ali Hafed's farm stumbled across a large rock in one of his streams and placed the rock on his mantel. A friend stopped by his house, noticed the large rock, and proclaimed that it "had to be" a diamond. The new owner was skeptical because the streams on his property had hundreds of those rocks, buried right beneath the ground. In truth, those rocks were real diamonds; and Ali Hafed's farm had acres and acres of diamonds. Over the next several decades, his farm proved to be the largest diamond field of his era; and many of the European crowns, those crowns that are found today in many museums, have diamonds from Ali Hafed's original land.

What is the moral of this story? You don't need to travel the world, seeking more wealth. You don't need to explore outside of yourself for some external reward. Think internal, not external. You just need to find those diamonds buried beneath your feet, the diamonds buried inside of yourself. To find something new, you often have to discard something old. Free yourself. Then find those diamonds, mine those diamonds, and share those diamonds with the people in your life. Those diamonds may be the habits within this survivor guide. So, mine and develop an improved understanding of the importance of your eating style and your exercise routine; mine and develop an improved mental clarity; and mine and develop a personal mission with a set of specific goals. Mine and develop a new spiritual component and more connections with people. Mine and develop continued personal development. Combine these habits with a better use of structure and time management; and employ a number of the guide's suggestions to lift your emotional mood. Then share these diamonds, this newfound wisdom, with the people in your life. With these new habits, you do not need more material wealth. The real wealth will be found in the quality of your relationships, the quality of your life, and the quality of your new freedom.

Chapter 89

Our Golden Moments

"When was the last time you looked at the stars
with the wonder they deserved."
Kris Kristofferson

We progress through life with a random series of golden moments of blissful happiness. Short-lived, but golden. In any relationship, I have believed that the number of golden moments for a pair of people was directly related to the love between the two people and the quantity of time the two people were able to spend with each other. The more time together, the more golden moments. Each of us has a special relationship with a small group of people. Each of us yearns for more golden moments. With this guide, I gained an additional insight. Our golden moments are related to more than love and time; they are related to the quality of our habits. The more you employ these habits, the greater your chance of creating an increased number of golden moments, and not just for yourself, but also for those people you love. You should be sharing this guide with the people you love, but especially with your children and friends, so they can experience a lifetime of their own increasing golden moments.

A great life would be an endless series of golden moments from childhood into adulthood and finally into your older years. If a person could learn the value of these habits at a young age, they could increase their golden moments, setting up a lifetime of those moments. Wouldn't a life well lived be a wonderful foundation for your golden years? That perspective explains my earlier line that you are never too young to read this book. Think of our parental responsibility. Each of us wants our child's life to be better than our own. With the increasing disparity of income, the increasing ethnic/religious conflict, and the changing economic tide (slipping away from America), the odds do not seem to be in your child's favor. Or your niece or nephew's favor. With our current poor medical health and longevity statistics, our broken health care system, and an increasing prevalence of psychiatric and developmental illnesses, that challenge seems to growing harder year-by-year. Truly, for our children, life does not seem to be growing any easier or less complicated. We need to do something, agreed?

One of the solutions is more love for our children and more time spent with our children. Unfortunately, Americans work longer hours than most countries through the world. You remember, I hope, the earlier statistics on the time we have left to spend with our loved ones. In America, the average parent spends four to thirty minutes a day talking with his or her spouse and one to twenty minutes a day talking to his or her children. That time allotment needs to be drastically improved. At the same time, there needs to be better modeling of the right behaviors, habits, and personal development. Share what you have learned with your children. Share what you have learned with all family members. Help them delete their negative thoughts and self-doubts. Support their dreams and personal missions, regardless of whether they conflict with your thoughts of what they should do. Help them with their goals, even if they are not your goals. Encourage them to develop more spirituality with more connection to others. Help them with their medical and emotional health, directing them toward a healthier style of eating and an improved exercise routine. From my perspective, all of these components, especially when started early in life, would give your children and family members a better chance for an improved relationship with you (and others), a better understanding of the world, and a much greater chance for an expanded number of those random golden moments. So, make that a priority. Simply stated, give them a better future and a greater sense of hope. Help them with their own footprints. Make it all part of your legacy. And theirs.

Chapter 90

How Giving Leads To Hope

"Hope is a good thing."
Andy Dufresne in 'Shawshank Redemption'

When my father developed dementia, we took care of him as well as we could, but eventually we had to place him in a nursing home. We would often visit him daily. Each morning, he ate breakfast, and then packed all of his belongings, setting them on his bed, ready to move out. This happened day after day, week after week. After several months, reality set in. He realized that he would not be leaving the nursing residence. He realized that he had no future beyond the enclosed walls. What did he do? Purposefully, he stopped eating. He might have lost his memory, but he had not lost his willpower. No one could convince him to resume eating and he died within three weeks. His friends did not understand his final act. I did. He hit a point where he could not control his life, where he could not create his future, where he could not find any chance for giving. All of us need to give; and fingers crossed, this guide will offer that chance.

When my father died, the minister offered the familiar metaphor that my father's spirit was like a sailboat, heading toward the horizon. Slowly, we were seeing less and less of that sailboat, finally seeing only the mast. The minister explained that just as we were sadly waving goodbye from our land, there was another group of people on the other side of the horizon who were cheering, applauding, and welcoming my father to their land. I have always liked that image, leaving one group of friends to join another group of friends. But for those of us among the living, for those of us left behind on our land, we need to expand that metaphor. As we sail into our golden years, we need to keep our eyes on our horizon. Did you know that the eyesight of the average human has worsened over the last couple of hundred years? It's because we don't watch the horizon enough. We are too focused on the smaller screens, the surfaces that are only inches from our eyes. A metaphor for our life? Regardless, that narrow focus creates poor vision. For your later years, as you implement your changes, you need to make certain that your vision stays sharp. You need to stay focused on your horizon, where you are going and what you want in your final years. You need to watch your progress and your direction, not paying attention to your wake. Stay in the present, not the past. And maintain your acts for giving. Without them, you may not want to keep moving forward.

Your golden years, as you can tell from my guide, require a resetting of habits, but they also require a resetting of priorities. There is a common saying that we each make a living by what we get, but we make a life by what we give. You need to be consistently focused on giving to yourself, your family, your friends, and your world. You can give more than you realize; and your giving is not restricted by the size of your wallet. For your happiness, giving is almost as necessary as breathing. That was the other hidden issue with my father's death. He had always been a giving man; and in the nursing home, there was no avenue for further giving. In fact, the only gift he could offer was stopping the cost of his nursing home. Do you know which day he died? He died on the last day of the month so my mother would not have to pay for one more month of his care. His death, in my eyes, was his final gift to her. He did not die depressed and empty. He died with the sense of connecting and the joy of giving. Despite the circumstances, it still came him hope over those final weeks. You could see it in his eyes. So, keep giving as you progress toward your future. My hope is that this survivor kit has laid a foundation for those three crucial components: connecting, giving and hope.

There is another point to consider. Your giving is your footprint. When my father died, I was flooded with long-forgotten memories. I remembered myself as a kid, just five years old, throwing up on the side of a winding mountain road. What part of that memory was the clearest? My dad's hands reaching around my waist, helping me bend over to empty my stomach. I also remembered a car accident at age nine. I was sitting in the front seat, wedged between my mother and father (and this was before seat belts), and a car roared through a red light, heading directly into our path. I do not recall the screech of our brakes, but I recall how my dad swung out his right arm, how he pressed his hand against my chest, and how he prevented me from flying forward into the windshield. You are not a captain of a college football team without some strength. One more forgotten memory? While body surfing in Poipu Beach in Kauai my dad and I spotted a large shark fin, probably ten yards from us, sharply turning in our direction. I remember how my dad's hand reached out, grabbed my shoulder, and yanked me into the breaking wave and pulled me back toward shore. With these memories, what was my point? Well, that was his legacy. Throughout my life he was always offering a helping hand, always offering security, always giving. Right to the end. For me, that was his legacy, something that I would not forget! The value of giving.

Chapter 91

So, Are You Sharing This Guide?

"When you learn, teach. When you get, give."
Maya Angelou

I once read that we remember 20 percent of what we read, 30 percent of what we hear, 40 percent of what we see, 50 percent of what we say, 60 percent of what we do, and 90 percent of what we read, hear, see, say, and do. My point? With this guide, you need to talk about it with others. You need to share it with others.

There's a story of a farmer with an old blind horse. Whenever he wanted the horse to drag the plow to till the land, he would attach the horse to the plow and then loudly call out the names of three horses, directing them to all "pull"! Of course, there was only one horse. But that farmer knew that the old blind horse would pull harder, thinking he was part of a team. That's true for all of us. No one succeeds on his or her own. Your golden years, even with a group of new habits, are not easy. However, it is far easier when you are part of a team. Perhaps, that team will be family members or friends who are helping you toward your mission. Perhaps, it will include more and more people as you progress through your later years.

So, whom should you include? As you develop the new habits and progress into your later years, I encourage you to progressively widen your circle, even beyond your family and children. I suggest that you even include some people whom you might have initially discounted. Think of Abraham Lincoln's approach. When you examine the list of America's best presidents, Lincoln comes to the forefront, with his willingness to appoint prior opponents to his cabinet and his willingness to appoint certain people to specific positions, even when there were easy reasons (negative judgments) for not appointing them. Many critics questioned Lincoln's selection of Ulysses Grant to lead the North in the Civil War. The critics of that era viewed Grant's alcohol abuse as a reason not to select him. Lincoln knew that most people tend to make the same fundamental mistake. He knew that most people judge others on their weaknesses, rather than appreciate their strengths. He was able to move past weaknesses; he was able to see a person's strengths. Without that ability, we might have lost the Civil War and never emerged as the United States of America. So, shed the burden of negative judgment. Try reaching out to some people whom you might have avoided, trying to improve their lives by sharing more of yourself.

If Lincoln's approach sounds too difficult, listen to Buddha's wisdom. He preached the value of letting go of your anger. Buddha used to say that we were not punished for our anger, but we were punished by our anger. Anger toward old events or other people harms you much more than it harms them. So, with your understanding of what you need to do to improve your mood and what you need to do to improve your life, can you move past old squabbles, old conflicts? Maybe, as you grow stronger with the new habits, you can enlarge your family of friends. When you scale a mountain, do you want to stand alone? To make it worthwhile, you need company at the top. Yes, make certain you are surrounded by those whom you love. But there is also an advantage in expanding your love and understanding to others. If you want to make these years a masterpiece, take that additional step. Give more than you ever anticipated. And even when your ship sails beyond the horizon, the beneficial effects of your masterpiece, your golden years and your giving, will be felt by many, not by just a few.

What have I done? There are many examples, but let me list one of my first steps. While writing this guide, I reached out to my old college roommate, another physician who lives in Los Angeles. On a monthly basis, we have been getting together for lunch, reestablishing our prior friendship. It has truly been fun. Are there other people who warrant an attempt for renewed friendship from me? Absolutely. When I was growing up in Southern California, from age three to age nine, I was considered the fifth child of our neighbors. I was always at their house, playing with their family. My best friend from that family? He was part of my class at Williams College. Consider those odds. Your best friend from childhood joins you at the same college? But since college, has he visited? Have any of those family members made contact? No. Now, do you have similar situations in which old friends, dear friends, have disappeared from your life? Well, there is no blame. There is no judgment. We have all stepped onto our own conveyor belts. Whose responsibility is it to reach out? Mine. Yours. And with this guide, I am doing just that. Imagine that scene in the movie *The Help* in which the lady screams in bed when reading about herself? Hopefully, that will not be my old friend's response when he reads these pages. Still, if you find yourself with a similar challenge, use your new habits. Take responsibility. Go for it. Expand your circle of friends.

Chapter 92

What If...?

"Facts are stubborn things."
John Adams

What if the unthinkable happens? You work hard to follow this guide; you successfully incorporate the necessary habits; and you become a better person with much to offer. Then, suddenly, an accident happens. Your life is cut short. Was it worth the effort? I remember when my uncle died. He had worked for the government for decades, building up a pension with a plan to retire at an early age. Well, just months before his planned retirement, he died. At his funeral, his wife offered a long soliloquy of all the trips and activities that they had saved for retirement. It was an impressive bucket list. But you know me. I am not a great fan of bucket lists (until you are ready). I am a fan of using your golden years first for improving yourself. So, in my view, was it worth it for my uncle to have sacrificed decades of his life for some bucket list? No. But would it have been worth it if he had spent time, a month or a year, changing himself and improving himself? The answer is absolutely yes. Do you know why?

If you think this scenario is hypothetical, think again. None of us is going to come out of this home stretch alive. That is one of those stubborn facts. So, in this final series of years or decades, what is the advantage of working on yourself as opposed to completing a bucket list? I would argue the following: if you change, even for a single day, it is worth it. Why? Because you gain the opportunity to learn the truth about yourself and you earn the opportunity to share that truth. I have pushed for little changes and small progressions. But changing who you are and then having the chance to share the real you? Well, there is nothing small about that achievement, even if it is for one single day. There is a saying that you cannot discover your goodness until you know who you are. There is also a saying that a person only becomes a person through other people. Isn't it more important for you to learn and appreciate yourself and others? Isn't it even more important for your family and friends to know and appreciate each other?

At my father's funeral, when I was speaking to the group of family and friends, I shared more than my surge of forgotten memories. I recounted the course of his life and his repeated sacrifices for his family. He used to say that you never learned anything while talking. Hopefully, he will make an exception for me with the writing of this guide. At the end of my testimonial, I shared how he was a wonderful father and a great friend who used to call me "his best buddy." I shared how much I loved the man and how much I will miss the man to my own dying day. I ended the speech with a simple, heartfelt promise: "If there is a heaven and I get to heaven and he is not there, ... well, I ain't staying." Now, isn't that something you would want your children to say? Isn't that something you would want your friends to say? When they finish their current life and progress to the next dimension, whatever is that dimension, don't you want them to come looking for you? Now, that is a legacy of value. That is a legacy of meaning. And that's what I want for my own legacy. I do not need a trip to some historic church or a visit to see some museum masterpiece. I don't want better scenery. I just want to be part of a great family and a great group of friends. Isn't that what most of you want? Gravity can help you fly to Rome, but gravity can also bring you back home to the real you. That's where I want to spend my time, home with family and friends. Creating my own golden moments. Creating my own footprints. Creating my own legacy. If those goals work for me (and they have been working beyond my expectation), they can work for you.

There's one final point. Remember my initial comments about our generation and our historic opportunity? I do not want the above legacy just for me; I want it for our generation. Through our individual footprints, let's reclaim our historic role as leaders. We stand strong, ready to make a contribution. Let's change the world's perception of us. Together, let's mentor the adults and defend the children. Let's showcase the value of things greater than money or fame. Let's highlight the importance of living in the world of being, not just doing. Let's underscore the importance of who you are, not what you do. Let's model the joy of giving, not just receiving. One by one, let's aim for a societal transformation. If can change ourselves in our golden years, we can redefine our role in society and we can gain increased regain respect for older people. We might even be able to reset some of the values of society. Now, how's that for a generation footprint?

Chapter 93

My Final Confession

"The world is not made up of atoms, it's made up of stories."
Muriel Rukeyser

At this point, as I conclude this guide, I think it is fair to ask: How much have I changed with this book? Financially, I am not as wealthy as I was when I started this writing process. So, if you are looking to fill your pockets with coins, I will repeat my earlier refrain that my survivor kit is not a financial map. But that was never the point. If fact, there was a stage in the writing process where I had a chance to sign with one of the traditional publishing houses. Guaranteed money. But I declined. Why? Because I did not want something commercial, I wanted something personal. Remember: this guide was written for a friend (who had already committed suicide) and for me. I wanted my guide to reflect me, not some formula. I wanted everything, from the narrative to the title to my confessions, to be mine. I did not care if the book were read by one person or seven people. I was just hopeful that it would place me on the right path. And the process, as expressed several times, has succeeded beyond my expectations.

You could take my word for that proclamation, but let me share some stories of my experience. For my most recent Christmas, I did not spend a fortune to give my two daughters extravagant presents. Nothing that I could have purchased would have been more special than something that I had created. So, what did I do? Over their four years of college (the younger daughter had just graduated last summer), I had written numerous emails. Okay. I could have texted and saved myself some time. But I wrote those emails, wanting to share the experience of having your child head off to college, the experience of having your child transform from a young lady to a grown woman. Parenthood is filled with many stages from the joy of pregnancy to the wonder of those first spoken words to the forgotten importance of those grade school teachers to the competitiveness of high school and to the chaos of college. But the transition from a daughter-father relationship to more equal relationship? That was something I wanted to capture. That was something I wanted to share. So, I saved all my emails, and I bound the emails into a book, titled *A Father's Letters*. I created a separate book for each of my daughters, filled with just my personal emails (and some emails from my wife). Both of them loved their books. I even caught them secretly reading it at times in the hectic Christmas Day. One daughter shared it with one of her best male friends, and even he cried while reading it. Now, for me, that gift was an extension of this guide, as it was an attempt to share more of myself and leave a clearer footprint.

Another story, which also made me poorer? When my older daughter was between her junior and senior college year (her last summer under our roof), I elected to take a full month off from my work. Income? Poof! Gone! I told my daughter to arrange a month-long vacation for the family with her making all the bookings for flights, hotels, and excursions. She was the parent; we were the children. It was not a high cost vacation; and it was not aimed to hit any bucket list items. She selected the cities and she arranged the itinerary from Spain to Greece to Turkey to Poland to Great Britain. For me, the goal was simple. I wanted an uninterrupted month with my wife and two daughters. And you know what? My daughter, Skyler, planned a better vacation than I could have planned. It was worth every penny! And we economized! But one highpoint? On my daughter's twenty-first birthday, she and I, after my wife and younger daughter had collapsed into their hotel beds, stole our way up to the hotel roof. One *mojitos* after another, one hour after another … well, I had the privilege of experiencing one of life's golden moments. Feeling as if I had risen above the constant rush of life, I was able to pause and appreciate the beauty of Florence and the beauty of my daughter, now a grown, independent, and lovely woman. By giving up income, by diverting myself from external reward, I had created a memory that was, as they say, priceless. I had created something special, something worthy of a legacy.

Before I started writing this book, I do not think I would have made the choices (and sacrifices) to establish those two stories. I do not think I would have been as focused on the importance of sharing, giving, and simply being. And during the trip (and while writing the Christmas gift), I would not have been so focused on sharing my view of the key habits that transform life into something far more meaningful. I am hoping that you follow my lead and perhaps go well beyond my own efforts. The final progression is to redefine your legacy. You cannot complete that simply through writing or traveling; it has to be accomplished by really connecting with those whom you love. And maybe that is the final confession. None of us can survive without love. We need each other. For many people, to reach that realization, they need to break old habits and old beliefs. They need to reenergize, refocus, and experience a rebirth of new habits, new passions, new priorities, and enhanced relationships (of all types). I can tell you that it is possible. It can happen to you. But to believe me, you are going to have to change and be amazed at your own transformation. Hopefully, this guide will start you toward that new destination. Just remember to enjoy the journey. Along the way, do me one favor. Create some memorable stories. Make some footprints. Live. Love. And make a difference.

Acknowledgements

I want to express my thanks to my best friend, my wife Priscilla (Ace). She has been my biggest supporter, patiently waiting for me to improve. I met her at 3 a.m. while I was a medical intern. She was signing the death certificate for one of my patients, not an unusual occurrence. Beside the corpse, she looked pretty good. As I asked her out, that was the only compliment that came to my mind. I remarked how good she looked next to the corpse. Since she was exhausted and clearly not seeing too straight, she accepted my invitation for a date. And I never dated another woman. Lucky me. I also want to thank my two wonderful daughters, Skyler and Austen. They have been my footprints on the world, and the world is far better with them in it. I would love to highlight all of their fine features, but they would kill me.

Nevertheless, I could not have asked for a better wife or two better daughters.

I want to express my thanks to my friend, Jeffrey Knight, who, before he died, embraced the purpose of this book and asked me to share his story. He is the individual who had the courage to give up his material possessions for something far greater, the wisdom that comes with living in a Buddhist monastery. He made an attempt to be a contributor, not just a consumer. He may have fallen to his own demons, but he represented some of man's better qualities. He is greatly missed by those of us who knew the real person beneath the illness. He wanted so much more for himself and the world. If he is watching, I hope he is pleased with my effort.

I want to thank the professionals who helped me publish this book. Jack Canfield and Steve Harrison's course on "Best Seller Blueprint" and Steve Harrison's "Quantum Leap" program were incredibly helpful. Those programs taught me the value of reaching people's hearts by sharing more of yourself. I want to express my appreciation for Steve Harrison's entire team, including such cohorts as Geoffrey Berwind, Debra Englander, Brian Edmonson, Raia King, Nick Ippoliti, and so many other professionals. The same sentiment applies to CreateSpace, the publisher of this book. Everyone, especially the editor Henry Gekonde, was outstanding. When you enter a physician's office, your care is not determined by just the quality of the doctor; it is determined, more than you realize, by the quality of the staff. The same truth holds for any book. The real credit should go not to the writer, but to those professionals who helped bring the vision of the book to fruition. Of course, if there are any misspellings, it's all their fault, right?

I also want to thank my long-term friends for their support. They know who they are. But I want to especially thank three outstanding physicians: Dr. Robert McWilliams for his camaraderie since our internship/residency days, Dr. Randy Ross for his habit of always giving, and Dr. Chris Selvage, my roommate at Williams College, for his constant friendship over the decades. Long-term, close friends: Where would any of us be without them? To be honest, I wish my list of life-long friends were even longer. But there is still time. For me and for you. Sharing and giving: it's what makes our lives more meaningful. I thank those people who have given me the chance to give (and receive).

Additional Acknowledgements

I want to thank those individuals whose wisdom contributed to my guide for your golden years. This guide is as much theirs as mine.

Barbara De Angeles
Joseph V. Bailey
Gene Baur
T. Colin Campbell
Dale Carnegie
Deepak Chopra,
Russell Conwell
Kenneth Cooper
Norman Cousins
Stephen Covey
Ronnie Cummins

Kathy Freston
Viktor E. Frankl
Benjamin Franklin
Rory Freedman
Joel Fuhrman
Donna Gates
Rick Hanson
Stephen Hawking
Louise Hay
Napoleon Hill
Abraham Lincoln

Earl Nightingale
Dean Ornish
N.V. Peale
Anthony Robbins
John Robbins
Ocean Robbins
Michelle Simon
Jeffrey Smith
H. D. Thoreau
Brian Tracy
Andrew Weil

Wayne Dyer   Nelson Mandela   Marcia Wieder
Thomas Edison   C. McDougall   Aurora Winter
Albert Einstein   Joseph Mercola   John Wooden
Caldwell Esselstyn Isaac Newton   Zig Ziglar

Website

BoomerHealthInstitute.com

This website is a resource that offers continued updates on additional habits to improve the quality of ourselves, our relationships, and our lives. It offers a variety of programs (speeches, teleseminars, and coaching) that may further expand your vision of a better future. It also offers a membership community where we can share ways to improve and redesign our lives while interacting with individuals who have the same pursuit. Join us. Together, we can make our lives less stressful, more balanced, and far more meaningful. Maybe, we can make the world a little bit better.

CPSIA information can be obtained at www.ICGtesting.com
Printed in the USA
LVOW10s1458061113

360255LV00015B/740/P